CONTENTS

ICT Infrastructure
Management

OGC
Office of Government Commerce

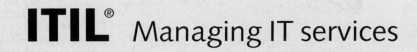
ITIL® Managing IT services

London: TSO

Published by TSO (The Stationery Office) and available from:

Online
www.tso.co.uk/bookshop

Mail, Telephone, Fax & E-mail
TSO
PO Box 29, Norwich, NR3 1GN
Telephone orders/General enquiries: 0870 600 5522
Fax orders: 0870 600 5533
E-mail: book.orders@tso.co.uk
Textphone 0870 240 3701

TSO Shops
123 Kingsway, London, WC2B 6PQ
020 7242 6393 Fax 020 7242 6394
68-69 Bull Street, Birmingham B4 6AD
0121 236 9696 Fax 0121 236 9699
9-21 Princess Street, Manchester M60 8AS
0161 834 7201 Fax 0161 833 0634
16 Arthur Street, Belfast BT1 4GD
028 9023 8451 Fax 028 9023 5401
18-19 High Street, Cardiff CF10 1PT
029 2039 5548 Fax 029 2038 4347
71 Lothian Road, Edinburgh EH3 9AZ
0870 606 5566 Fax 0870 606 5588

TSO Accredited Agents
(see Yellow Pages)

and through good booksellers

For further information on OGC products, contact:

OGC Service Desk
Rosebery Court
St Andrews Business Park
Norwich NR7 0HS
Telephone +44 (0) 845 000 4999

First published 2002
Third impression 2004

ISBN 0 11 330865 5

Printed in the United Kingdom for The Stationery Office
164448   c15   02/04

Titles within the ITIL series include:

Service Support (Published 2000)
Service Desk and the Process of Incident
Management, Problem Management, Configuration
Management, Change Management and
Release Management   ISBN 0 11 330015 8

Service Delivery (Published 2001)
Capacity Management, Availability Management,
Service Level Management, IT Service Continuity,
Financial Management for IT Services and
Customer Relationship Management   ISBN 0 11 330017 4

Planning to Implement Service Management (Published 2002)   ISBN 0 11 330877 9
Application Management   ISBN 0 11 330866 3
Security Management   ISBN 0 11 330014 X

ITIL back catalogue – an historical repository available as PDF downloads from www.tso.co.uk/ITIL

The managers' set
The complementary guidance set
Environmental management, strategy and computer operations set

3 Deployment

FOREWORD

Organisations are increasingly dependent on electronic delivery of services to meet customer needs. This means a requirement for high quality IT services, matched to business needs and user requirements as they evolve.

OGC's ITIL (IT Infrastructure Library) is the most widely accepted approach to IT Service Management in the world. ITIL provides a cohesive set of best practice, drawn from the public and private sectors internationally, supported by a comprehensive qualification scheme, accredited training organisations, implementation and assessment tools.

Bob Assirati

OGC

PREFACE

The ethos behind the development of the IT Infrastructure Library (ITIL) is the recognition that organisations are increasingly dependent upon IT to satisfy their corporate aims and meet their business needs. This growing dependency leads to growing needs for quality IT services – quality that is matched to business needs and user requirements as they emerge. ITIL provides the guidance that will help to match that quality against the needs and cost in order to provide the best IT match for the business.

This is true no matter what type or size of organisation, be it national government, a multinational conglomerate, a decentralised office with either a local or centralised IT provision, an outsourced Service Provider, or a single office environment with one person providing IT support. In each case, there is the requirement to provide an economical service that is reliable, consistent and fit for purpose.

ICT Infrastructure Management is concerned with the processes, organisation and tools to provide a stable IT and communication infrastructure, and is the foundation for ITIL Service Management processes, promoting a quality approach to achieving business effectiveness and efficiency in the use of information systems. ITIL Service Management processes are intended to be implemented so that they underpin but do not dictate the business processes of an organisation. IT Service Providers will be striving to improve the quality of the service, but at the same time they will be trying to reduce the costs or, at a minimum, maintain costs at the current level.

For each of the ICT Infrastructure Management processes described in this book, one or more roles have been identified for carrying out the activities and producing the deliverables associated with the process. It should be recognised that it is often possible to allocate more than one role to an individual. Conversely, in larger organisations, more than one individual may be required to fulfil a role. The purpose of a role, as described in this book, is to locate responsibility, not to suggest an organisation structure.

The authors

The guidance in this book was distilled from the experience of a range of authors working in the private sector in ICT Infrastructure Management. The material was written by:

Paul Graham	Amplecom Ltd
Sjoerd Hulzinga	PinkRoccade
Colin Rudd	IT Enterprise Management Services Ltd
Annemieke van Dijk	Hewlett Packard
Rob van Winden	Perot Systems

with contributions from:

Bert Bekenkamp	Perot Systems
Ivo Doeff	Perot Systems
David Hinley	D S Hinley Associates
Carol Leigh	AXA Shared Services Ltd
Ian Stringfellow	Co-operative Wholesale Society
Robert Wielinga	Perot Systems

The project was managed and coordinated by Annemieke van Dijk of Hewlett Packard.

A wide-ranging national and international Quality Assurance (QA) exercise was carried out by people proposed by OGC and *it*SMF. OGC and Hewlett Packard wish to express their particular appreciation to the following people who spent considerable time and effort (far beyond the call of duty!) on QA of the material:

Graham Barnett	Fujitsu
Chuck Bies	Maryville Technologies
Derek Cambray	Amdahl
David Cannon	ManageOne
Martin Carr	OGC
Jack Churchill	BMC Software
Michael Davies	ProActive Services PTY Ltd (Australia)
Wim Dubois	SX Consultants
Kevin E Ellis BA MBA	Emfisys, Bank of Montreal
David Hinley	D S Hinley Associates
Jule Hintzbergen	Cap Gemini Ernst and Young Nederland B.V.
Kevin Howe	Maryville Technologies
Phil Ives	Yell Group Ltd
Tom Ivison	Siemens Business Systems
Tony Jenkins	Parity Training Ltd
Chris Jones	Optus
Vladimir Kufner	Hewlett Packard
Angela Layaerts	SX Consultants
Adrian Leach	Parity Training Ltd
Steve Mann	Sysop
Jurgen Muller	Cartesian Service Management Group (S. Africa)
Rene Posthumus	Ultracomp B.V.
David Pultorak	Pultorak and Associates Ltd, USA
Linda Rodgers	D S Hinley Associates
Fiona Rosier	Yell Group Ltd
Ed Tozer	Edwin E. Tozer Ltd
Capt. Steve Tremblay	Department of National Defence, Canada
Aaron van der Giessen	Maryville Technologies
Jan Maarten Willems	SX Consultants

Contact information

Full details of the range of material published under the ITIL banner can be found at www.itil.co.uk.

For further information on this and other OGC products, please visit the OGC website at www.ogc.gov.uk/. Alternatively, please contact:

OGC Service Desk
Rosebery Court
St Andrews Business Park
Norwich, NR7 0HS
United Kingdom
Tel: +44 (0) 845 000 4999
E-mail: ServiceDesk@ogc.gsi.gov.uk

1 ICT INFRASTRUCTURE MANAGEMENT OVERVIEW

1.1 Introduction

Knowledge and information are recognised as two of the most important strategic resources that any organisation manages. The quality of the Information and Communications Technology (ICT) systems are paramount to collecting, analysing, and disseminating information throughout the organisation. Therefore, organisations need to invest appropriate effort in their design, planning and management, in order to get the best value from ICT. Unfortunately, these aspects of ICT are, in too many cases, addressed only superficially by organisations.

It is widely recognised that ICT is evolving rapidly, with increasingly complex and sophisticated systems and services being introduced in ever-shorter time intervals. The range of options now available, coupled with the lack of comprehensive ICT Management process standards, represents a daunting challenge for ICT Management. ICT components are increasingly deployed throughout the organisation, which makes the management of such distributed resources both important and difficult. The onus is on ICT Management to ensure that the distributed ICT resources underpin Information Systems (IS) and facilitate decision-making, yet are managed as transparently as possible.

Information and Communications Technology Infrastructure Management (ICTIM), encompassing the processes, organisation and tools, aims to provide a stable IT and communication infrastructure, and is the foundation for the ITIL Service Support and Service Delivery processes.

This book covers all aspects of ICTIM from identification of business requirements through the tendering process to the testing, installation, deployment, and ongoing support and maintenance of ICT components and services. The book discusses:

- what ICT infrastructure is
- what ICTIM is
- why it is important.

It also provides a general approach and framework for ICTIM based on best practice guidance on the planning, design, deployment and ongoing technical support and management of ICT components and services. In defining the management processes necessary for the provision of quality ICT services, it is recognised that customers require a service, and the means of providing that service should be driven primarily by their requirements. ICTIM should ensure that business needs are met in a sustainable manner at a cost that the business can afford.

Good planning, administration and control are key to ensuring that Information Services are built and that they continue to meet business needs in a cost-effective manner. These aspects need to be managed throughout the ICTIM process in order to ensure that the process is aligned to the needs of the business. Planning, administration and control are essential to ensure that suitable resources, with the right skills and competencies, are procured and retained to undertake the necessary roles in infrastructure Design and Planning, Deployment, Operations, and Technical Support.

1.2 Business context

There are several underlying reasons why effective, proactive management of ICT is becoming more important, namely:

- dependency – organisations are increasingly dependent on ICT (see Figure 1.1)
- pervasiveness – ICT is now a significant channel for delivery of the organisation's products or services
- complexity – ICT infrastructures are becoming larger, more distributed and complex (see Figure 1.1)
- flexibility – changing business requirements mean that users are demanding new services; often these have to be provided using the existing infrastructure
- customer satisfaction – customers have become less tolerant of poor services owing to the severe impact that failures have on mainstream business functions
- investment – for many organisations ICT forms a substantial portion of the budget, and there is growing demand for ICT to demonstrate and deliver the long-term value from an investment perspective
- time to market – movement towards global competition, and shorter lifecycles for technologies that afford competitive advantage, increase the necessity to deliver products and services to market in shorter time-frames.

The challenges facing Business and ICT Managers are both diverse and extensive. It is acknowledged widely by the business community that their organisations have a significant dependency on ICT for business operations. Indeed, ICT components are often an integral part of business services and products. This dependency necessitates alignment of strategic planning between the business and ICT. In turn, this requires good communication and the alignment of ICT with business goals.

To achieve this alignment it is important that good working relationships are established between executives, for example, the Chief Executive Officer (CEO) and Chief ICT Officer (CIO). Executives need to demonstrate both vision and leadership to ensure that the business direction is supported by firm strategies for achieving business aims.

For effective, proactive management of ICT, the onus is on ICTIM to develop business and ICT partnerships and improve ICT project delivery in a demonstrable way.

The ICTIM process should be managed effectively, and in order to manage it, it is necessary to select appropriate measures, covering the process, the products and the resources. The measures should facilitate both prediction, i.e., for planning purposes, and comparison, for instance, to demonstrate process improvement. A balanced set of measures is required by management so that they might, for example, improve process efficiency and performance, and reduce ICT costs, including the Total Cost of Ownership (TCO) – see Figure 1.2. A balanced set of measures can also provide valuable management information on which to base decisions, and be used to inform the business about service value for money and comparative costs.

The distributed, powerful and complex ICT infrastructure is placing more stringent demands upon ICT Management and its processes and tools, and hence a demand for more investment. Such demands have contributed to an increase in the TCO of ICT. TCO is a concept that was originally developed by Gartner, and can be defined as all the resources and costs involved in the deployment and support of desktop computing within an organisation. This includes not just the

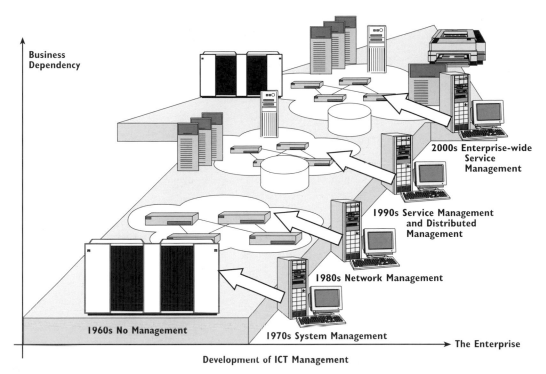

Figure 1.1 – Development of ICT Management

purchase cost of the hardware and software, but also the hidden costs of the supporting mainframes, databases, backup systems, networks, installation, support, maintenance, upgrade, etc.

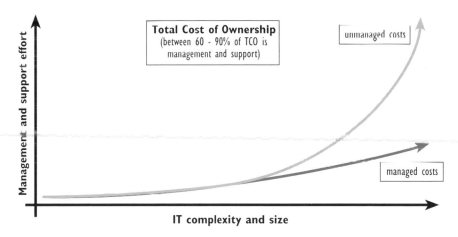

Figure 1.2 – Increase in management costs

The pressure is on ICT Management to reduce all these additional costs as well as reducing the cost of the hardware and software. However, this cannot be addressed in isolation; therefore the real goal is:

> … to reduce the overall Total Cost of Ownership (TCO) of ICT, while maintaining the overall quality of the ICT services provided.

Measurements are necessary for ICTIM to be able to monitor and control performance, for example, in the quality of IT service provision; they are also necessary to demonstrate the business value attained through ICT.

Service Level Agreements (SLAs) are often created without due regard to the effects of ICT on customer services. For example, it is common to see a transaction response time defined as 'within two seconds (excluding network transmission time)'. It is imperative that the impacts of networks are fully analysed and assessed in the provision of customer services and that Service Management does not abdicate responsibility for managing network services, i.e., these services are considered to be an integral part of service provision.

The majority of issues and problems arising between business and ICT are caused by poor communication. Poor communication can arise early in the process lifecycle, for example, in strategic planning; strategies may be developed that remain known to only a chosen few or sit on the shelf gathering dust! It is essential that strategic information is disseminated widely and that the organisation is fully committed to the strategies. In disseminating and communicating strategies, it should be remembered that they are devised to provide competitive advantage and that there is a business risk through overexposure. There are many ways of communicating strategic information. Staff should be made aware of the importance of the organisation's strategies and ensure that sensitive information is not disclosed in case competitors gain an unfair advantage.

There is often much scope within an organisation for improvement in the communication mechanisms used between the business and ICT. With the communication facilities afforded through the technology available today, there remains little justification for both the business and ICT not to communicate with each other in an effective manner. A vital element of this business–ICT communication process is the exchange, mutual appreciation and understanding of each other's strategies.

Key issues that can arise relating to strategies, and which require tactical consideration, include:

- changing ICT needs, acquiring and retaining the right resources and skill sets
- use of ICT to gain competitive advantage
- lack of coordination and control with the move from centralised organisations to distributed systems and mobile environments
- the range of ICT applications and infrastructure
- ever-increasing demand in the volume and speed of change
- Supplier Management and management of the supply chain
- validating and proving effectiveness in relation to spending and investment.

Many of these issues are associated with the quality of the ICT Design and Planning process and are discussed further in Chapter 2.

In general, ICT Management must recognise the importance of their role in underpinning the operation of the business. They must coordinate and work in partnership with the business, facilitating growth, rather than let the technology and ICT dictate and drive the business.

However, it is equally important that the business does not dictate to ICT. This could lead to the situation where ICT is never empowered to make decisions and is always on the 'back foot' in trying to deliver all-embracing solutions to impossible time-scales as illustrated below:

> The business projects within a large financial organisation were viewed either as 'another major business success' or 'yet another ICT failure'.

Key message

Projects should be seen as jointly owned partnership ventures between the business and ICT that either succeed or fail together.

The use of a suitable formal project method and approach can help to develop good business–ICT relationships.

The importance of achieving good working relationships between the CEO and the CIO has been mentioned in terms of understanding the business direction and in ensuring the alignment of key strategies. In fact, the relationship between the CIO and all the major stakeholders within the organisation is crucial to a successful ICT unit and in facilitating business growth.

1.3 The benefits of managing ICT

Effective ICT Infrastructure Management (ICTIM) has benefits for both the business and ICT. Many of these benefits are tangible and can be measured, thus demonstrating the efficacy of ICTIM processes.

1.3.1 Benefits to the business

The business benefits arising from effective ICTIM generally relate to the reliable and consistent matching of ICT services to user needs (i.e., service quality), which in turn contributes to the overall success of the organisation's business through higher productivity. This benefit is achieved through:

- increased service availability and quality to users
- better match of capacity to users' requirements
- less adverse impact of changes on the quality of ICT
- more efficient handling of problems
- lower costs of ICT service provision
- reduced risk of failure, minimising the effect of such failure.

1.3.2 Benefits to IT services

ICTIM helps ICT services become more efficient and effective by:

- managing changes to ICT infrastructure – reducing the resources needed to cope with the adverse effects of changes
- managing problems – monitoring service levels enables trends and problems to be identified and dealt with quickly, reducing the number of problems and the resources required to deal with them
- anticipating problems – anticipating potential performance, capacity, and availability problems, and initiating corrective action to prevent a crisis

- helping the ICT directorate to understand their ICT infrastructures, leading to better informed decisions

- increased productivity of key ICT personnel (less fire-fighting)

- reduced risk of not meeting ICT and business commitments

- identifying new technology which could reduce costs, improve service levels or facilitate improved and innovative business processes and solutions

- planning expansions and upgrades − maintaining a close match between demand and capacity enabling the organisation to make more efficient use of resources.

1.4   ICTIM in relation to the other ITIL books

In today's organisations, ICT infrastructures are the foundations on which business services are built. Within ITIL, the processes and best practices for providing IT services to the line-of-business functions and the user are described in the *Service Delivery* and *Service Support* books. These processes rely on a solid and stable ICT infrastructure as described in this book.

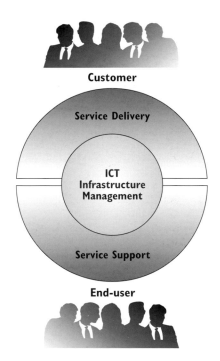

Figure 1.3 − ICTIM in relation to Service Delivery and Service Support

Figure 1.3 shows how ICT infrastructure relates to IT Service Delivery and IT Service Support, whilst Figure 1.4 depicts the full set of ITIL publications, and how they provide a bridge between the business and technology. Best practice guidance and detailed information on the processes can be found in the appropriate sections of the individual publications. This book covers all aspects of ICTIM and its dependencies and interfaces with the other areas, especially the *Service Delivery* and *Service Support* books.

The other books contained within the framework are:

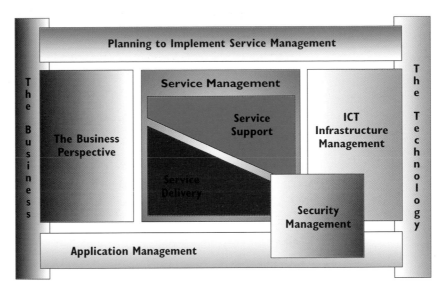

Figure 1.4 – The ITIL Publication Framework

1.4.1   Service Delivery

This book covers the processes required for the planning and delivery of quality ICT services:

- Service Level Management
- Financial Management for IT services
- Capacity Management
- IT Service Continuity Management
- Availability Management.

1.4.2   Service Support

This book describes the function of the Service Desk and its responsibilities as well as the processes required for the ongoing support and maintenance of ICT services:

- Incident Management
- Problem Management
- Configuration Management
- Change Management
- Release Management.

1.4.3   Planning to Implement Service Management

This book examines the issues and tasks involved in planning, implementing and improving Service Management processes within an organisation.

1.4.4   The Business Perspective

The Business Perspective aims to familiarise Business Management with the underlying components of ICTIM, Service Management and Application Management that are necessary to support their business processes. The book aims to enable Business Managers to gain an understanding of the benefits of best practice in IT Service Management in order that they can be better informed and more able to manage relationships with Service Providers for mutual benefit.

1.4.5   Application Management

Application Management addresses the complex subject of managing applications from the initial business need, through the application lifecycle, up to and including retirement. In addition, *Application Management* includes the interaction with IT Service Management disciplines and ICTIM. The book places a strong emphasis on ensuring that IT projects and strategies are tightly aligned with those of the business throughout the applications lifecycle, so as to ensure that the business obtains best value from its investment.

1.4.6   Security Management

This book details the process of planning and managing a defined level of security on information and ICT services, including all aspects associated with reaction to security incidents.

1.5   Structure and scope of this book

Figure 1.5 presents the main ICTIM processes described in detail in the following chapters of this book. The relationships to each other and with Service Management and Application Management are also shown.

The main ICTIM processes as shown in Figure 1.5 are:

■ **Design and Planning** – concerned with the creation and/or improvement of the ICT solution

■ **Deployment** – concerned with the implementation and rolling out of the business and/or ICT solution as designed and planned, with minimum disruption to the business processes

■ **Operations** – concerned with the daily housekeeping and maintenance of the ICT infrastructure

■ **Technical Support** – concerned with structuring and underpinning other processes to guarantee the services delivered by ICTIM.

1.5.1   The Design and Planning processes

The Design and Planning processes within an ICT organisation are concerned with providing overall guidelines for the development and installation of an ICT infrastructure that satisfies the needs of all aspects of the business.

Definition – Design and Planning processes

The development and maintenance of ICT strategies and processes for the deployment and implementation of appropriate ICT infrastructure solutions throughout the organisation.

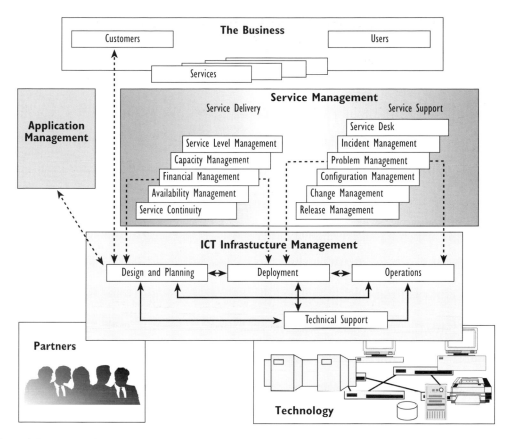

Figure 1.5 – The interfaces of ICTIM

The processes are concerned with:

- coordinating all aspects of ICT design and planning
- the interface between ICT and business planners.

Design and Planning takes input from the business, for example, from business planners, to develop appropriate plans and strategies for all areas of ICT, including:

- technology (e.g., mainframes, distributed systems, networks, desktop and mobile devices)
- architectures and frameworks
- processes and procedures
- management methods and systems.

The objectives of the Design and Planning processes are to:

- develop and maintain strategies for the deployment and implementation of ICT solutions throughout the organisation
- coordinate all aspects of design and planning within ICT
- provide a coordinated ICT planning interface to all business and service planners
- assist in the development of policies and standards in all areas of design, planning and ICT.

1.5.2 The Deployment process

The Deployment process within an organisation is concerned with the implementation and rolling out of the ICTIM as designed and planned.

Deployments are often undertaken using a project lifecycle, in which the project team starts with a plan specifying the scope of the deployment, the resource requirements and a time schedule for the deployment of the IT Infrastructure components.

> **Definition – Deployment process**
>
> **Concerned with the implementation and roll-out of the business, and/or ICT solution as designed and planned, with minimum disruption to business processes.**

From the technical perspective, the Deployment process creates or modifies a technical solution made up of one or more technical components. It should be remembered that a fundamental part of the deployment comprises the technical services that must be – or become – available within the technical infrastructure in order to support this new or changed technical solution.

The Deployment process provides guidance and structure for the adaptation of these technical solutions within the current infrastructure. This has to be done within the context of international standardisation, company standards and solutions that are capable of surviving the foreseeable future.

The Deployment process must embed the solution in a structure that facilitates its management and maintenance in accordance with the guidelines from Design and Planning. The solution should also integrate within the existing operations and monitoring framework.

It is also important to consider the effects on staff and the organisation itself as part of the Deployment process. When new or modified technology solutions are being deployed, it is necessary for the success of the Deployment process that changes within the organisation, and the way people within the organisation behave, are managed under the guidance of the Deployment process.

1.5.3 The Operations process

The Operations process ensures effective operational management of the ICT infrastructure, including the necessary housekeeping and maintenance of the infrastructure.

> **Definition – Operations process**
>
> **All activities and measures to enable and/or maintain the intended use of the ICT infrastructure.**

The Operations process provides the basis for a stable and secure ICT capability on which to provide IT services. The Operations process establishes and maintains this capability.

The Operations process is technology focused with a strong element of management concerned with monitoring and control. Although Operations has a technology bias, the service aspects are not ignored, in that effective Operations Management ensures the stability of the ICT infrastructure, for example, through the definition and application of operability standards.

The Operations process is usually perceived to be in the 'back office' of the organisation, i.e., in the background or of a general supporting nature to the 'front-line' customer-facing roles. Operations may therefore have a fairly low profile within an organisation. However, Operations is a speciality in its own right, and the essential nature of Operations in support of the business is slowly being recognised, particularly in situations that dictate the need for a continuous process, covering 24 hours, 365 days a year.

Operations interfaces with other ICTIM and Service Management processes on a number of levels and at various times. For example, other ICTIM and Service Management processes may develop the standards that are incorporated into the Operations process. Operations provides information (status and usage) to other ICTIM and Service Management processes, as well as being concerned with the managed objects (MOs, representations of ICT infrastructure resources as seen by Management) on a day-to-day basis.

Operational Level Agreements (OLAs) define the levels and standards to which the Operations process adheres. The Operations process is bound by the prerequisites of the supplier of the ICT infrastructure elements. The Design and Planning process provides the management methods and systems employed by Operations.

1.5.4 The Technical Support process

The Technical Support process within an organisation is concerned with structuring and underpinning other processes to guarantee the services delivered by ICTIM.

> **Definition – Technical Support process**
>
> **The development of knowledge for the evaluation, support and proofing of all current and future ICT infrastructure solutions.**

The objectives of Technical Support are to be the centre of technical excellence in Operations and Deployment, and to assist in the provision of end-to-end services. It should provide resource scheduling and administrative support underpinning all other ICT processes. Using analysed and interpreted data from ICT Management tools, it will continually report on the quality of the ICT services to the Design and Planning function in order to influence the overall business planning process.

The process is concerned with:

- research and development of new technologies
- third-line Technical Support
- budget planning and control
- procurement
- Supplier Management
- liaison with Design and Planning on production of Statement Of Requirements (SOR) and Invitation To Tender (ITT)
- tactical implementation of overall service improvements

- liaison with Deployment on release methodologies, mechanisms and operational acceptance

- acting as the technical reference point for all areas of IT and third parties

- technical planning, scheduling and management for support, administration and Operations functions and tools

- provision of analysis and management reports on all aspects of the ICT infrastructure

- maintenance of documentation and procedures.

1.6   The roles, responsibilities and interfaces

ICTIM is concerned with the flow of work arising from the definition of the business requirements through to the deployment and delivery of the final ICT business solution. Figure 1.6 shows the logical flow of work through an ICT organisation. The diagram also reflects the need within ICTIM for an administrative function for the overall control and coordination of ICTIM, and a resource for procurement, audit and accounting system support, update and administration of Design and Planning, Deployment, Operations, and Technical Support.

The ICTIM and administration area may also be involved in management reporting and liaison with, for example, Service Management regarding Service Improvement Programmes, service performance measures, etc.

The stages of a service lifecycle

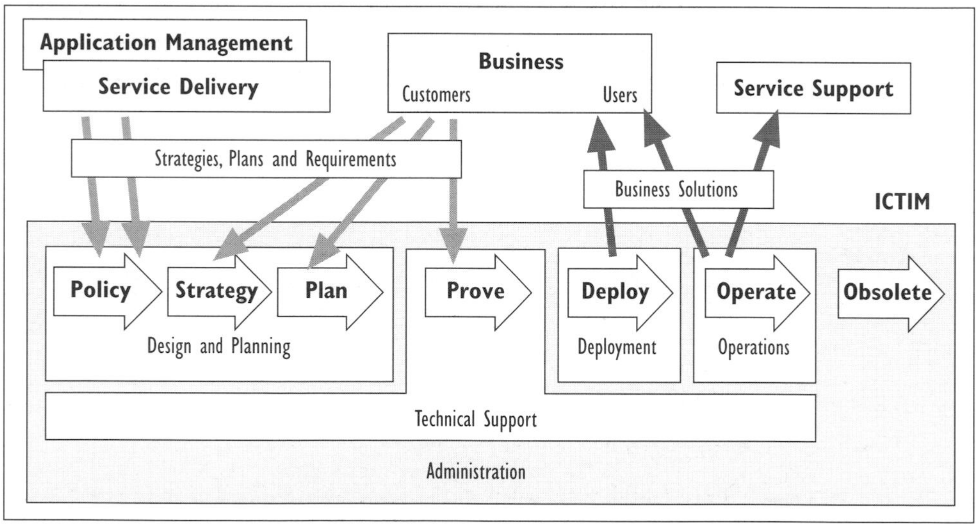

Figure 1.6 – Workflow through ICTIM

The roles and responsibilities of staff within the ICT organisation should be closely aligned to the workflow and the processes involved within ICT.

1.6.1   Organisational structure

The structure of an ICT organisation can assist the staff involved within the ICTIM processes to function efficiently and effectively. The structure of the ICT organisation should be based on a process or functional structure rather than a technology, technical or a support role basis. This ensures that the ICT organisation is more closely aligned to the business and its requirements rather than organised in 'technical silos'. This also helps to break down the artificial barriers that so often occur within ICT organisations and minimise the interfaces required both within ICT and to other areas outside ICT.

Key messages

1   **Organisational structures can often impede the implementation of new strategies.**

2   **Organisational structure can either inhibit change and the implementation of strategy, or facilitate and encourage it.**

Increasingly, organisations are evolving the structure of the ICT organisation to align more with the ICTIM and IT Service Management (ITSM) processes rather than the older, more traditional technology or support team structure.

Centralised and distributed support and management responsibilities

Generally speaking, the majority of ICT Management staff and responsibilities are centrally located within a business. However, in many organisations there is a need to locate ICT staff and functionality on a distributed basis throughout the organisation. This may be on a campus, regional, national or global basis. It is essential that the roles and responsibilities of centralised and distributed staff are realistic, clearly defined, agreed and documented. In most organisations, the principal role of the distributed staff is concerned with day-to-day operational aspects of the local infrastructure and services. However, the distributed staff may also get involved in assisting in the Technical Support, Deployment and Administration processes from time to time. However, it is rare for organisations to use distributed staff in the Design and Planning (D and P) processes.

The ICT infrastructure is rapidly moving away from the traditional concentration in central facilities and data centres. This move to locally distributed systems seems set to accelerate in the future, and managers with responsibility for ensuring the efficient and effective use of distributed systems are, therefore, under increasing pressure within organisations. However, the requirement to operate and manage concentrated data centres will remain a priority for many large organisations. Indeed, with the increased speed and capacity of today's networks they may actually grow in importance to many organisations.

The establishment of a function within ICT Management to manage the use of local ICT infrastructure helps to prevent problems occurring as a result of a lack of coordination and control. The environment to be addressed is necessarily complicated, spanning as it does the various business units of an organisation. The function must be flexible enough to address with equal validity all the differing demands arising from the range of business units to be supported.

The aim is to retain a corporate approach to ICT service provision without placing unnecessary restrictions on the development of local solutions to local problems. Distributed planning and purchasing of ICT systems could be very attractive to a number of organisations. However, some corporate guidance and direction is essential to ensure that local systems can inter-operate with corporate ICT systems and other regionally distributed systems. Care must be taken to ensure that corporate guidance and planning does not lose sight of local needs. For example, distributed systems could be planned as regionally fault tolerant but this factor could be overlooked if planned at a corporate level.

Locally sited ICT equipment has become more powerful and more popular in recent years. In many organisations, such equipment has been allowed to proliferate in response to locally perceived needs. In some organisations, there has been no single plan to ensure consistency of approach or to avoid expensive repetition of mistakes, and little consideration of future requirements, either local or corporate. This is particularly true in relation to the use of mobile access devices. The planning, distribution, use and support of these devices are major problem areas for many large organisations.

Example

A major national organisation lost 30% of its mobile phones due to poor planning and management processes. The majority could not be tracked down or located and therefore had to be written off.

The responsibility for deciding the split in roles and functionality should reside with overall ICT Management and the D and P function. The factors affecting this decision include:

- size, complexity and geographical distribution of the organisation
- culture of the organisation
- diversity of the services, the business and the business functions
- availability of staff resources, skills and knowledge in both ICT and the business units
- current power, complexity and distribution of the ICT infrastructure
- planned power, complexity and distribution of the ICT infrastructure
- remote management capability of the distributed infrastructure
- need for local support and assistance
- costs associated with installing and operating centralised and distributed staff and systems.

It is important to establish appropriate ICTIM controls as, in some organisations, up to half of the components may be unaccounted for.

1.6.2   External interfaces

There are several major interfaces with areas outside the ICTIM function. The principal ones are:

- Corporate Management
- Business Management
- the ICT Steering Group (ISG)
- the Service Management processes
- Application Management
- Security Management.

There are also partners, suppliers, legal, commercial, and corporate procurement functions. A Human Resource (HR) function may provide ICTIM with assistance on skill sets, personal development plans, training plans and approved training service suppliers.

These interfaces are essential to the smooth operation of an ICT department and, as such, need to be agreed, well established, effective and efficient.

The crucial link is the ISG. A well-organised and supported ISG provides the vital bridging function between the business and ICT, ensuring that the key ICT projects and programmes are driven by business needs and business priorities.

The influence of Corporate Management, Business Management and the ISG within an organisation are illustrated in Figure 1.7.

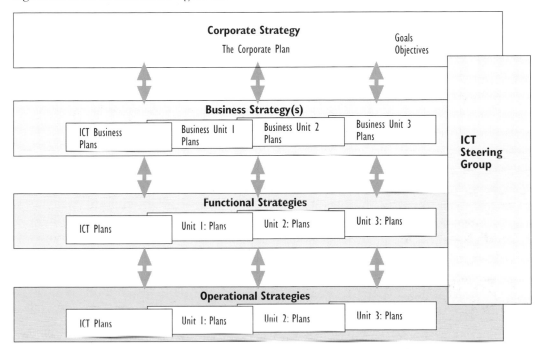

Figure 1.7 – Business and ICT alignment

Corporate Management

If the organisation as a whole has a clear vision of where it is going and what it is trying to achieve, this will enable the ICT function to clearly understand its role in underpinning and enabling the organisation's ambitions to be realised.

> **Key message**
>
> **The most vital consideration for any ICT strategy is that its type and content should be closely aligned with the type and content of the business strategy or strategies of the organisation.**

Business Management

The ICT function is often run as a business within a business. In these circumstances, ICT needs to have business, functional, and operational strategies, objectives and plans. All the ICT documents should be coordinated and integrated with the business plans, functional plans and operational plans of all the other business units within the organisation.

Key message

This activity of aligning ICT business, functional and operational plans with those of the business is often missing or poorly addressed in many organisations. It is essential that if ICT services are genuinely going to be aligned with business requirements this activity is given full focus and commitment at senior level.

ICT Steering Group (ISG)

The ISG is instrumental in this process of coordination and integration of all business plans, functional plans and operational plans. The ISG provides the vital coordination of all business projects and programmes with ICT projects and programmes. It should also ensure that all ICT projects and programmes are driven by business needs and business priorities, within the capabilities and resources available to the ICT function. The ISG should be staffed with senior Business Managers and senior ICT Managers.

Service Management

The Service Management processes are concerned with developing a 'service culture' within ICT and for coordinating a process of continual improvement within ICT. The D and P processes within ICTIM need principally to interface to the more proactive Service Delivery processes and plans, as indicated in Figure 1.5, although there is also a need to be aware of Service Support processes and plans.

Application Management

Application Management addresses the complex subject of managing applications from the initial business need, through the Application Management lifecycle, up to and including retirement. Application Management has a number of interactions with both Service Management and ICTIM, and the latter has a specific need for coordination and interaction in relation to application strategy, design, and development.

Security Management

Security Management interacts with ICTIM over security requirements and security policies and procedures. Security is an important aspect in all ICT plans, as ICT services with a weak security foundation are likely to experience a security breach with possible detriment to the business.

1.6.3   Internal interfaces

The internal interfaces occur between all the ICT Management processes, namely:

- **ICTIM and administration functions** – the ICTIM and administration functions support the other processes and receive reports of ongoing activities and progress
- **Design and Planning** – provides strategic design and planning direction, advice and guidance on all aspects of ICT to all of the ICTIM processes

- **Technical Support** – provides the overall technical support for all ICT systems in use within the organisation, and provides any assistance and support required on ICT technical issues for other ICTIM processes
- **Deployment** – is concerned with the deployment and implementation of business solutions and provides advice and guidance on all aspects of deployment
- **Operations** – is concerned with providing effective and efficient operational management for all live ICT systems, and provides information and advice on all operational aspects.

1.7 Layout of each chapter

The following chapters of the book describe ICTIM processes, providing an overview of the basic concepts, the process goals and scope and detailed description of the process, including inputs, activities and deliverables.

There are specific sections within each chapter to consider:

- the potential benefits, costs and possible problems
- the key roles, responsibilities and both internal and external interfaces
- process details including deliverables, and process management
- tools and techniques to support the process.

1.8 Purpose of the book

The purpose of this book is to give best practice guidance on the planning, design, deployment and ongoing technical support and management of ICT components and services. Good planning, administration and control are key to ensuring that ICT services provide the information flows necessary to implement the effective Information Systems upon which organisations depend to meet business needs cost effectively. This book arranges ICTIM in a practical and structured manner. It presents a framework and the processes surrounding that framework, which can be used to develop appropriate, efficient and effective ICTIM for each specific organisation.

1.9 Target readership

This book is aimed primarily at:

- Business Managers (management summary only)
- business planners and strategists
- business and ICT analysts
- directors of ICT (management summary only)
- ICT Managers and senior managers and their staff
- Network Services Managers and their staff (data and voice teams)

- ICT project managers, implementation project leaders and team members
- ICT Service Managers and their staff
- Service Management Managers, process owners and their staff
- ICT infrastructure planners and designers
- ICT strategists and solution architects
- ICT Deployment Managers and their staff
- ICT Support Managers and their staff
- ICT Operations Managers and their staff
- ICT Administration Managers and their staff
- ICT Development Managers and their staff
- ICT Risk and Security Managers, planners and strategists
- Supplier and Procurement Managers
- ICT supplier and outsourcing organisations
- e-commerce Managers and their staff
- e-business Managers and their staff
- ICT auditors and consultants.

Readers should be aiming to 'adopt and adapt' the practices described in the book, on a scale appropriate to the size and complexity of their organisation, and the services and infrastructure to be managed. It is not essential that all aspects of this book be implemented. It is essential that all aspects are considered and evaluated with reference to the organisation and its requirements. Different elements of the book may be used and adapted in different ways to suit the requirements of specific organisations.

Annex 1A   The role and responsibilities of the ICT Infrastructure Manager

ICT Infrastructure Managers are responsible for the management and overall control of the ICTIM process. Their main objectives are to ensure that the ICTIM processes are defined, adequately resourced, and are effectively governed. They ensure that good relationships are developed with both the business and Service Management to ensure that the scope and overall objectives of ICTIM are defined and agreed.

It is important that the roles and responsibilities of ICTIM personnel are defined and that the interfaces and procedures for interactions between ICTIM and other business and IT disciplines are defined.

ICTIM staff are involved in bringing awareness of the benefits and advantages of effective processes for Design and Planning, Deployment, Operations, and Technical Support. They ensure that ICTIM issues are identified and addressed from the early stages of eliciting business requirements through the procurement process to the testing, installation, deployment, and ongoing support and maintenance of ICT components and services.

An ICT Infrastructure Manager ensures that:

- ICT plans are produced and circulated to the appropriate IT Service Management and Business Management on a regular basis
- changes to architectures, plans, designs, configurations are reviewed and approved
- any changes that impact on the ICT services are appropriately assessed and the risks and impact made clear
- ICT components and services are adequately managed and administered
- ICT components and services are appropriately monitored and that there is adequate funding for the necessary tools to support diagnostic and performance monitoring
- there is adequate monitoring of security and supporting procedures
- there are appropriate plans for recruitment, training and development of ICTIM staff
- the quality and cost of ICT services are monitored and controlled to ensure that they are matched to business needs and are provided within budget
- appropriate regulations and standards are enforced
- regular audits and risk analysis of the ICT infrastructure are conducted
- relationships with suppliers and partners are developed accordingly, with compliance to contractual commitments
- regular reviews of ICTIM processes are performed.

ICT Infrastructure Managers may play a key coordination role as part of a business change programme and in crisis management.

■ ■ ■ ■ ■ ■ ■ ■ ■ ■ ■ ■ ■ ■ ■

2 DESIGN AND PLANNING

2.1 Introduction

The Design and Planning (D and P) processes within an ICT organisation are concerned with providing the overall strategic guidelines for the development and installation of an ICT infrastructure, which satisfies the current and future needs of the business. However, the infrastructure alone cannot deliver quality services, and it is essential that the processes surrounding the technology are also considered by D and P, especially those of Service Management.

In essence, the Design and Planning activities can be defined as:

> **Definition – Design and Planning processes**
>
> **The development and maintenance of ICT Design and Planning strategies and processes for the deployment and implementation of appropriate ICT infrastructure solutions throughout the organisation.**

The work of ICT infrastructure Design and Planning needs to assess and reconcile many types of need, some of which may be in conflict with one another. The work should ensure that:

■ the ICT infrastructure serves the needs of the business, its products and services, and the needs of the IS architecture and strategy

■ the right balance is struck between innovation, risk and cost whilst seeking a competitive edge, where desired by the business

■ there is a good fit with the infrastructures of customers, partners and peers

■ there is compliance with relevant frameworks and standards

■ a coordinated interface is provided between ICT planners and business planners

■ all ICT processes are considered strategically, especially the Service Management processes.

The process should use input from the business, its plans and planners to develop appropriate policies, plans and strategies for all areas of ICT. These plans and strategies should cover all aspects of ICT, including roles and responsibilities, architecture and frameworks, processes and procedures, and management methods.

2.1.1 Basic concepts

Information technology has been widely utilised for the last 40 years but it is only in recent years that the Internet has had a real impact on the business community. That impact has been quite dramatic for some organisations:

'IT is the business.'

and

'The business is IT (or ICT).'

It is essential, therefore, that ICT systems and services are designed, planned, implemented and managed appropriately for the business as a whole.

This is especially true of those businesses that are built and depend upon e-business processes and revenue. However, for all organisations the Internet has had a dramatic impact upon the operation of both the business and ICT. The requirement then, is to provide business processes and ICT services that:

- are flexible and adaptable, yet complete
- can absorb an ever-increasing demand in the volume and speed of change
- provide '24x7' operation
- are responsive with high availability
- are customer oriented, focused and driven.

With all these pressures on both ICT and the business the temptation, and unfortunately the reality in some cases, is to 'cut corners' on the planning processes or to miss them out completely:

'Fail to plan and plan to fail.'

However, in these situations the planning activity is even more essential to the overall delivery of quality services. Therefore, more time should be devoted to the process rather than less.

In general, the key to a successful ITIL project is an appropriate level of planning to determine which projects will have the greatest impact or benefit to the organisation. With the appropriate level of thought, preparation and planning, effort can be targeted at the areas that yield the greatest return rather than those areas where it will be wasted.

Most projects and strategies fail through a lack of planning and preparation. The implementation of ITIL processes is all about the preparation and planning of the effective and efficient use of the three Ps: People, Processes and Products (tools and technology), as illustrated in Figure 2.1.

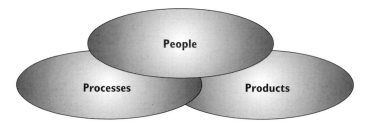

Figure 2.1 – The three Ps: People, Processes and Products

The D and P function should be responsible for developing strategies and plans covering all three areas within this diagram with due regard to the business drivers, Service Level Agreements (SLAs) and Service Level Requirements (SLRs).

However, there is no benefit in producing plans and keeping them to yourself. Plans must be published, agreed, circulated and used. Acceptance and progression of the plans is also important. Therefore, another critical aspect of the planning process is 'the three Cs':

Communicate....
Communicate....
and...Communicate !!

2.1.2   The goals

The specific goals of the D and P processes are to develop and maintain strategies, policies, plans, architectures and frameworks for ICT that can:

- meet the existing ICT requirements of the business
- innovate more effective ICT and business solutions
- be easily developed and enhanced to meet the future business needs of the organisation, within appropriate time-scales and costs
- develop the soft skills within ICT by moving strategy into everyday operational tasks
- make effective and efficient use of all ICT resources and secure ICT environments
- contribute to the improvement of the overall quality of ICT service within the imposed cost constraints
- reduce, minimise or constrain long-term costs.

2.1.3   The scope

The D and P processes should cover all areas of ICT and be closely linked to the overall business planning and design processes. If this is to be accomplished effectively and economically, the documents, processes and activities of business and ICT D and P should be coordinated and synchronised as illustrated in Figure 2.2.

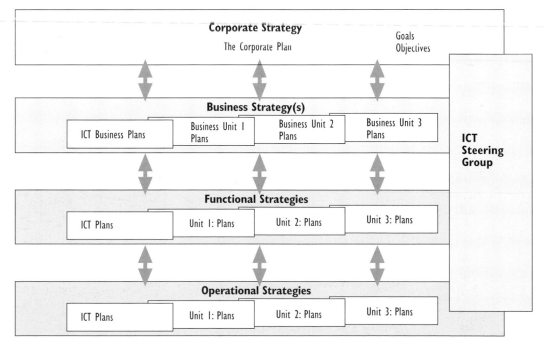

Figure 2.2 – Business strategy and ICT strategy

In order to ensure that business and ICT strategies and plans remain synchronised, many organisations form a joint coordinating body called an IT or ICT Steering Group (ISG or ICTSG). This body consists of senior management representatives from various business areas and ICT. The function of the ISG is to meet regularly and review both the business and ICT plans and strategies to ensure that they are aligned as closely as possible to one another. The ISG should ensure that unrealistic time-scales, which could jeopardise quality or disrupt normal operational requirements, are not imposed or attempted by either the business or ICT.

The scope of the D and P processes can be further refined and developed by considering the inputs required by the process, the supporting processes that contribute to the overall process and the outputs and deliverables generated by the process.

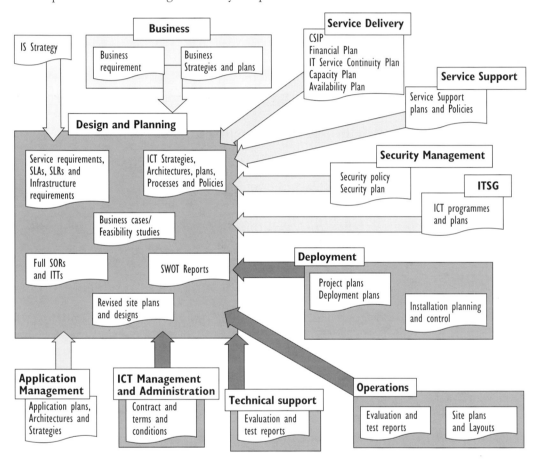

Figure 2.3 – The inputs and deliverables

As shown in Figure 2.3, the complete list of inputs, activities and outputs are:

Inputs

- corporate visions, strategies, objectives, policies and plans
- business visions, strategies, objectives and plans
- existing IS and ICT infrastructure strategies:
  - IS strategies and plans
  - ICT strategies and plans
  - the overall ICT architecture
  - ICT Management architecture and framework

- Service Management visions, strategies, objectives and plans especially:
  - Service Level Management plans, Service Catalogue, service plans and the Continuous Service Improvement Programme (CSIP)
  - Financial Plan
  - Capacity Plan
  - Availability Plan
  - IT Service Continuity Plan
    Service Support and Service Desk plans (incident, problem, change, Configuration and Release Plans)
  - security policies, handbooks and plans

- the current ICT environment:
  - the current enabling technology
  - the current processes and procedures
  - the current staff knowledge and skills
  - the procurement policy, supplier strategy and Supply Chain Management processes
  - the applications strategy and architecture
  - ICT business plan
  - business and ICT Quality Plans and policies.

Processes

- review all input plans and documents
- liaise with all other design and planning activities
- produce and maintain ICT policies and plans
- produce and maintain ICT architectures
- produce and maintain ICT strategies.

Deliverables

- ICT strategies
- ICT policies
- ICT plans
- overall ICT architectures
- Design and Planning processes and procedures
- ICT Management architecture and framework
- ICT D and P standards and policies
- SWOT analysis reports
- business cases and feasibility studies
- Statements of Requirements (SORs) and Invitations to Tender (ITTs)
- project plans
- site plans, schematics and topology diagrams
- comments and feedback on all other plans.

2.1.4 Objectives

The main objectives of the D and P processes are to:

- produce and maintain ICT plans, strategies, policies, architectures and frameworks for the development and implementation of ICT solutions throughout the organisation
- coordinate all aspects of Design and Planning within ICT
- provide coordinated ICT planning interfaces to all business and service planners
- assist in the development of policies and standards in all areas of design, planning and ICT
- receive and act upon feedback from all other areas incorporating the actions into a continual process of improvement.

2.2 Benefits, costs and possible problems

The benefits, costs and possible problems associated with establishing effective Design and Planning processes are provided in this section.

2.2.1 Benefits

The benefits of good ICT Design and Planning practices manifest themselves in two ways:

1 Benefits to the business

- ICT services more closely aligned to business requirements
- improved quality of service and service availability, leading to improved business productivity and revenue
- faster and improved quality of ICT response to business needs
- cost-effective provision of ICT services
- reduced Total Cost of Ownership (TCO) leading to long-term reduction of costs
- planned purchase, development and implementation
- better management information of business processes and services
- improved working relationships with ICT
- faster and better quality projects, deployments and changes (delivered on time, to cost and quality).

2 Benefits to ICT

- ICT services more closely aligned to business requirements
- increased productivity of key ICT personnel, with more efficient use of resources, leading to reduced incident and problem resolution times
- more proactive development and improvement of technology and services
- reduced risk of service failure
- ability to handle higher volumes of projects and changes with better management, coordination and reduced adverse impact on the delivery of ICT services

- faster exploitation of appropriate ICT technology, driven by business needs
- better and more informed planning and acquisition of ICT components and services
- services and systems designed to meet achievable business and operational targets and time-scales
- better management of suppliers with improved supplier performance
- reduced risk of failure in meeting commitments
- improved working relationships with business.

2.2.2 Costs

The costs associated with an effective and efficient ICT Design and Planning process are:

- an increased need for management time and planning resources
- staff recruitment, development, training and accommodation
- the development of processes, procedures and documentation
- procurement of additional tools, hardware and software
- communication strategies, publication, deployment and training
- the implementation of cultural change programmes.

2.2.3 Possible problems

Some of the principal problems that may be associated with the establishment of an ICT Design and Planning process are:

- lack of management commitment
- inadequate resources, budget and time
- a resistance to planning and a reluctance to be proved wrong ('hindsight is a wonderful thing')
- a lack of corporate objectives, strategies, policies, and business direction
- inefficient use of resources causing wasted spend and investment
- lack of knowledge and appreciation of business impacts and priorities
- diverse and disparate technologies and applications
- resistance to change and cultural change
- lack of planning leading to knee-jerk reactions and unplanned purchase
- poor relationships, communication and a lack of cooperation between ICT and the business
- ICT dictating to the business, or the business dictating to ICT. It must be a balanced partnership to succeed, with the business leading the partnership
- lack of training or inadequate management of the succession cycle in the replacement of staff
- constraints posed by old technology and legacy systems and networks
- unrealistic business perceptions and expectations with a low success rate in ICT delivery
- lack of tools, standards and skills

- tools too complex and costly to implement and maintain
- lack of information, monitoring and measurements
- unreasonable targets and time-scales, e.g., service targets, Service Level Agreements (SLAs) and Operational Level Agreements (OLAs)
- over-commitment of resources with an associated inability to deliver (e.g., projects always late or over budget)
- poor Supplier Management and/or poor supplier performance
- lack of customer awareness and cost consciousness within ICT.

2.3 The roles, responsibilities and interfaces

The D and P processes are concerned with establishing the effectiveness and efficiency of the overall ICTIM process with due regard to interfaces, thus ensuring an overall productive quality workflow.

2.3.1 The roles and responsibilities

The roles and responsibilities of staff within D and P should be closely aligned to the overall workflow and the processes involved within ICT.

The two key roles and responsibilities within D and P are those of the ICT Planner and the ICT Designer:

- The **ICT Planner/Strategist** is concerned with the coordination of all ICT plans and strategies. Their main objectives are to develop ICT plans and strategies that meet and continue to meet the ICT requirements of the business, and coordinate, measure and review the implementation progress of all ICT strategies and plans.
- The **ICT Designer/Architect** is concerned with the overall coordination and design of the ICT infrastructure. Their main objectives are to:
  - design a secure and resilient ICT infrastructure that meets all the current and anticipated future ICT requirements of the organisation
  - produce and maintain all ICT design, architectural, policy and specification documentation.

To perform these roles, it is necessary for staff to have good knowledge and practical experience of Project Management, methods and principles. Full definitions of these two roles are contained in Annex 2A.

2.3.2 Organisational structure

In Section 1.6.1, centralised and distributed ICTIM was discussed. ICTIM staff are normally centrally located within a business, although it is not uncommon for some ICT staff to be distributed in order to provide localised operational support on a day-to-day basis. However, D and P staff are normally located centrally, but are involved in establishing plans for any distributed resources.

The planning process is vital to the successful operation. D and P are likely to be involved in planning any distributed support roles. Such plans must be realistic and agreed by all parties.

The first steps in producing viable plans are to agree a centralised coordination function and to recognise the need for agreed working practices to be implemented between central and distributed staff. To be beneficial these agreed working practices must have the support of all ICT Management and staff and all Business Management and staff. It is necessary to recognise the need for two different functions:

- **Distributed Service Administrators (DSAs)**: these are the staff located in the vicinity of the distributed users and services, with administrative responsibility for their local ICT service and infrastructure. Good liaison with customers and users, and high-quality local service provision is of paramount importance to the DSAs.

- **Distributed Service Administration Coordination (DSAC)**: this is a centrally located function concerned with providing coordination and guidance for all DSAs within an organisation. If consistency throughout the organisation is to be achieved, it is vital that good methods of management, planning and communication are established between DSAC, DSAs and the business units.

The responsibility for deciding the split in roles and functionality should reside with overall ICT Management and the D and P function. The factors affecting this decision include:

- size, complexity and geographical distribution of the organisation
- culture of the organisation
- diversity of the services, the business and the business functions
- availability of staff resources, skills and knowledge in both ICT and the business units
- current power, complexity and distribution of the ICT infrastructure
- planned power, complexity and distribution of the ICT infrastructure
- remote management capability of the distributed infrastructure
- need for local support and assistance
- costs associated with installing and operating centralised and distributed staff and systems.

The typical areas of the ICT infrastructure administered by the DSAs are:

- distributed networking equipment
- distributed PABX equipment
- distributed server equipment
- desktop systems (hardware and software)
- mobile access devices, e.g., laptops, mobile phones, palmtop and hand-held equipment
- telephones, pagers and faxes
- equipment used for home working
- specialist front office equipment (e.g., Electronic Point-of-Sale (EPOS) and Electronic Funds Transfer (EFT) equipment).

These areas of the ICT infrastructure are typically the least likely to be accurately controlled and managed. Therefore, there is an urgent requirement for most organisations to establish these roles and responsibilities, as some organisations may have up to half of the components within these areas unaccounted for. Examples of the responsibilities of DSAs and DSAC have been included within Appendix E.

2.3.3 External interfaces

There are several major interfaces with areas outside the ICTIM function. The principal ones are:

- Corporate Management
- Business Management
- Service Management
- Application Management.

These interfaces are essential to the smooth operation of an ICT department and, as such, need to be agreed, well established, effective and efficient. The ISG is a crucial link, providing a vital bridging function between the business and ICT, ensuring that the key ICT projects and programmes are driven by business needs and business priorities.

The influence of Corporate Management, Business Management and the ISG within an organisation are illustrated in Figure 2.2.

Corporate Management

Clear and effective corporate strategy, vision, objectives and management are vital to the planning of a successful ICT function. The production of the corporate strategy, vision and objectives, provides important information and explicit documentation that should trigger other planning review cycles. This will ensure that all other strategies are kept in line with the overall corporate strategy, vision and plans.

Organisations differ in their strategic planning activities and cycles, and in the types of strategy produced. Some organisations prefer 'hybrid strategies' based on a combination of different types, whereas others make a conscious decision to develop a specific type of strategy. In some organisations, the strategy evolves and develops organically over time.

> **Key message**
>
> **The most vital consideration for any ICT strategy is that its type and content should be closely aligned with the type and content of the business strategy or strategies of the organisation.**

Business Management

Business Management should have a shared vision and set their management objectives. Each business unit within the organisation should develop their own business, functional, and operational plans to achieve their objectives.

The D and P function within ICT plays a key role in aligning the ICT business, functional, and operational plans with those of the business – see Figure 2.2.

Key message

This activity of aligning ICT business, functional and operational plans with those of the business is often missing or poorly addressed in many organisations. It is essential that if ICT services are genuinely going to be aligned with business requirements this activity is given full focus and commitment at senior level.

Many organisations are appointing e-business Managers or functions within their organisations. These functions are charged with developing strategies, visions and objectives for all e-business and e-commerce operations within the organisation. These Business Managers need to actively engage and work closely with ICT Management, and liaise with D and P.

Service Management

The D and P processes within ICTIM principally need to interface with the more proactive Service Delivery processes and plans, as indicated in Figure 2.4, although there is also a need to be aware of Service Support processes and plans.

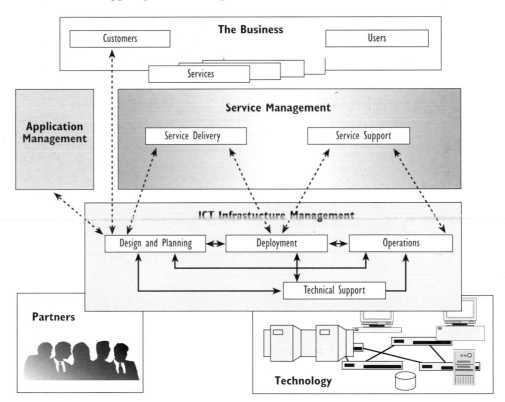

Figure 2.4 – Design and Planning interfaces

The principal aspects of the interfaces are as follows:

- **Service Level Management (SLM)** is the process concerned with managing the quality and level of ICT service delivered to the business. The main areas of interest to D and P are:
  - the Service Catalogue

- SLAs and SLRs
- service plans, reviews and reports
- the Continuous Service Improvement Programme (CSIP)
- supplier contract and support OLA information, such as details of Service Level targets

The D and P function will need to work closely with SLM to ensure that the infrastructure provides and continues to provide the quality and level of service documented within agreed SLAs and SLRs. The CSIP should be used to continually improve the levels of service delivered.

- **IT Service Continuity Management** is the process for ensuring that the ICT service resilience and recovery is appropriate to the business impact and disruption caused by the loss of the service. It is one of the most valuable Service Management processes and provides:

  - the IT Service Continuity Plans
  - Business Impact Analysis (BIA) information
  - risk analysis and Management information

- **Financial Management for IT services** is the process of management and control of all financial resources within the ICT function. It principally supplies D and P with:

  - the financial plan
  - costs, budgets and charges
  - the cost of functions and processes
  - the cost of failures

- **Availability Management** is concerned with ensuring that the availability targets agreed within SLAs are met or exceeded. The main value to D and P is in the:

  - Availability Plan
  - Availability measures and guidelines for new services
  - Availability reviews and reports
  - identification of weak or failing components within the ICT infrastructure
  - Component Failure Impact Analysis (CFIA) information

- **Capacity Management** produces plans for the capacity and performance of all services and ICT components to support the existing and predicted service levels. In order to do this Capacity Management will provide:

  - the Capacity Plan
  - the Capacity Management Database (CDB)
  - infrastructure usage and trends
  - capacity reviews and reports
  - facilities for modelling and prototyping of new services and existing services and systems
  - the current workloads and schedules

- **Service Desk** provides a single point of contact for all customers and users on all aspects of the usage of ICT functions. It is principally of value in supplying D and P with:

  - a valuable set of management information
  - customer satisfaction feedback

- **Incident Management and Problem Management** provide integrated processes for the management of all incidents, problems and known errors associated with the ICT infrastructure and services. The processes supply:

- valuable management information on incidents, problems and known errors
- areas of proactive improvement

■ **Configuration Management** provides a single process for the control of all ICT assets and configuration information, including:

- the Configuration Management Database (CMDB)
- Configuration Management plans
- status information on all components of the ICT infrastructure
- topology and schematic connectivity and relationship information
- service and component impact information

■ **Change Management** provides a single process for the control and management of all changes and provides:

- the Forward Schedule of Change
- details of all changes, change status and change plans

■ **Release Management** is a single process for the control and management of all releases and provides:

- Release Plans, policies and contents
- the Definitive Hardware Store (DHS)
- the Definitive Software Library (DSL)
- Release implementation plans and schedules.

More detailed information on the Service Management processes can be found in the ITIL books, *Service Delivery* and *Service Support*.

Application Management

Application Management is concerned with all aspects of the application lifecycle including: Requirements Management, design and development, and maintenance. The main points of interest to D and P within this area are:

- applications strategy
- application design architecture and concepts
- application development plans and policies
- applications requirements
- applications work programmes
- applications development projects and schedules

2.3.4   Internal interfaces

The D and P processes have internal interfaces with all the other ICT Management processes, namely:

- ICTIM overall functions, including administration
- Technical Support
- Deployment
- Operations.

An overall schematic diagram of the various processes involved in ICTIM is shown in Figure 2.4 and the internal interfaces with D and P are described below:

■ **Overall ICTIM and Administration** is concerned with the overall management and administration of all ICT issues. D and P would report to the overall ICTIM function and would require knowledge of, and be supported by, the ICT administration function and processes.

■ **Technical Support** is concerned with providing the overall technical support for all ICT systems in use within the organisation. D and P would require assistance and support on ICT technical issues from this area.

■ **Deployment** is concerned with the deployment and implementation of business solutions. D and P would require advice and guidance on all aspects of deployment within the organisation.

■ **Operations** is concerned with providing effective and efficient operational management of all live ICT systems. D and P would require information and advice on all operational aspects from Operations.

D and P would provide strategic design and planning direction, advice and guidance on all aspects of ICT to all the ICTIM processes.

2.4   The management processes involved

Good management systems make effective and efficient use of the people, processes and products. For truly effective management, the interaction between these must be understood in order for the management system to meet its objectives. The interactions between the components of a management system are illustrated in Figure 2.5.

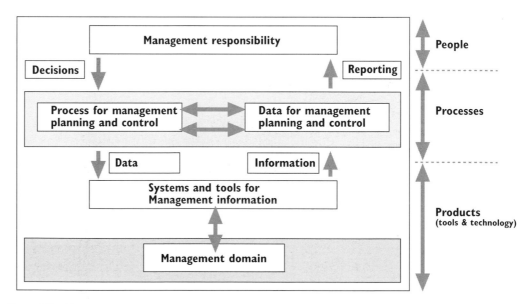

Figure 2.5 – Management system components

The quality of the information and the reporting delivered by a process will greatly influence the quality of the decisions made. However, each management process and domain cannot function in isolation. It is essential that all the management systems and process within an organisation be integrated with each other. In order to make quality decisions, reports and information are often required from many different management domains and processes. Therefore, in the most effective ICT groups, the people, the processes and the products of each ICT Management system are fully integrated; indeed, the best of all are those where the ICT Management systems are fully integrated with management systems throughout the organisation.

It is essential that the ICT D and P processes are inherently linked to all other D and P processes within the organisation, and that improvements and developments are reflected across corresponding processes.

2.4.1   Strategic management

There are four key tasks of strategic management:

1   reviewing the current position

2   defining the required or desired state

3   designing and implementing a plan to migrate to the desired state

4   reviewing and evaluating the progress of the plan.

These are ongoing tasks and should be completed on a regular basis as illustrated in Figure 2.6. These are the adaptation of the fundamental concepts of a continual process of improvement: Review, Revise, Plan, and Implement.

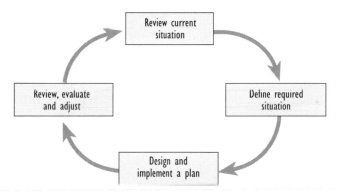

Figure 2.6 – The four key tasks of strategic management

These key tasks are covered in detail in the following four sections.

2.4.2   Reviewing the current position

This task consists of reviewing all aspects of the current ICT organisation. It can be completed in many different ways, for example:

■ internal review and/or internal audit

■ external review and/or external audit

■ internal benchmarking and/or external benchmarking.

It may use any one of the above mechanisms, and often a combination of techniques is employed. A review should consider all aspects of the ICT operation including:

■ the organisation, its culture, its goals and its businesses including where ICT fits within the overall structure

- all ICT Management and planning aspects
- all technological aspects
- the ICT services and the quality of the delivery of those services
- people issues covering resource levels, skills, knowledge
- processes, policies and procedures
- all aspects of documentation
- geographical aspects, locations and environments
- external influences and factors, e.g., industry trends and market developments.

One of the most common techniques used for this review is the SWOT analysis. This technique focuses on the internal and external influences and factors, and is named after the four perspectives that are analysed, namely the strengths, weaknesses, opportunities and threats. It focuses on the influences and factors, for example, industry trends and market developments, and their effects by examining:

- **Strengths** – e.g., assets, image, brands, skills, expertise, attributes and alliances, quality of service

- **Weaknesses** – e.g., high costs, low quality, lack of capacity, loss of skills, old technology, out-of-date processes

- **Opportunities** – e.g., additional potential customers, new services or products, changes in regulations or standards, social or cultural change, new technology

- **Threats** – e.g., shrinking market, new competition, new legislation, economic change, new methods.

This analysis can be used as a basis for developing the future direction of ICT within the organisation, as shown in Figure 2.7.

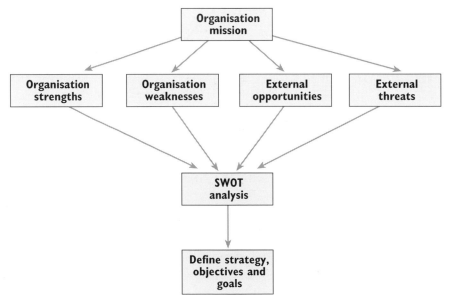

Figure 2.7 – SWOT Analysis

The information gained from a SWOT analysis can be used to determine the areas that need to be focused on within an organisation in order to achieve its mission.

2.4.3　Defining the required or desired state

This involves analysing the information contained within the review of the current situation and identifying areas that need to be addressed and improved. This should include some form of prioritisation of these areas so that improvement activities can be ordered into an appropriate schedule. Once the current situation has been fully understood, the future desired position can be defined. This will consist of three distinct but related activities:

- producing a strategic vision of the future
- setting goals and objectives
- developing a strategy to achieve the objectives.

Targets, goals and objectives will need to be defined in measurable terms and often there will be a conflict between the desired state and the available budget, invariably leading to a compromise between available funds and the desired position.

Senior ICT Management and an ICT strategic planning team often complete these tasks jointly.

Producing a strategic vision

This sets out the senior ICT Management vision of where ICT is intended to go. It involves the development of a 'road map' of the future direction of ICT and identifies the capabilities and competencies that ICT plans to develop or acquire. In its simplest form, this may consist of a mission statement but in other cases, it may be a more detailed document containing details of a two- or five-year plan.

> **Key message**
>
> **Successful designers and planners often use the information obtained from the SWOT analysis to:**
>
> - **develop and exploit the organisation's strengths**
> - **reduce, minimise or remove weaknesses**
> - **exploit and grow opportunities**
> - **manage and reduce threats**
> - **create new strategies, set objectives and goals and assess their likelihood of being achieved.**

Setting goals and objectives

The purpose of this task is to develop the goals and objectives that underpin the achievement of the strategic vision. These should be the overall performance targets for ICT and can be expressed in terms of:

- defined goals and objectives
- deliverables and Critical Success Factors (CSFs)
- metrics and Key Performance Indicators (KPIs).

There should be clear and measurable targets that relate to the ICT organisation as a whole. They should consist of short-term, medium-term and long-term goals that can facilitate the development of a results-oriented culture throughout the ICT organisation.

All ICT Managers should then develop objectives and goals within their own areas that underpin the strategic goals and objectives of the ICT organisation as a whole. This will ensure that all the groups and teams involved within ICT are working together to achieve common goals and objectives rather than pulling in opposite directions and working against each other to achieve individual objectives.

Developing a strategy

Once the strategic vision, the goals and objectives have been agreed, a corresponding strategy can be produced. This strategy needs to cover:

- organisation, culture and business units
- culture and values within ICT
- ICT products and services
- functions, roles and responsibilities
- processes.

It should utilise the SWOT analysis of ICT and endeavour to:

- build on the strengths
- minimise the weaknesses
- develop and take advantage of the opportunities
- reduce or counteract the threats.

The strategy should be a clear and concise, dynamic document. It should not be allowed to become stale or stagnate. A strategy enables the organisation to proactively plan for future improvement and development of the ICT business and react and adapt to changing situations. Therefore, the strategy must not only be reviewed on an annual basis in line with business and organisational strategies and plans, but also whenever there is significant change in any of the aspects affecting its production. The best ICT strategies are those driven from the organisation, customer and business perspective, rather than those that simply focus on ICT issues.

All ICT strategies should, like good business strategies, be based on prudent business risk. It is only by taking justifiable risk that ICT organisations can develop, grow and support the developing business needs of the organisation. In some cases, the growth of ICT can actually lead to growth and expansion of the business or organisation itself. Often the development and implementation of an ICT strategy will necessitate the restructuring of the ICT group in order to succeed. In some cases, it can actually require restructuring of the organisation itself.

2.4.4   Designing and implementing a plan

Managing the implementation of the strategy is simpler and easier to achieve if the internal ICT processes and strategic objectives are closely aligned to the organisation's processes and strategic objectives. It is the most time-consuming and complex of all the activities associated with strategic management. Management of the implementation process requires assessment of what it will take to implement the project and what must be done to create the most appropriate plan for efficient and effective implementation. The project and its plan should be subject to appropriate Risk Management and will need to be adjusted and refined within its lifecycle. All managers and staff within ICT need to be aware of their obligation and contribution to the success of the implementation process.

Managing the implementation process is an intensive activity that requires to be run as a carefully managed project, namely by:

- developing an ICT group capable of successful implementation of the strategy
- raising the awareness and the profile of the strategy within and outside ICT and the need for its success
- securing the budget and resources to support the implementation of the strategy
- developing processes and procedures to support the strategy
- creating a supportive working environment and culture
- ensuring that leadership is provided to continually improve the quality of the implementation and that all ICT Management supports the strategy and implementation leadership
- making strategy part of 'everyone's everyday job' and motivating all members of the ICT group to support and assist the implementation of the strategy and reduce and remove processes that inhibit or obstruct the implementation
- implementing best practice and continual improvement programmes.

> **Key message**
>
> **The secret to the successful implementation of a strategy is to plan small measurable steps with regular deliverables, measurements, milestones and reviews.**

2.4.5 Reviewing and evaluating progress of the plan

Reviewing and evaluating the progress of the implementation project is a regular and continual activity. All managers within ICT should be responsible for evaluating progress towards strategic objectives. This should consist of:

- evaluating overall ICT group performance
- evaluating individual team performance
- evaluating individual performance
- assessing external developments outside ICT
- obtaining and acting upon feedback from all areas.

These progress reviews will trigger corrective action where:

- the business or organisational strategy changes
- the plan fails or starts to fail
- circumstances change
- targets need raising or lowering.

These corrective actions or adjustments to the plan will need agreement and sign-off, and will necessitate the commitment of additional resources, budget or time. A Balanced Scorecard (BSC) (see Section 2.7.1) can be used as a mechanism for reviewing and evaluating progress against the overall strategy.

> **Key messages**
>
> 1   It must be recognised that the BSC only measures the implementation of strategy. It does not actually create the strategy, nor does it indicate whether the strategy is the right one for the organisation. The strategy must be continually appraised to ensure that it is the most appropriate for the organisation.
>
> 2   If the content of the strategy is allowed to change freely, the rate of change could exceed progress and could get out of alignment with the BSC.

2.4.6   Planning issues

The ICT infrastructure is the physical vehicle for providing ICT services. Its scope, scale and architecture should, therefore, be determined by the level of service to be provided. The objective of planning is to create the environment in which the agreed service levels can be provided.

The planner is required to anticipate the services required in the medium and longer term. Therefore, planning should start with the view of the future contained in the corporate and business strategies of the parent organisation. These should be complemented with the details of specific requirements, articulated in programme and project requirements, as they emerge.

The issue facing business organisations is the extent to which corporate ICT infrastructure investment will bring benefits unobtainable when ICT infrastructure is split between business areas. If central corporate investment is justified, questions may remain as to the commitment of all the managers involved. It is essential that, whatever approach is taken to investment, it is undertaken with full agreement and commitment from all concerned at the corporate and business unit levels.

Many senior Business Managers are aware of how important ICT infrastructure has become to their organisation. Like the services built on it, the infrastructure must be cost-effective, lean, secure, resilient yet adaptable; the ICT strategy and subsequent planning work will define the nature of the infrastructure.

The business may wish to retain control over the technical policy for the ICT infrastructure and ownership of its architectural design.

Various initiatives, particularly within Government, such as 'market testing', have drawn attention to the question of who is to provide the ICT capabilities. Not only is there a need to achieve value for money, but also there is a legitimate questioning of the ability of ICT directorates to respond to changing needs within the required time-scales, at affordable prices and with appropriate services and systems of the desired quality.

The provision of ICT infrastructure is a joint responsibility of the ICT provider and the business. While the provider is likely to be responsible for the day-to-day provision and satisfactory operation of the ICT infrastructure, the business or 'informed customer' should agree technical policies governing the standards to which the infrastructure must adhere. In addition, management policies that set the rules for changes to the infrastructure should also possibly be agreed.

The depth of coverage of these policies depends on the extent to which the business wishes to control the make-up of the ICT infrastructure. Such control may be needed by the business for a number of reasons:

- to manage change
- to decide the user interface at workstations
- to ensure software is portable, compatible and consistent
- to ensure the customer's systems are not locked into proprietary architectures
- to ensure conformance to international or European standards
- to give confidence that infrastructure capacity will be matched with demand and business need
- to give the customer confidence that systems supporting different parts of the business can be linked to the extent required.

Where ownership of the infrastructure is transferred to the provider, the provider is likely to be free to accommodate other business's services on any spare capacity. In such circumstances, compromises may be needed to obtain a best fit of the infrastructure to the various needs of a number of business units or customers. If ownership is transferred to the provider, the business or 'informed customer' needs to take steps to ensure its systems can continue to run at the end of the contract.

Ownership of the infrastructure can of course remain with the business or customer. In these circumstances, a single function may exist in the business or customer organisation to take responsibility for all aspects of ICT service provision; or that responsibility can be devolved to the various business units. In either case, the owning authority – the organisation or the business units – will take their own decisions about the make-up of the infrastructure. Usually, it is desirable for there to be some coordination at the centre and some policies that apply across the whole organisation to the infrastructure. Generally the provider is required to provide information, for instance, on demand for ICT capacity and advice, or on infrastructure developments to help the business make decisions on future infrastructure needs. However, it is recommended that advice on infrastructure advances also be obtained independently.

The SLA or contract will specify quality requirements for the service to be provided, which means that the quality of infrastructure and of its operation, maintenance and support are covered implicitly. The respective responsibilities of provider and customer need to be defined clearly in the contract.

Expenditure on ICT infrastructure is an investment, because it involves spending money in the short term in order to gain long-term benefits. Therefore, it is normal to subject it to an investment appraisal as part of the process of gaining authority to proceed. In the course of undertaking such investment appraisals a number of issues usually arise, namely:

- approval for expenditure is often given on a project-by-project basis
- economic benefits are often not directly attributable to infrastructure projects
- accurately forecasting capacity requirements may be difficult
- the relatively large scale of ICT infrastructure investments makes such investments the object of considerable analysis.

2.5   The processes and deliverables of strategic planning

The purpose of an IT Infrastructure is to support the attainment of business goals through efficient and effective use of ICT systems. Consequently, business needs have to be translated into supporting technology. This section describes a model of how this process might be viewed.

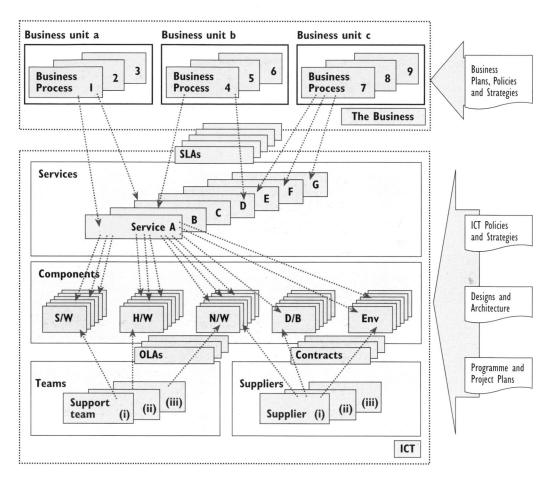

Figure 2.8 – ICT infrastructure model

Figure 2.8 illustrates the fact that business units and processes are dependent upon ICT services, ICT services are dependent upon the technology infrastructure and its constituent components, and these components are supported by internal support teams and external suppliers. The interfaces between the ICT services and the business are documented within SLAs, and the interfaces between support teams and suppliers are documented and agreed within OLAs and Underpinning Contracts. The contents and use of these documents is described within the *Service Delivery* and *Service Support* books of the ITIL library.

Key messages

1   Planning should not be a last minute exercise, but the result of forward thinking made possible by the involvement of ICT planners at all levels of planning and policy-making.

2   ICT infrastructure should not be planned in a piecemeal manner, but in total and in a way that supports the ICT strategy as a whole, strategically, tactically and operationally. This makes it possible to achieve the benefits of a good infrastructure by achieving economies of scale and optimisation.

The aim of strategic planning is to design the ICT services and infrastructure required to support the business and its needs. This requires a process of identifying the customers with shared business interests, determining the technical capability required to support the IT services demanded, designing the appropriate architectures and selecting the IT components to form the 'provided' infrastructure.

A business community may be business-unit-based (in which case, applications and data, as well as technical infrastructure, typically are shared), or it may exist only to share technical resources for reasons of proximity, coincidence of technical need or by needs arising from a departmental strategy. The concept of business community increasingly extends beyond the organisational and legal boundaries of many enterprises in order to facilitate the integration of ICT into external business processes.

ICT infrastructure can also be shared among client organisations of a Facilities Managed (FM) provider or outsourcing organisation. The motivation, in this case, is the cost effective use of the infrastructure and its support personnel to allow the FM provider or outsourcer to offer an economic service to its clients.

It is important that the ICT strategy is:

- aligned with the business strategy and plans
- appropriate, realistic and achievable
- business focused
- balanced between short-term and long-term objectives
- timely and feasible
- cost-effective
- includes implementation milestones that are measurable.

As shown in Figure 2.9, ICT planning takes place at many levels, from strategy through to operational infrastructure planning and is greatly influenced by all levels of business strategy and planning.

An ICT strategy is considered a prerequisite to coherent ICT infrastructure planning, tactical planning and operational planning. The overall planning process should progress through the levels shown in Figure 2.10.

Figure 2.10 illustrates that the strategies, policies and architectures are not only active and proactive documents, but are also reactive. These documents should be aligned to the strategic corporate and business documents and provide forward direction for the development of ICT, but

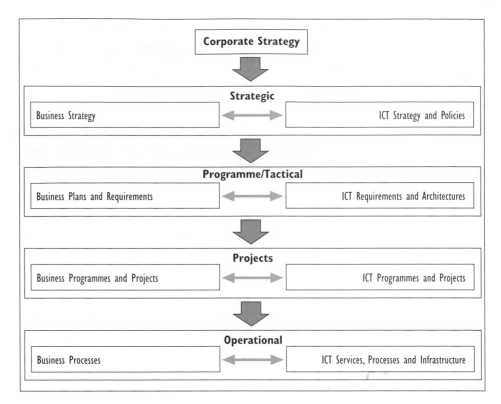

Figure 2.9 – Business and ICT planning levels

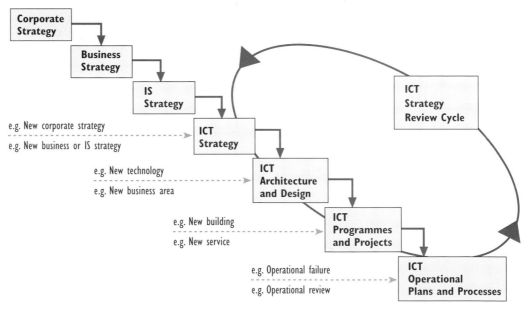

Figure 2.10 – Planning levels and triggers

they must also react to the relevant events and triggers to ensure that ICT is developed in an appropriate way, learning from its experiences.

It should be recognised that ICT infrastructure is a long-term investment, which will evolve with changing business needs and changes in the levels of demand for existing services. Thus, as shown previously, there will be different entry points to ICT planning when it becomes necessary to:

- support a new business unit
- provide a new business service

- improve performance of systems and services
- meet increasing demand or rectify shortfalls in required operational characteristics
- substitute components within agreed operating budgets.

A strategic approach should be adopted with regard to the planning of an ICT infrastructure. This implies creating '*architectures*' or '*blueprints*' for the long-term framework of the ICT infrastructure required to support an ICT strategy. The investment involved can be considerable and great care should be taken to adopt the right approach for securing financial approval to invest in ICT infrastructure. Planners should understand that they need to build confidence in, and backing for, any proposed business case.

At the outset, it is worth ensuring that the appropriate financial approval process is understood. To begin with it is important to identify the approval process and body or bodies concerned. Having determined where the authority for approval lies it may be useful to discuss the case for ICT infrastructure expenditure with that authority before a case is submitted.

ICT planners should be aware of the difference between an overall business approval, as can be given to a business programme, an ICT strategy or an infrastructure plan, and a business case approval. It is only the latter which is an approval to spend money. In the case of ICT it is normally given at the project level. Therefore, it is best if the architectures for ICT infrastructure can be implemented in stages so that funds are requested only for what is clearly necessary.

Key message

Financial approval bodies are not primarily interested in technical arguments. To be successful a business case must relate costs to business benefits, using sound methods of investment appraisal.

The development of an ICT strategy is a complex and demanding task. It is vital, therefore, that the appropriate time and resources are invested into the development of the strategy. The best ICT strategies are driven by the business and business needs. Therefore, as shown in Figures 2.10 and 2.11, the triggers for the development and revision of the ICT strategy should be the development and revision of business strategies and plans.

Strategic planning is a valuable mechanism for realising integration and alignment between ICT and the business. It is imperative that it is used to facilitate convergence of ICT and business people and processes rather than divergence. ICT needs to be driven and directed by the business – although in some cases it is necessary for ICT to lead and stimulate the business – but not in a dictatorial or prescriptive manner. ICT and the business need to work together in partnership to support the creation, evolution and development of new business opportunities, business models and business processes. ICT has a responsibility to the business in the explanation and justification of how new technology can contribute to the transformation of business processes and efficiency.

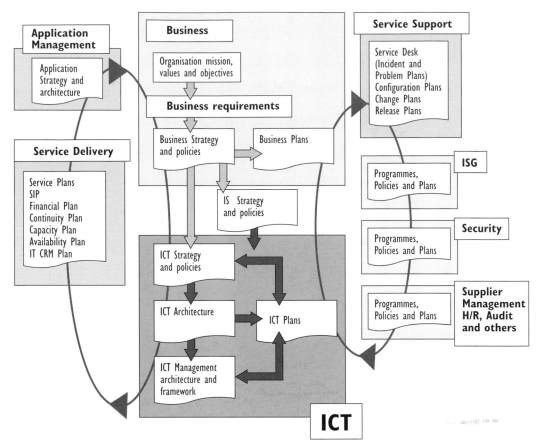

Figure 2.11 – The development of ICT strategies and plans

Key messages

1   The strategic documents should be coordinated between the business and ICT to ensure that they are aligned and integrated.

2   The strategic ICT documents should be used to coordinate, plan and manage all aspects of the ICT infrastructure.

3   The strategic documents should be subjected to Change Management and full impact assessment.

Sometimes other external events will trigger the re-evaluation and modification of the ICT plans and strategies (see Figure 2.10). All the available inputs should be reviewed each time the ICT plans and strategies are revised.

In situations where planning is being carried out at the strategic, tactical and operational levels and re-evaluation is being triggered by external events, the plans can lose their alignment to the overall detriment of the planning process. It is important that there is an effective ICT strategy review cycle and Change Management process.

Having established consistency between strategic and infrastructure planning, the IT planner remains faced with the need to present a sound case. Essentially, the problems are the same as those of any planner wishing to justify investment. When expenditure and benefits occur over time one has to make quantitative judgements about future events that become less certain the further in the future they occur. Therefore, the first task is to address the uncertainties inherent in making a case for investment expenditure, and to do so in a way that avoids the temptation to minimise the costs and unrealistically inflate the benefits.

It has been typical of ICT infrastructure investments that their profiles of expenditure and benefits have shown high initial costs arising from the use of corporate resources (such as mainframes, networks and databases). It is not uncommon for the initial costs to swamp the projected benefits arising from the first one or two business projects using the infrastructure. Moreover, when ICT infrastructure is designed for sharing between business areas, often in the interest of economies of scale, the more likely it is that heavy initial costs will arise.

Such patterns of cashflow present problems of justification because it is easier to justify a case in which the balance between benefits and costs occurs sooner rather than later. Therefore, from an investment appraisal point of view it is sensible to plan the build-up of infrastructure in an incremental manner wherever possible, for example, by installing equipment that can be upgraded on site. Fortunately technical developments, such as the use of high speed LANs and the technology of distributed processing, may distribute or even remove some of the 'major spends' of IT Infrastructure investments.

It is the nature of investment that costs are incurred in the relatively predictable short term in order to achieve benefits that, because they occur later, are less predictable. A business case will be strengthened if the uncertainties of estimating are made clear and squarely faced. Such an approach will help to reinforce confidence. A case in point is the issue of the Capacity Plan. Capacity is planned to meet immediate and anticipated demands, and ICT Service Providers are only too familiar with the experience of running out of capacity at inconvenient times. These problems arise from the uncertainties surrounding estimates of both demand and capacity. Regarding the latter, it must be admitted that, in spite of modelling and other mathematical techniques, the ability to predict the behaviour of a complex system remains inexact, or at best difficult to achieve. Quite sensibly, a contingency allowance is incorporated into the planned capacity. To be acceptable this should be quantified in terms of the uncertainties surrounding the estimates of demand and capacity. It should never represent a purely speculative investment in infrastructure.

2.5.1   The ICT business plans

Every ICT organisation should be run as a business within a business. It should, therefore, have a business plan. The principal aims of an ICT business plan are to:

- provide a justification for investment from Business Managers, senior management and the board in ICT
- give direction and motivation to everyone working within the ICT organisation
- set ICT performance targets and measurements.

Therefore, an ICT business plan should:

- be clear, concise, structured, honest and achievable
- contain a marketing plan for the development of ICT services
- make reference to all ICT strategies
- clarify visions, goals and objectives for the short, medium and long term
- describe the products and services offered and their corresponding customers and markets

- outline internal and external, organisational, structural and cultural issues
- summarise the strategies to be implemented
- contain summaries of budgets and recoveries, with preferred courses of action and possibly costed alternatives
- have clear measurements, targets, CSFs and KPIs with associated time-scales, for ICT as whole ICT teams and individuals
- refer to and detail dependencies on strategic partners, suppliers and outsourcers
- list key risks that must be mitigated to ensure success.

2.5.2   The ICT architectures

As mentioned previously, a strategic approach should be adopted with regard to the planning of an ICT infrastructure. This implies creating '*architectures*' or '*blueprints*' for the long-term framework of the ICT infrastructure. ICT planners, designers and architects need to understand the business, the requirements and the current ICT infrastructure in order to develop appropriate ICT architectures for the short, medium and long term.

Architectures need to be developed within the major areas of:

- technology
- management of the technology.

These architectures are discussed in the following sections:

Technology architectures

Architectures are needed in all areas of ICT infrastructure. Where relevant they need to be developed in:

- overall infrastructure design and architecture
- information security measures, including firewalls, authentication and security systems
- Knowledge Management and data management
- Application Management
- e-commerce and e-business
- central server and mainframe architectures
- distributed regional servers, including local file and print servers
- data networks (LANs, MANs, WANs, protocols, etc.)
- Internet, intranet and extranet systems
- voice networks (PABXs, Centrex, handsets, mobiles, faxes, etc.)
- client systems (desktop PCs, laptop PCs, etc.)
- mobile access devices (handheld devices, mobile phones, palmtops, scanners, etc.)
- storage devices, Storage Area Networks (SANs), Network Attached Storage (NAS), data warehousing and data mining
- backup and recovery systems and services (servers, robots, etc.)
- document storage, handling and management
- e-mail, groupware applications, office automation and other desktop applications

- specialist areas of technology such as EPOS, ATMs, scanning devices, GPS systems, etc.

This will result in a hierarchy of architectures, which will need to be dovetailed together to construct an integrated set of technology architectures for the organisation.

Management architectures

There are two separate approaches to developing a management architecture:

- **selecting a proprietary management architecture:** this is based upon selecting a single set of management products and tools from a single proprietary management solutions supplier. This approach will normally require less effort but will often mean that compromises will have to be made with management functionality and facilities, which may result in gaps and disappointments

- **selecting a 'best of breed' architecture:** this approach involves the selection of a set of 'best of breed' management tools and products from a number of management solutions suppliers and then integrating them to provide a comprehensive management solution. This will generally require more effort in the integration of the tools into a single comprehensive management solution but will often provide greater management functionality and facilities leading to long-term cost savings.

The challenges for ICT Management are to coordinate and work in partnership with the business in the building of these management solutions. This has to be achieved while reducing the overall Total Cost of Ownership (TCO). The main method of realising these goals is the reduction of the overall network management and support costs, while maintaining or even improving the quality of service delivered to the business. In order to do this the correct processes need to be developed and implemented.

To gain the greatest benefit from the use of the three Ps, organisations should determine the roles of processes and people, and then implement the tools to automate the processes, facilitating people's roles and tasks. The best way of achieving this is to develop a model or architecture based on these principles.

However, ICT faces a big challenge in developing and maintaining the soft skills required to perform the roles and processes effectively. In the truly efficient organisations, these roles and processes are aligned to those of the business. This ensures that the business and ICT Management process and information have similar targets and goals. However, all too often, organisations devote insufficient time and effort to the development of the soft skills necessary for the processes and the business alignment to be effectively achieved.

The architecture that should be adopted is a development and refinement of the three Ps – see Figure 2.12.

These five areas can be briefly defined as:

- **Business:** the needs, requirements, processes, objectives and goals of the business units and managers within the organisation
- **People:** the scope, tasks and activities of the managers and staff involved in the support and delivery of ICT services
- **Processes:** the processes and procedures used to support and deliver ICT services to the business and its customers

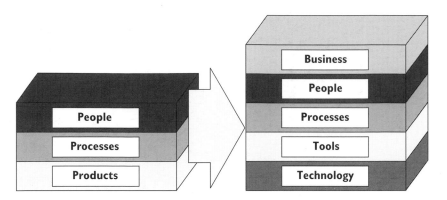

Figure 2.12 – The expansion of the three Ps

- **Tools:** the management and support tools required to effectively manage the ICT infrastructure

- **Technology:** the ICT infrastructure used to deliver the service and information to the right person, in the right place at the right time.

Such an architecture can be used to design and implement efficient, effective and integrated management solutions that are aligned to the business requirements of the organisation and its Business Managers. This management architecture can be applied within an organisation to:

- **design from the top down,** ensuring that the management processes, tools and information are aligned with the business needs and goals

- **implement from the bottom up,** ensuring that efficient and effective management processes are fully integrated with the tools and technology in use within the organisation

- **integrate processes and tools,** ensuring greater exploitation of products and technology and end-to-end processes and responsibilities.

The key to the development of a management architecture is to ensure that it is driven by business needs and not developed for ICT needs in isolation:

> Management architectures need to be …
> '… business aligned, NOT technology driven'.

Within this overall structure, a management architecture is needed that can be applied to all areas of ICT Management and not just to individual isolated areas. This can then be implemented in a coordinated programme of inter-working, to provide overall end-to-end Enterprise Management so essential to the effective management of today's ICT infrastructure. If only individual areas buy into the architecture, then individual 'islands of excellence' will develop and it will be impossible to provide the complete end-to-end solutions required to support today's e-business solutions.

As well as ensuring that all areas of the ICT are integrated, it is vital that the management architecture is developed from the business and service perspective (i.e., 'top down'). Therefore, the key elements to agree and define before developing management architecture are:

- management of the business processes: what are the business processes and how do they relate to network and IT services and components?

- management of service quality: what is service quality, how is it going to be measured and where will it be measured?

These are the key elements that need to be determined by Service Level Management and ICT Management. They provide crucial input to the development of business-focused management architectures.

A Seven Layer Model (see Figure 2.13), developed for the implementation of Network Services Management (NSM), is applicable, in that it provides a useful extension to the management architecture shown in Figure 2.12.

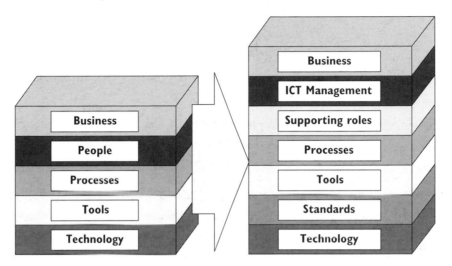

Figure 2.13 – The Network Services Management Seven Layer Model

This extension expands two of the areas into more detail:

- **People:** the scope, tasks and activities of the managers and staff involved in the support and delivery of ICT networked services are expanded in terms of:

  - management roles: the definition of the scope, roles and ownership of the various ICT Management processes – this will involve the definition, measurement, reporting and review of targets
  - supporting roles: the definition, scope and responsibility of the various areas and teams involved within the delivery and support of ICT services

- **Tools:** the management and support tools required to effectively manage the ICT infrastructure and services are expanded into:

  - tools: the actual management tools themselves, in terms of their facilities and functionality
  - standards: the management standards required to ensure inter-operability of the management tools. These should include details of the protocols, interfaces and data formats for the exchange of information between management tools.

The architectures described suggest that the future of network and Systems Management will be less focused on the technology and become more integrated with the overall requirements of the business and ICT Management. These new systems and processes are already starting to evolve as the management standards for the exchange of management information between tools become more fully defined, by organisations such as the Distributed Management Task Force (DMTF). In essence, management systems will become:

- more focused on business needs
- more closely aligned to business processes

- less dependent on specific technology and more 'service-centric'
- more integrated with other management tools and processes as the management standards evolve. This will involve the integration of Systems Management, operational management and Service Management tools and processes, with fewer 'technology silos' and 'islands of excellence'
- part of end-to-end management systems and processes, more focused on provision of quality and customer services
- less rigid and more flexible. There will be a move away from some of the more rigid, single supplier frameworks to a more open 'best-of-breed' approach.

It must be recognised that this is a two-way process and requires a two-way communication and working relationship.

Several organisations have used this approach to significantly improve the way ICT services are delivered to the business. The benefits gained have included:

- ICT services being more closely aligned to business needs, processes and goals
- support staff being more aware of business processes and business impact
- a reduction in overall management and support costs leading to a reduced TCO
- improved service availability and performance, leading to increased business revenue
- improved service levels and quality of service.

2.5.3   Strategic focus

The majority of issues and problems arising in today's ICT are caused by poor communication. Indeed, strategic documents are sometimes developed and then never used. These problems can be avoided by meeting regularly to review the strategy and making everyone aware of their contents. Kaplan and Norton advocated the principle of 'making strategy everyone's everyday job' and linking this to the measurement of strategy using the Balanced Scorecard.

A strategy owned by senior executives and Management should become a part of everyday operational activity for everyone within the organisation. In order for this to happen, policies and strategies should be distributed and accessible to all staff within the organisation. The other major use of these deliverables is by Management and D and P themselves, in the monitoring and reporting of the progress of strategy implementation.

2.6   The design and development of ICT standards and policies

The ICT design activities should cover all aspects of ICT policy and operation including:

- technological aspects
- environmental aspects
- process and procedures
- security aspects
- supplier and procurement aspects
- aspects of documentation
- staff and employee aspects.

These need to be considered in isolation and in terms of their interfaces and dependencies on one another. A central ICT document library should be established, preferably a centrally available, electronic document library containing all ICT policy and standard documentation. It would be advantageous certainly in large organisations if this documentation also contained relevant corporate, organisational, industry, national and international standard documents.

2.6.1 Infrastructure design

Certain design philosophies should be adopted in the design of all ICT systems. Wherever possible the design adopted towards all ICT systems should attempt to be:

- usable, easy to use
- modular
- scalable
- flexible
- secure
- manageable
- resilient to failure
- quick to recover
- easy to support and diagnose failures.

Guidelines on all aspects of technology should be provided, including design considerations for all the areas of technology architectures contained in Section 2.5.2.

All design documents, policies and architectures should be concise and active documents that are regularly used and reviewed.

In individual projects, systems and services, the design process attempts to match the business, customer and user requirements with the available technology and resource limitations as effectively and efficiently as possible. This match must be achieved while taking into account the issues of cost and the 'Service lifecycle' (i.e., from business requirement, through implementation until obsolescence and decommissioning – see Appendix K) and the requirements of management and support.

Achieving this requires a structured approach to design; however, it must be appreciated that ICT design is somewhat of a 'black art' that is highly dependent on the skills of the design team, and unless the ICT infrastructure is very simple, it is not possible to evaluate all potential options. The best that can be achieved is to produce a draft design and cost it, and then introduce a number of modifications to the design to see if any are cheaper and/or more effective. If they are, then incorporate these changes into the design as a basis for further modifications.

As the first step, it is important to develop a good Statement Of Requirements (SOR) that accurately reflects the business requirements. This needs to be a joint process and needs to contain details of the basic functionality required in both business and technical terms. It is important for both the business and ICT to recognise that time spent 'up front' developing a good quality SOR is essential and is time well spent. If this is not done the solution obtained will not provide what is required by the business, and extensive time, money and effort will be wasted both by the business and ICT trying to recover the situation for the lifetime of the solution.

Key message

A national organisation within the UK procured a business solution with an inadequately defined and documented SOR. The delivered solution cost £300,000 and took three months to implement, but never provided the full functionality required by the business. An additional three months and £250,000 was then spent in developing a system that was useable. However, this system never fully satisfied the business requirement and was replaced 18 months later. If time had been spent initially in defining the requirements more precisely many of these issues could have been avoided.

The SOR will thus allow the technological requirements and the range of viable options to be identified. These include, for example:

- centralised data systems – a mainframe host, applications, networks and terminals
- decentralised client server system, using local data networks – the networking of PCs, LAN-LAN, or LAN-Host based services
- voice systems – PABX or networked Centrex services or VPNs
- global solutions using Internet- or intranet-based solutions and technology
- combinations of all of these.

Constraints in design may already exist due to:

- the characteristics of the applications software or of supporting services and systems that are part of live ICT services
- the organisation's policies, strategies or in-house standards.

This may lead to overall designs that are less than optimal, but that are nevertheless suited to the business and practical and cost-effective in the medium term.

Design decisions must be based on the core requirements and the traffic volumes associated with them. In most cases, there will not be a 'best' solution, and several ways of meeting the requirements will be possible. Each potential design must be evaluated in terms of meeting business requirements and costs.

A wide range of skills and expertise is necessary to achieve an effective and practical solution. Designers must be aware of the danger of being led by the technology of the latest networked system or service. An effective way of saving resources on design (and on subsequent redesign and management) is to carry out Reference Site Visits (RSVs). Appendix J contains more details on the use and preparation for RSVs.

Designers should call on the expertise of others to gauge the impact of design decisions on the existing ICT infrastructure, services and related ICT functions. This will involve consulting with specialists from, for example, Operations, Technical Support, Service Continuity, Security, Financial, Capacity and Availability Management. More strategic issues, such as moving to e-commerce or an integrated private network, may also have a major impact on design.

In the next section, some of the basic issues for ICT infrastructure design are highlighted.

Design issues

ICT infrastructure design is driven by a number of factors, of which cost is important but not the predominant issue.

Business issues

The design of the ICT infrastructure will inevitably be constrained by characteristics of the services and systems owned by the business it is supporting. For example, it may be necessary to implement two separate LANs in a single floor of a building in order to meet the business performance and security requirements of a small number of users in a cost-effective manner. The use of a 'gateway' between the two LANs could provide the required connectivity without subjecting all users to a common (lower) level of performance.

Topology issues

A principal design issue is infrastructure topology. The customers, the users, the geography, the buildings, the technology and the services used within the infrastructure often influence the topology of the infrastructure. The designer needs to address all these issues within all areas of technology used within the organisation, while making economies and savings wherever and whenever possible. Some of these savings may accrue from the use of outsourced or hosted services.

Often designers will consider a number of options. This will necessitate evaluating the advantages and disadvantages of each topology, from the point of view of:

- fitness for purpose
- usability, scalability and flexibility
- availability, reliability and maintainability
- capacity/performance (amount of data and response time required)
- cost
- security
- support and management of the technology.

These issues must be taken into account in the design of all aspects of the overall ICT infrastructure, including not only the infrastructure itself, but also the environmental and cabling issues.

Technological issues

Designers must also consider the impact of failures and errors on the design of the infrastructure. This is particularly important in the design of networks, storage and server technology. A logical hierarchical approach to design should be adopted so that errors or failures within areas of the infrastructure are limited by design or segmentation to the local section of the infrastructure and do not impact the complete infrastructure.

Many infrastructure components have significant processing and storage capability inherent in their architecture. In many cases this processing capacity enables the system to exhibit 'intelligent' behaviour. An example of this is the ability of a group of network switches to analyse and localise the cause of a network failure and then derive the best overall re-routing strategy or strategies to restore service. Some network protocols and technologies have inherent recovery techniques built into them that can be used to automatically invoke alternative network connections with minimal impact on overall service. Designers should evaluate the use and advantages of intelligent network components. These design considerations need to be evaluated in conjunction with availability and IT Service Continuity requirements.

Security issues

The logical and physical security of the infrastructure must also be quantified. Security is of particular importance for communications networks because of the physical distribution – networks are the most vulnerable parts of ICT systems and facilitate access to all other areas of ICT.

When designing additional connections or services to an existing infrastructure it should be borne in mind that the security of the existing infrastructure may have to be improved in order to meet the requirements of the new or enhanced components or services. Detailed guidance about security is available within the ITIL book, *Security Management*.

Designers should be familiar with Risk Management to an approved and appropriate standard. Risk Management consists of the processes of identifying assets, threats and vulnerabilities and the use of justifiable countermeasures to protect the confidentiality, integrity and availability of IT systems. This method should be applied to all major new infrastructure designs to ensure that the risk and impact of failure to the existing and new infrastructure and services is minimised.

Ownership issues

The ownership of the infrastructure will also influence the design of the infrastructure. If sections of the infrastructure or even the entire infrastructure are outsourced, or even owned by external suppliers, the design will need to recognise this. In these instances complete areas of the infrastructure will be separately run and managed by other organisations. These external design processes and technology will need to be integrated with the internal design processes and technology. This will ensure that there are no discontinuities or incompatibilities in the design or the infrastructure itself. Similar problems can also arise where business units own their section of the infrastructure and have decentralised purchasing power.

Modelling issues

Each design should be subject to modelling and trending of the expected traffic volumes and their expected growth, to ensure that the planned infrastructure will support the anticipated business volumes.

Service Management issues

Designers of infrastructure should continually discuss and evaluate their designs with all the Service Management processes to ensure that the designs address their issues and concerns.

For each alternative potential design, alternative solutions must be properly considered:

- are there better or more cost-effective ways of achieving the same business aims using new or different infrastructure and services?

■ can existing systems and services be integrated advantageously with the proposed new systems and services?

■ can the new infrastructure be integrated without adversely affecting the existing services and service levels and either improve the functionality, performance or availability at no additional cost, or produce overall cost savings?

2.6.2   Environmental design and space planning

Every ICT organisation should have policies and standards to be applied to the environmental areas to be used for the housing of ICT equipment. Guidelines on the typical contents of these standards are contained in Annex 2B and details on environmental policies and standards can be found in Appendix D. These should ensure that appropriate actions are taken to install suitably secure equipment environments based on business impact and risk. This information on risk and impact should be obtained in conjunction with the Availability Management and IT Service Continuity functions.

Although the management and control of the ICT environment is performed by ICT Operations, they often require assistance in the planning and preparation of such areas, and D and P may be involved.

In larger ICT organisations there may be a person or a function tasked with the responsibility of 'space planning'. This consists of ensuring that there is sufficient amount of the suitable environmental space available in the appropriate locations. This would mean that this function would need to know the environmental requirements for all ICT equipment including:

■ size and equipment footprints

■ power requirements and circuit-breaker ratings

■ uninterruptible power supply (UPS) and generator loadings

■ temperature and humidity requirements

■ heat outputs and air-conditioning requirements

■ door clearance and engineering access requirements

■ cabling requirements

■ electromagnetic interference (EMI) and radio frequency interference (RFI) requirements

■ air quality requirements

■ weight and false floor loadings

■ network considerations

■ any additional Health and Safety requirements.

These activities are often completed in conjunction with the IT Service Continuity and Availability Management processes, as these areas will have valuable information concerning the risks and business impacts of the services and systems involved.

2.6.3   Processes and procedure design

It is essential to the efficiency and effectiveness of an ICT organisation that all of its processes are correctly designed and fully integrated. Management and operational processes cannot work in isolation. Therefore, the overall design and integration of ICT processes are crucial activities. D and P have the responsibility of continually reviewing and improving all ICT Management and operational processes to ensure that they are fully integrated. This would include:

- all ICTIM processes
- all Service Management processes
- System and equipment installation processes. Guidelines on these are contained in Appendix C
- Security Management processes
- Procurement and disposal processes.

Plans should also be developed to ensure that staff are trained in the use of and kept up to date with all relevant processes and procedures.

2.6.4   Security

Security standards and policies are often designed by security specialists, even ICT standards and policies. In some organisations, separate security or ICT security functions exist. However, in smaller organisations, these functions do not exist and the D and P processes have to develop the ICT security standards and policies. Guidelines on completing these activities are given in the ITIL *Security Management* book and the BSI standard BS 7799.

It is essential that ICT security processes are tightly integrated with organisational security processes and policies. This is achieved by:

- good inter-working practices between the Security Officer within the business and the ICT Security Manager
- regular joint meetings and reviews
- common employee guidance, handbooks and working instructions
- shared and integrated business and ICT security standards and policies
- common and integrated business and ICT security plans.

The security policies should also cover the use and misuse of ICT components and services.

2.6.5   Suppliers and procurement

Ideally each organisation should have both supplier and procurement policies. The supplier policy should provide details of preferred components and services – it should contain the list of suppliers from whom those services and components should be procured. The procurement policy should cover how these components and services are procured from the preferred suppliers. These policies are often combined into one overall supplier and procurement policy.

Many organisations are developing strategic partnerships and/or alliances enabling them to focus on the key core activities of the organisation and its business. This can often mean aspects of ICT functionality are run by Outsourcing, Application Service Providers (ASPs), Hosting or Facilities Management organisations.

A critical aspect to be considered within the strategic planning cycle is *'which capabilities are core to the business's future capacity to exploit ICT successfully and need to be retained within the organisation?'* The integrity and track record of potential external sourcing organisations must be carefully examined and quantified before entering into long-term engagements. There are many start-up companies that offer hosting services that do not have the process maturity and experience of running *'mission-critical'* systems and services, and many organisations carry the scars from involvement with such organisations.

It is also paramount that good policies and procedures are developed, implemented and maintained for the ongoing management of suppliers and contracts.

2.6.6 Documentation

Every ICT organisation should have standard policies and procedures for all documents, which should be in line with overall corporate organisational standards. Documentation should cover:

- formats, layouts (style) and templates
- version control, numbering and ownership
- quality review, approval procedures and frequency.

All essential documentation and information should be centrally stored and generally available for viewing, ideally in electronic format, although it must be remembered that off-site hard copies of IT Service Continuity Plans are still vital. Central storage of key documentation and its general availability will ensure that all staff use the latest version of documentation and that all personnel are using standard methods and procedures.

Ideally, a document management solution should provide the following benefits:

- the elimination of report reruns
- a reduction in printing costs
- error-free, automatic report distribution
- an increase in the productivity of ICT staff and end users.

All essential documents should be recorded in the CMDB as prescribed by Configuration Management. Using the CMDB to control documents in this way will ensure that that they are authentic, valid and controlled.

2.7 The techniques, tools and technologies (the three Ts)

It is essential within ICTIM that the techniques, the tools and the technologies used to plan, design, deploy, operate, support and administer the infrastructure components and services are compatible and integrated. This will help to ensure that high quality services are provided cost-effectively to the business. This section discusses some of the measurement techniques, categories of tools, and technology requirements.

2.7.1 The techniques

There are many techniques used today to measure the effectiveness and efficiency of the ICT planning processes. Often organisations use a combination of methods rather than just an individual technique. D and P should assume responsibility for ensuring that the quality of service required by the business is provided effectively and efficiently within the imposed cost constraints and that the progress of the implementation of the strategy is compared on a regular basis against planned targets.

However, it must be remembered that although the measurement of progress is vital it is not the end product, but merely a means to an end. Often people produce and gather measurements, metrics and reports as a full-time occupation. It is essential that the production of statistics is not seen as the sole objective of the strategy implementation but merely an indication of its progress and success.

> **Key message**
>
> **The implementation of strategy is a change project NOT a measurement project.**

Balanced Scorecard (BSC)

This is a technique developed by Kaplan and Norton and involves the definition and implementation of a measurement framework covering four different perspectives, namely that of the customer, the internal business, learning and growth, and the financial perspective. The four linked perspectives provide a Balanced Scorecard to support strategic activities and objectives, and can be used to measure overall ICT performance.

Management By Objectives (MBO)

This technique is based on aligning individual managerial objectives and performance with overall corporate objectives. This is achieved by setting and measuring key results of individual managers derived from strategic plans. This will evolve in a hierarchical way as shown in Figure 2.14.

Figure 2.14 – Management By Objectives (MBO) hierarchy

Care must be taken in the selection and setting of objectives because, if objectives are not integrated and consistent, sections of the business and ICT could be working against each other. It should also be recognised that metrics and measurements can influence behaviour, both positively and negatively.

Strengths, Weaknesses, Opportunities and Threats (SWOT)

This technique involves the review and analysis of four specific areas of an organisation: strengths, weaknesses, opportunities and threats. Once analysed, actions should be taken to:

- develop and exploit the organisation's strengths
- reduce, minimise or remove weaknesses
- exploit and grow opportunities
- manage and reduce threats.

Regular SWOT analysis exercises should be conducted to ensure that the actions taken are having the desired effects.

Total Cost of Ownership (TCO)

The TCO is becoming a key metric in the measurement of the effectiveness and the efficiency of ICT Management. TCO is defined as all the costs involved in the design, development, deployment, management and support of desktop computing within an organisation. For example, estimates of the TCO for desktop computing vary from £2,000 to £10,000 per PC per annum, with support and management accounting for anything between 25% and 75% of the overall costs.

> **Key message**
>
> **TCO is a useful way of reducing overall costs but only when it is linked to the overall quality of ICT service delivered, and all other performance measurements.**

2.7.2 The tools

Essential components of efficient processes are the tools that enable the processes to be automated and integrated. D and P must ensure that all the management tools in use within an ICT organisation are integrated wherever possible, leading to a fully integrated ICT organisation.

In order to achieve this level of integration, D and P must recognise the need to develop an architecture or framework for management processes and tools. This consists of reviewing the processes and tools that exist within an organisation and identifying what gaps currently exist within their capability.

As shown in Figure 2.15, the focal point of any ICT Management processes and tools is that of event management and correlation. This is the vital hub on which all process and tool integration is developed. It is essential that the event management tools provide flexibility and support of many interfaces allowing as many tools and processes as possible to be integrated into the overall architecture.

Other aspects that should be considered essential components of the overall management architecture are:

- agent requirements
- interfaces between the management platforms and the agents
- networking and security requirements on the management systems
- deployment of the tools and agents
- domains, responsibility and scope of the management platforms.

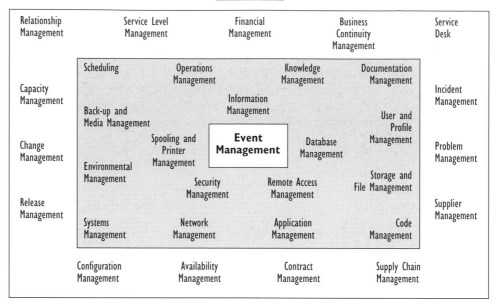

Figure 2.15 – The Enterprise Management architecture

A strategy can then be developed that builds on the exploitation of the existing processes and tools, reducing the gaps in their capabilities. This is effectively the first stage of a four-stage process:

- reviewing and assessing current position

- defining a future state

- planning the transitions necessary to achieve the future state

- defining measures of achievement.

Part of the process of reviewing the current situation is not just assessing what processes and tools that are in use but also assessing their value to the business and ICT.

A hierarchical view of management tools and processes can be developed, consisting of:

- **Strategic tools:** critical to the organisation, providing one or more essential functions or vital core processes

- **Tactical tools:** important to the organisation and generally satisfying one or more ICT functions, e.g., a Service Desk

- **Operational tools:** used to manage the operational domains and help ensure operability and availability of individual domains, objects and components, e.g., network management and Systems Management tools

- **Technology:** the bottom layer consisting of the actual objects and ICT infrastructure technology and components that provide the services delivered to the business, e.g., database and Application Management.

Wherever possible, steps should be taken to develop, exploit and expand the capabilities of tools.

It is often better to concentrate on a small number of effective management tools than to use a multitude of ineffective ones.

Specific requirements for tools to facilitate D and P processes are varied and need to be assessed and selected on an individual basis by each organisation. The major tools used by D and P processes and functions are:

- planning tools
- design tools
- risk assessment tools
- modelling tools
- statistical analysis tools
- reporting tools.

2.7.3 The technologies

The technologies, particularly the network technologies, need to facilitate and support the inter-operation and working of the management techniques, processes and tools. It is vital that the components within the infrastructure support the minimum functionality, requirements and information required by the management processes and tools, otherwise there will be gaps in the management controls.

2.8 The planning and implementation of new technology and services

The planning of new technologies and new services should include all aspects of the lifecycle of both services and infrastructure. This will require that due consideration is given to all stages from requirements and design to obsolescence. The issues involved in the areas of planning and implementation are considered in the following sections.

2.8.1 Introducing new technologies

The design, planning and implementation of new technology should be carried out using a formal project method such as PRINCE2®[1] (PRojects IN Controlled Environments). Before new technology is considered for implementation within an organisation, it must be considered against all ICT strategies, policies, architectures and plans to ensure that it is consistent with them. If the technology is not currently covered by these documents, either the technology will need to be rejected as incompatible or the documents will need to be revised to incorporate the new technology. If the documents are to be revised, all areas of the business and ICT will need to be involved in order to fully assess the impact of implementing the new technology on the organisation.

The implementation of new ICT technology is generally the time when most disruption of ICT services is caused. Therefore, it is vital that proper time and consideration are given to the challenge. All aspects of the implementation need to be assessed:

- business benefits to be obtained from the adoption of the new technology
- requirements and needs of the new technology

---

1. PRINCE is a registered trademark

- the cost of the change
- impact on the organisation of the new technology
- stability of the new technology and its anticipated life span
- assessment and management of the risks associated with the new technology
- impact on the ICT infrastructure of the new technology
- integration of new technology with the existing technology
- installation, testing, deployment, operation and support of the new technology
- decommissioning of obsolescent technology.

All of these issues should be considered in conjunction with all aspects of the organisation. Only when the issues have been fully considered and evaluated can documents be revised and the new technology incorporated into the overall ICT strategy. All of the documents listed in Annex 2B will need to be reviewed for possible revision for accommodation of the new technology. Once this has been completed, all the issues contained in Appendixes C, D and F will need to be considered. Hence the importance of Change Management.

In selecting ICT solutions, the designers always have to balance:

- the value of innovative solutions
- the need to comply with relevant standards
- the need to ensure continuity of existing systems and services
- pressure from suppliers, partners and peers
- value-for-money pressures
- the need to maintain the integrity of the infrastructure
- the need for service performance and reliability.

This means that there is constant evaluation of the risks and rewards of the level and type of change to undertake.

2.8.2   The process for implementing new services

An outline schedule of the steps involved in the implementation of a new service is included in Appendix F. All stages in the lifecycle of a service should be catered for within the project plan. The service lifecycle is considered in detail in Appendix K and a suggested checklist of activities for service acceptance is contained within Appendix M.

Annex 2A   ICT Planner and Designer roles

2A.1   ICT Planner

An **ICT Planner/Strategist** is responsible for the coordination of all ICT plans and strategies. The main objectives of the role are to:

- develop ICT plans and strategies that meet and continue to meet the ICT requirements of the business
- coordinate, measure and review the implementation progress of all ICT strategies and plans.

An ICT Planner/Strategist:

- produces and maintains the overall set of ICT standards, policies, plans and strategies, encompassing all aspects of ICT required to support an organisation's business strategy – ICT planning includes participation in the creation of Service Level Agreements and the planning of all aspects of infrastructure, internal and external, public or private, Internet and intranet, necessary to ensure that the provision of ICT services satisfies business needs
- assumes responsibility for all aspects of ICT standards, policy and strategy for ICT as a whole and for significant projects or major new strategic applications
- recommends policy for the effective use of ICT throughout the organisation and works with ICT Designers to ensure that overall plans and strategies are developed in conjunction with ICT design for all areas of ICT
- reviews ICT costs against budgets and new developments, initiating proposals to change ICT plans and strategies where appropriate, in conjunction with Financial Management
- assumes full responsibility for the management, planning and monitoring of the deployment of all stages in the lifecycle of ICT systems, including investigation, analysis, specification, design, construction, testing, maintenance, upgrade, migration and operation. It is essential that while performing these activities that the business, ICT Management and all the Service Management processes are kept up to date with the progress of the project
- obtains and evaluates proposals from suppliers of equipment, software, transmission services and other services ensuring that all business and ICT requirements are satisfied
- identifies internal and external influencing factors, forecasts strategic needs and sets policy for strategic and effective use of ICT within the organisation
- sponsors and monitors research, development and long-term planning for the provision and use of ICT architectures, products and services
- reviews ICT performance and initiates any improvements in organisation to ensure that service levels and targets continue to be met in liaison with Service Level Management
- takes ultimate responsibility for major decision-making in ICT, accounting for quality, security, availability, integrity and safety ensuring that all ICT and Service Management roles are consulted

- works with senior management and other senior specialists and planners in formulating policy and making procurement decisions applicable to all areas of ICT

- recognises the key business drivers and those areas of business need which are not adequately supported by current and planned ICT services within the strategic planning time-frame, developing the strategic ICT response to the business requirements

- identifies suitable applications, services and products, together with their environments, to meet business needs within the required planning time-frame

- develops plans for the implementation of authorised new ICT services, applications and infrastructure support, identifying budgetary, technical and staffing constraints, and clearly listing costs and expected benefits

- monitors the existing ICT strategy in relation to business needs, to determine opportunities for improving business processes through the use of new technology, and to identify unforeseen risks to the achievement of forecast business benefit

- investigates major options for providing ICT services effectively and efficiently and recommends new innovative solutions based on outsourcing, new approaches to recruitment and retention, and global supply contracts

- produces feasibility studies, business models, ICT models, business cases, SORs, and ITTs for recommended new ICT systems, identifying the business impact, the probability of satisfying business needs, the anticipated business benefits and the risks and consequences of failure

- oversees and coordinates the programme of planned ICT project implementations and changes, taking appropriate action to identify and overcome problems and resolve conflict

- conducts Post Implementation Reviews (PIRs) of those information systems introduced in pursuit of the strategy, to assess the extent to which expected business benefits were realised

- liaises with Support, Deployment and Operational teams to plan for their immediate and future needs

- provides authoritative advice and guidance on relevant national and international standards, regulations, protocols, and tariffs

- documents all work using required standards, methods and tools

- ensures that all ICT planning processes, roles, responsibilities and documentation are regularly reviewed and audited for efficiency, effectiveness and compliance

- maintains a good overall knowledge of all ICT product capabilities and the technical frameworks in which they operate.

2A.2 ICT Designer

An **ICT Designer/Architect** is responsible for the overall coordination and design of the ICT infrastructure. Their main objectives are to:

- design a secure and resilient ICT infrastructure that meets all the current and anticipated future ICT requirements of the organisation

- produce and keep up to date all ICT design, architectural, policy and specification documentation.

An ICT Designer or Design Architect:

- produces and maintains all aspects of ICT specification, including the overall designs, architectures, topologies, configuration databases and design documentation of all ICT systems – this should include not just the technology but also the management systems, the processes, the information flows and the external services

- recommends proactive innovative ICT solutions for the improvement of ICT design and operation whenever and wherever possible

- translates logical designs into physical designs taking account of business requirements, target environments, processes, performance requirements, existing systems and any potential safety-related aspects

- creates and maintains minimum ICT design policies, philosophies and criteria covering connectivity, capacity, interfaces, security, resilience, recovery, access and remote access, ensuring that all new services meet their service levels and targets

- reviews ICT traffic volumes and requirements, identifying trends in traffic flows and levels of service

- proposes design enhancements to ICT infrastructure, capacity changes, contingency and recovery arrangements as required and is aware of operational requirements, especially in terms of service levels, availability, response times, security and repair times. All these activities are performed in liaison with all of the Service Management disciplines

- reviews ICT costs against external Service Providers, new developments and new services, initiating proposals to change ICT design where appropriate cost reductions and benefits can be achieved, in consultation with Financial Management

- provides advice and guidance to management in the design and planning phases of ICT systems, to ensure that requirements (particularly capacity, recovery, performance and security needs) are reflected in the overall specifications

- provides advice and guidance to all areas of ICT and Business Management, analysts, planners, designers and developers on all aspects of ICT design and technology

- interfaces with designers and planners from external suppliers and Service Providers, ensuring all external ICT services are designed to meet their agreed service levels and targets

- plays a major role in the selection of any new ICT infrastructure or technology solutions

- assumes technical responsibility for ICT standards, policy and design for all significant projects or major application areas, assisting with the impact assessment and evaluation of major new ICT design options

- provides technical advice and guidance on relevant national and international standards, regulations, protocols, and tariffs

- reviews and contributes to the design, development and production of new services, SLAs, OLAs and contracts, covering ICT equipment and services

- takes full responsibility for the design aspects of all stages of the lifecycle of ICT systems, including investigation, analysis, specification, design, construction, testing, maintenance, upgrade, migration and operation

- reviews and possibly produces and maintains the ICT security policy in conjunction with any business or ICT Security Management roles

- works with ICT colleagues where appropriate, producing or updating ICT and corporate documentation and models

- updates or provides input to cost-benefit analyses, risk analyses, business cases, SORs/ITTs and development plans, to take account of design decisions

- obtains and evaluates proposals from suppliers of equipment, software, and other ICT Service Providers

- constructs, interprets and monitors test plans to verify correct operation of completed systems against their design objectives

- assists in the assessment and selection of suitable ICT solutions to meet all or part of specified requirements

- documents all work using required standards, methods and tools

- ensures that all ICT design processes, roles, responsibilities and documentation are regularly reviewed and audited for efficiency, effectiveness and compliance

- maintains a good technical knowledge of all ICT product capabilities and the technical frameworks in which they operate.

Annex 2B   The contents of ICT policies, strategies, architectures and plans

This annex contains suggested details of the types of policy and standard documents that should be produced and maintained by ICT, and also outlines the minimum contents of ICT technology strategies, architectures and plans. However, it should be stressed again that all these documents should be frequently and regularly reviewed and revised and should be actively used within everyday ICT processes and procedures.

They must also be maintained in alignment with all similar documents in use within the business and the overall organisation.

2B.1   ICT policies and standards

The policies and standards developed and maintained by ICT should include:

- access policies and standards
- acceptance criteria standards and policies
- applications policies and standards
- business case standards
- business requirements standards
- cabling standards and policies
- contract policies and standards
- communications policies and standards
- data policies and standards
- database standards and policies
- design standards and policies
- desktop and laptop policies and standards
- development standards, methods and policies
- document and document library standards and policies
- e-commerce and e-business standards and policies
- e-mail and groupware standards and policies
- environmental policies and standards
- functional requirements standards and policies
- handover standards and policies
- ICT security policies and standards
- ICT systems use, misuse and abuse
- ICT technology standards and policies
- information standards and policies
- intranet standards and policies
- ITT standards
- network standards and policies
- network addressing standards and policies

- planning standards and policies
- procurement standards and policies
- programme standards and policies
- project methods
- project planning policies and standards
- project review standards and policies
- prototyping standards and policies
- quality standards and policies
- remote access standards and policies
- sign-off policies and standards
- SOR standards
- storage policies and standards
- supplier standards and policies
- testing policy and standards
- user access policies and standards
- user account and password management standards and policies
- user interfaces and standards.

2B.2 ICT strategy

The strategies developed and maintained by ICT should include:

General

- strategic plan:
  - mission, vision, values, goals and targets
  - actions and performance objectives
  - core activities, and non-core activities
- strategic ICT objectives
- long-term ICT objectives
- short-term ICT objectives.

The business

- business relationships
- business interfaces
- business communications.

The culture

- business knowledge and awareness
- service quality
- customer focus.

Communications

- internal communications and awareness
- external communications.

Organisation/structure

- team structures
- team building
- inter- and intra-team communication.

Information and data

- information flows, Knowledge Management
- information security and access
- database systems
- data management, data storage, data warehousing
- data analysis and mining.

Environment

- internal ICT environmental considerations
- external environmental considerations
- industry developments
- equipment environments.

People

- roles and responsibilities
- tasks and activities

Processes

- Design and Planning, Deployment, Operations, Support, Administration
- Service Delivery, Service Support.

E-business

- processes
- the Internet
- technology: interfaces, e-commerce and payments, security, encryption.

Technology

- hardware
  - mainframe servers, mid-range servers, regional servers, local servers
  - desktop, laptop, hand-held devices: palmtops/organisers
  - specialist devices

- software
    - application, operating systems, virus checking
- networks
    - data networks: LAN, WAN, Internet, intranet, extranet
    - voice networks: PABX, handsets, mobiles, cordless
    - protocols
    - cabling: office, backbone, campus
- ICT security
    - servers, networks, applications and the Internet
- e-mail
    - servers, software, gateways, fax, messaging, office and groupware applications
- backup systems
    - servers, software, robots, tapes.

Development

- methods and standards
- processes
- tools.

Management of the technology

- management requirements and architecture
- interfaces
- message and event formats and management
- management protocols
- alarm handling
- roles and responsibilities
- processes and procedures
- management tools and platforms.

Strategic partnerships

- strategic partners and relationships
- alliances and joint strategies.

2B.3   ICT architectures

The architectures developed and maintained by ICT should include:

Management architecture

- people's roles and responsibilities
- processes and procedures

- management tools: agents and management platforms
- functionality, scope and interfaces
- automation and alerting.

Technology architecture

- servers: mainframes, mid-range, PC servers
- clients: desktop, laptop and hand-held devices
- networks: data, voice and multimedia
- operating systems and systems software.

Applications architecture

- business requirements and priorities
- functionality, scope and interfaces
- applications platforms and environments
- roles and responsibilities
- processes and procedures.

E-commerce architecture

- business requirements and interfaces
- the customer interface
- security
- the Internet technology and platforms
- the tiers, their scope and functionality
- partnerships and peering relationships.

Information and data architecture

- business requirements
- business and ICT information flows
- data analysis and mining
- data storage and warehousing.

2B.4   ICT plans

ICT should produce and maintain a number of plans in order to coordinate and manage the overall development and quality of ICT services. These should include:

ICT business plans

- the business plans for the development of ICT services.

Strategic plans

- providing plans for the achievement of the long-term vision, mission and objectives of ICT.

Tactical plans

- providing plans for the achievement of the short- and medium-term vision, mission and objectives of ICT.

Functional plans

- providing plans for the achievement of the vision, mission and objectives of key ICT functions.

Operational plans

- providing plans for the development and improvement of operational procedures and methods.

Project plans and programmes

- ICT and business programmes
- ICT projects.

Processes plans and programmes

- objectives and targets
- process improvement
- roles and responsibilities.

Development plans

- development schedule
- development tools.

Service Management plans

- Service quality plan(s)
- Service Improvement Programme
- Financial Plans and Budgets
- IT Recovery Plans and Business Continuity Plans
- Capacity Plan
- Availability Plan
- Service Support Plans: Release Plans and schedules, Configuration Management plan and the Forward Schedule of Change, Service Desk plans.

All ICT plans should be developed, maintained and reviewed in line within the business and the overall organisation. This should be achieved using the impact assessment process of a suitable Change Management system.

3 DEPLOYMENT

3.1 Introduction

For the elegance of the ICT infrastructure design to be realised and the quality of the planning to come to fruition, the Deployment process must be managed effectively to transform the designs and plans into ICT solutions. Deployment is a linchpin, without which the ICT infrastructure design is unlikely to be implemented effectively, and Operations may be burdened with high levels of incidents and support requirements, and the achievement of target service levels is likely to be compromised.

The Deployment process creates or modifies an ICT solution made up of one or more technical components, and ensures that the necessary technical and supporting services are in place to enable the new or modified technical infrastructure to become fully operational.

It is the responsibility of the Deployment process to ensure that the ICT solution is embedded in such a way that it can be managed and maintained according to the guidelines laid down by the planning and design process. Furthermore, in terms of the management of the solution, it should be embedded in such a way as to facilitate its seamless integration within the existing operations and monitoring process.

> **Definition – Deployment process**
>
> **The Deployment process is concerned with the implementation and rolling out of the business, and/or ICT, solution as designed and planned, with minimum disruption to the operations of the business processes.**

Deployment involves a high degree of logistics management of all the new infrastructure components, and requires good medium term tactical planning skills, including Change Management, and Project Management competencies. To ensure that the migration to the new or modified ICT infrastructure is as smooth as possible, the Deployment process must ensure that adequate guidance and support is provided for the adaptation and adoption of the ICT infrastructure.

There should be sufficient liaison between the Deployment process and Design and Planning processes to ensure that the ICT solution being proposed has taken into account applicable international and company standards and is sufficiently robust and flexible to be of benefit to the business for the foreseeable future.

An important aspect of deployment, which may be overlooked whilst considering the technical aspects in terms of the rolling out of ICT components, is the consideration of the effects or impact the new or modified ICT infrastructure will have on the existing staff and on the organisation generally. As ICT solutions are being deployed, it is necessary for the success of the Deployment process that changes within the organisation, and the way people within the organisation need to interact or coordinate their activities, are considered, and any behavioural changes necessary are managed as part of the Deployment process.

However, before an ICT solution can be rolled out, it is necessary to undertake the detailed design and also the build of the ICT infrastructure solution. An example from the construction industry may provide a useful analogy to illustrate the building of an ICT solution, as given below:

> A building project often starts with the gathering of the needs and functional requirements of the prospective owner, including ideas on the architectural styles most liked by the owner and the preferred environmental location. These needs and wants of the prospective owner are gathered by the architect and considered, together with the demands and standards set by the various planning, building and governing authorities. The architect is then able to assess the feasibility of the ideas of the prospective owner.
>
> The architect produces a blueprint, which is reviewed by the various planning and building control authorities and other governing bodies to ensure that the architectural style proposed is sympathetic to the environmental location selected and that the proposed building will be constructed in accordance with the necessary standards and building regulations.
>
> When the blueprint has been ratified and all the necessary approvals have been obtained, the prospective owner can normally get the necessary funds released for the scheme to be deployed and the building phase to be initiated.

A similar process is often followed for ICT solutions. The needs of the business are expressed by management and are translated into high-level ICT requirements. These requirements are validated and ratified to ensure that they can be accommodated within an ICT solution that can meet the standards and requirements laid down for the architectural components while recognising the environmental constraints of the organisation. If there are architectural or technical anomalies between the proposed solution and the existing architecture and/or ICT environment, these are usually identified early in the planning cycle. The consequences for the current ICT environment and for future ICTIM should be identified and discussed with all relevant stakeholders. In order to understand fully the consequences or impact of a proposed solution, it may be necessary to undertake a pilot study, i.e., through the Technical Support process.

The Deployment process is suited to Programme and/or Project Management disciplines. For example, the deployment of an ICT solution is most likely to be carried out as a project in which a team starts with a plan specifying the scope of the deployment, the necessary resources in terms of quantities, resource hours, and a schedule to complete the deployment of the ICT infrastructure components. At the end of the project, the newly deployed ICT solution is brought under the responsibility of the Operations process.

A deployment programme/project should:

- recognise and maintain the standards and procedures used for programmes/projects within the organisation
- define and maintain the roles and responsibilities necessary for the Deployment process
- ensure that documentation and guidance regarding standards, procedures and architectures used by the organisation are made available from the Design and Planning process

- provide suitable documentation, guidance and direction so as to coordinate effectively with the Operations process
- provide guidance and direction to support the interfaces with existing Service Support and Service Delivery processes
- define and maintain suitable management reporting in order to monitor and track progress.

3.1.1   Basic concepts

The Deployment process can be envisaged in terms of four key phases: initiation, planning, execution, and close-down. Figure 3.1 depicts these four phases and the interface with the Technical Support process. The Deployment process may rely on established Service Management disciplines, for example, Change Management, to provide wider control mechanisms and to ensure the business change programme.

The business requirements are shown as input to the feasibility stage within the Technical Support process. However, they will have also been considered by Design and Planning and a number Service Management disciplines, including: Service Level Management, Capacity Management, and Availability Management.

Early consideration of feasibility provides some of the prerequisites to facilitate the initiation of the Deployment process. Design and Planning should have been involved in advising on appropriate standards and in providing architectural blueprints and frameworks. Limited pilot studies may also be carried out in order to demonstrate the feasibility prior to deployment.

Actual deployments are often carried out as projects, and the business priorities and acceptance criteria are input into the project initiation stage. The Deployment process must be cognisant also of other constraints, primarily installation and operability standards. Technical information on the infrastructure components and their assemblies should be contained within the Configuration Management Database (CMDB), and physical components such as software and hardware should reside in the DSL and DHS respectively. These libraries and stores are generally maintained by Release Management, who are responsible for ensuring that the necessary ICT components are made available for the deployment of the ICT solution.

Programme Management or indeed Change Management may be responsible for triggering and monitoring the deployment project.

In any complex deployment, it is likely that the early stages of execution will yield lessons that need to be fed back into the deployment plan for future sites or phases. Such experiences gained during the execution phase may highlight system or procedural flaws that require rectification and these may be fed back to Application Management and Service Support.

3.1.2   The goals

The main goals of the Deployment process are to deploy ICT solutions in an efficient, effective and value-for-money way so that they:

- meet the existing needs of the business
- provide a suitable and stable ICT environment that can evolve or adapt to meet the future needs of the business
- contribute to overall improvements in the quality of ICT services.

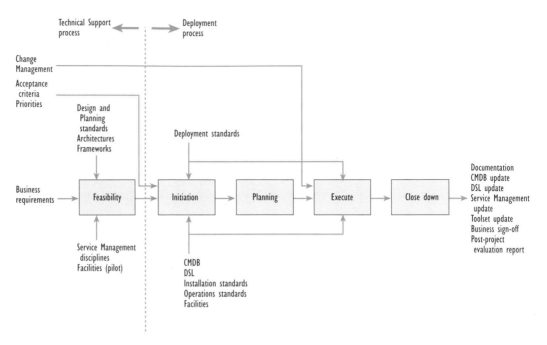

Figure 3.1 – Overview of the Deployment process

3.1.3   The scope

The Deployment process within an organisation is usually organised as a change programme and/or deployment project. For example, the deployment of a particular ICT solution may be conducted as a specific project within a wider business change programme. In these circumstances, the deployment may be carried out by a temporary organisational unit responsible for developing, delivering and rolling out the ICT solution. The Deployment project manager will report into an overarching Programme Management role that is responsible for ensuring that the business benefits from the ICT solution are realised and are monitored on a continuing basis.

The Deployment process starts with an initiation and planning phase where the project objectives, the necessary resources, a project plan, etc., are created and approved. After the approval, the project starts in accordance with the plans and is managed by Project Management.

The Deployment process is concerned with embedding the ICT solution in such a manner that facilitates its management and maintenance in line with organisational guidelines and standards. The Design and Planning process should play an active role in setting these standards.

When the ICT solution has been built, properly tested and accepted, it is ready to be brought into the live environment, and the ICT solution is delivered to the part of the organisation responsible for the Operations and administration process.

3.1.4   Objectives

The main objectives for Deployment are to:

■   create, maintain and manage a plan that contains clear statements on scope, schedule and resources necessary for the overall deployment programme or project

■   set up a team of professionals with the right skill set and cultural outlook for the execution of the programme or project

■   address Risk Management throughout the whole lifecycle of the programme or project

- ensure that the deliverables of the programme or project meet the requirements
- execute the programme or project as specified in the plan including the transition from the old situation to the new situation
- ensure that the knowledge that is built up within the team is transferred to the Operations organisation
- report the status of the programme or project in accordance with the organisation's standards and methods
- ensure that the necessary documentation is available for Operations and Technical Support.

3.2   Benefits, costs and possible problems

Deployment of an ICT solution is, in most cases, a temporary process that can be best achieved through the disciplines of Programme and/or Project Management. These management frameworks can help in realising the benefits from a successful deployment and also reduce the likelihood of problems affecting the deployment of the ICT solution.

3.2.1   Benefits

The Deployment process and management practices described in this chapter can help an organisation to develop or improve the deployment of their ICT solutions and to ensure that the role of Deployment is clear within ICTIM and to other parts of the organisation. Specific benefits that can be expected from using the guidance in this chapter include:

- greater alignment of project objectives with the business requirements
- improved communications with the business, for example, in terms of project sponsorship and commitment
- improved management and control of the Deployment process
- release and implementation of the ICT solution in accordance with project plans and delivery schedule
- smoother handover to Operations in accordance with operability standards
- ICT solution fully documented to facilitate Operations and Technical Support
- ability to handle more deployment projects with less risk of adverse impact on the delivery of ICT services
- better management information on deployment and the status of projects.

3.2.2   Costs

The main costs associated with adopting the guidance on effective and efficient deployment are likely to be:

- an increased need for competent project managers able to manage an ICT deployment project
- the development of processes and procedures to conduct deployment projects in a repeatable, and defined manner

- adoption and tailoring of tools to support the defined process, for example, Project Management tools, test tools, etc.

- the establishment and maintenance of appropriate test environments

- the implementation of process improvement and cultural change

- appropriate training and professional development of staff involved in deployment projects.

3.2.3   Possible problems

A number of problems have been recognised in defining, managing and supporting Deployment processes, and in conducting deployment projects. These include:

- a lack of management commitment

- inadequate resources in terms of skills and competencies

- a lack of proper planning and reluctance to accept predicted time-scales

- poor relationship management and the lack of necessary role interaction and task coordination

- inappropriate tools or inadequate training in their effective use

- lack of project monitoring and inappropriate project metrics

- over-commitment of resources and the inability of the deployment project to deliver to planned time-scales and budget.

Performing an ICT deployment as a project with a discrete organisational entity (project team) assumes that there are sufficient resources within the general resource pool to form a suitable team with the necessary skills and competencies to deploy the ICT solution. The use of additional resources, for example, those sourced externally, may lead to additional problems in team building and in transferring skills and competencies. External resources may also be unfamiliar with the organisational standards, procedures and guidelines, and a 'learner curve' may need to be considered during project planning.

Some ICT deployments may run the risk of severe adverse impact on the existing ICT services; it is therefore essential that Deployment undertakes the necessary risk identification and management activities, including contingency planning, in order to ensure that the ICT solution does not adversely affect existing services.

3.3   The roles, responsibilities and interfaces

Deployment of an ICT solution is, in most cases, a temporary process that can be best achieved through the disciplines of Programme and/or Project Management. Deployment projects, like any other projects, require core skills and competencies in Project Management, for instance, in project planning, estimating, Risk Management, monitoring and control. Soft skills are required to build and motivate a team and establish and maintain good relationships with the various stakeholders and process participants.

3.3.1   The roles and responsibilities

There are a number of specific roles associated with the Deployment process, which are needed to participate in, and undertake, specific activities in order to accomplish the deployment of an ICT solution, namely:

- **Deployment Process Owner** – responsible for the Deployment process and for improving the efficiency and effectiveness of the process
- **Deployment project manager** – responsible for the development of suitable plans for the deployment of the ICT solution and for managing the deployment on a day-to-day basis
- **Deployment Coordinator** – responsible for coordinating deployment activities with those of business development and ensuring that deployment projects meet their acceptance criteria and achieve a suitable handover
- **Deployment Analyst** – responsible for ensuring that suitable environments exist within the designated locations, and that the ICT solution components adhere to the agreed standards, during testing and deployment
- **Deployment Team Member** – responsible for building the ICT solution and working environment, and for supporting the acceptance testing process.

Further details of the scope and responsibilities of these specific roles are provided in Annex 3A.

3.3.2 Organisation

The structure of an ICT organisation can affect the functioning of ICTIM processes. Ideally, the ICT organisation should be process or functionally based and be focused on the business requirements, rather than technology. However, as far as the Deployment process is concerned, the merits of a temporary organisational unit, such as a project team, has been recognised.

The Deployment process starts with an initiation and planning phase in which the project objectives are made more explicit, and the authority is vested in the Deployment project manager to develop, deliver and roll out the ICT solution. The project manager establishes a suitable plan and determines the necessary resource requirements to realise the plan. After the plans have been approved and the team has been built, the project organisation is established and responsibilities are given to this organisational unit.

In some circumstances, the project to create a unique ICT solution is one of a group of projects or part of a larger business change programme. A programme may contain a group of projects managed in a coordinated way to obtain benefits not available from managing them individually.

The advantage of having a separate project – or programme – organisation is that it provides a better business focus, with the project objectives being aligned to the business needs. Also, it can more readily secure the commitment of stakeholders, and provide management information on the achievement of objectives and the realisation of business benefits.

3.3.3 External interfaces

The Deployment process has essential interfaces with Business Management, the Service Management processes, and Application Management. Because of the nature of the Deployment process, where many of the activities are transient, the relationship with Service Delivery and Service Support processes is also temporary.

As the requirements of the business become specified and are incorporated into the business or ICT solution, each of the Service Management processes contributes specific acceptance criteria for the newly deployed service or solution. Details of these acceptance criteria are contained in Appendix M.

Key Service Management processes that have direct interfaces with the Deployment process during the execution of a programme or project are as follows:

- Configuration Management
- Change Management
- Release Management
- Service Desk.

Configuration Management

Configuration Management (which includes Asset Management) is the process that is concerned with the identification of items of business value – Configuration Items (CIs) – managing changes to them, and reporting on their status, and Configuration Management Auditing. It provides the organisation with the visibility it needs in order to make informed business decisions by means of Status Accounting – on the status of a CI or a baseline – and the relationships that exist between the various components within the ICT infrastructure. Configuration and Asset Management also ensures that changes in the ICT infrastructure can only be made in an accountable manner. Therefore, no CI must be changed without an approved change being associated with it.

During the Deployment process, reference is made to relevant CI information for various reasons, for example:

- gathering information on current configurations of systems during the design of an ICT solution
- to obtain network parameter settings to set up the test environment and application settings.

The Deployment process may lead to updates of CI information due to a change that is being executed in the roll-out phase of a project. For example, a network configuration might be changed when an ICT solution is rolled out, or the system configuration of several systems may have to be changed. These changes, related to the deployment of ICT solutions, are always controlled by the Change Management process.

Change Management

The goal of the Change Management process is to control and manage all changes concerned with CIs. While the Deployment process is the process that is concerned with the rolling out of ICT solutions, the Change Management process is, by definition, used within the Deployment lifecycle, specifically in the roll-out phase.

The Change Management process is initiated by the completion of a Request for Change (RFC). The Change Manager is concerned with the execution of the change process. Inputs for the process include the roll-out plan and the acceptance test report. Care has to be taken when planning the migration to ensure adequate, tested back-out procedures are in place. During the change process, the CI data is updated in the CMDB, under the control of the Configuration and Asset Management process. The principal output of the process is an evaluated and approved change. The full change process flow is depicted in Figure 3.2.

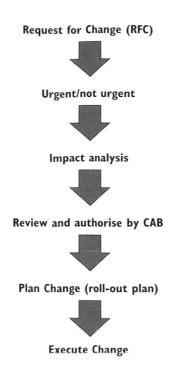

Request for Change (RFC)

Urgent/not urgent

Impact analysis

Review and authorise by CAB

Plan Change (roll-out plan)

Execute Change

Figure 3.2 – Change process flow

Release Management

The Release Management process is used for the control and management of the release of new ICT solutions. Input for this process is an authorised RFC from the Change Management process. It is the goal of Release Management to update the DHS and DSL so that the ICT solution can be deployed within the ICT infrastructure. The DHS is the physical storage of controlled hardware components, whereas the DSL is a repository that contains the correct, recognised, registered, legal and authorised set of software CIs.

The Release Management process is supported by a set of procedures and work instructions. These reflect how the organisations handle changes that are initiated by the Deployment process through the change procedures. It is important for the Release Management process to review the acceptance test plan to make sure that the requirements regarding software CIs are met.

There is also an onus on the Release Management process to specify the requirements regarding software CIs in terms of acceptance criteria used within the Deployment process.

Service Desk

The Service Desk is a single point of contact with customers. It is responsible for the communication of planned deployments and it keeps customers informed about equipment moves, release planning, availability, time-scales, etc.

3.3.4   Internal interfaces with other ICTIM processes

The Deployment process interfaces with the other ICTIM processes as described below.

Design and Planning

The Design and Planning process specifies the guidelines, architectures and frameworks on which the ICT infrastructure solutions are built. Specifically, in the Feasibility phase the ideas for an ICT infrastructure solution have to be checked against current Design and Planning standards. Following each subsequent project phase, the ICT infrastructure solution is checked and evaluated against these standards, which are then employed in acceptance testing to verify whether all the requirements related to Design and Planning are met.

When a project is being evaluated during the close-down phase, it is important that the knowledge that has been gathered during the Deployment phase is documented and, where necessary, is used to update current standards and practices.

Operations

The Deployment process for an ICT infrastructure solution is, in most cases, a temporary process, and it is important to prepare from the start of the project for the moment when the Operations process will take over the end product. The identification of the organisational unit, gaining involvement of the responsible personnel, and structured communications are important factors in gaining and sustaining commitment from Operations for the ICT solution.

It is advisable that Operations be involved in the process of the development of an ICT infrastructure solution from the initiation phase. It is important to adhere to existing Operations standards during all the Deployment phases, and during acceptance testing. This practice prevents the risk of developing an ICT solution that causes operational difficulties in the live environment.

In the execution phase, Operations becomes more concerned with the developed ICT solution. The solution development team hands over responsibility for the newly deployed ICT solution immediately after the migration. However, establishing an after-care period allows Operations time and assistance to get used to the new ICT solution, while at the same time, knowledge is being transferred between the project team and Operations staff.

When the Deployment process reaches the handover phase Operations standards are updated with the newly developed Operations procedures and guidelines.

Technical Support

The Technical Support process facilitates the Deployment process during the project or programme. In the Feasibility phase, staff associated with the Technical Support process gather information on the attainability of the business request. Technical Support investigates options in relation to Design and Planning standards. A pilot test is an approach that can be a helpful part of this investigation.

When business drivers, acceptance criteria and priorities are clearly defined, the Deployment phase can begin. From this point forward, the Deployment process is concerned with the ICT infrastructure solution. The Technical Support process is providing the facilities necessary for the correct execution of the project or programme. Examples of these facilities can be testing and acceptance resources, certain knowledge of current infrastructure components, standards, and also a place where questions can be asked.

3.3.5 Additional interfaces

There are a number of interfaces to various parts of the organisation, including:

- **Application Management** – this process is concerned with all aspects of the justification, procurement, design, development, and evolution of applications for use within the organisation. Application Management should provide Deployment with details of the:
  - application design architecture
  - application development plan and policies
  - application requirements
  - development projects and schedules

- **Human Resources** – provides information on skill sets, personal development plans, training

- **Quality Management** – to conduct an audit programme and ensure the compliance with the Quality Management System (QMS)

- **Security Management** – provides information on security plans and settings, for example, those necessary for building the ICT infrastructure solution

- **Supplier Management** – liaison with the Deployment process is necessary to ensure that the necessary ICT components are procured and are available for build and testing.

3.4 The management processes involved

Deployment of an ICT solution is, in most cases, a temporary process that can be best achieved through the disciplines of Programme and/or Project Management. Deployment projects, like any other projects, require core skills including the managerial abilities to plan, schedule, monitor and control the project. Project management with specific regard to Deployment projects is discussed in Annex 3B.

The Deployment process model, presented in Figure 3.1, depicts five phases that are necessary to transform an idea into an implemented and successful ICT solution, capable of delivering the business service required.

The Deployment process starts with initiation, in which management is concerned with formulating and agreeing the project objectives and terms of reference. Management processes are established for Requirements Management and high-level plans are produced to profile the type of project, often based on existing project frameworks and standards. Other processes in the initiation phase include Risk Management, in which the business, organisational and technical risks involved with the Deployment are recognised and addressed in the planning. Management is also concerned during project initiation in recognising all of the stakeholders and making sure that they are sufficiently aware and involved in the Deployment process.

Detailed project plans and resource schedules need to be developed and maintained during the Deployment process, and these should be approved by the Project Board. The plans are then used to monitor and report progress as the Deployment process proceeds.

A key aspect of the management of a deployment project is measurement and management reporting. These aspects need to be embedded within the project during the initiation and planning phases. Metrics are discussed further in Section 3.4.1.

The measurements taken during the execution form the basis of management reporting during deployment and also for post-project evaluation. The execution phase, consisting of the elements of design, build, test, and rolling-out, is discussed in detail in Section 3.5. This is followed by the handover stage, also discussed in Section 3.5.

3.4.1   Metrics

The objective of metrics is to identify variances and trends that may have an impact on the project. The benefits of these metrics are that they:

- provide early warning of risks and problems
- become a catalyst for corrective action
- communicate variances and trends to stakeholders.

Different types of metrics that can be gathered, reported upon, and acted upon are outlined below.

Progress metrics

Progress metrics measure the progress of a delivery engagement by comparing actual activity and product delivery dates against planned targets.

Performance metrics

Performance metrics measure delivery performance by comparing actual costs and elapsed time against planned targets.

Quality metrics

Quality metrics measure product and service fitness by comparing defects at various stages of the lifecycle against planned targets and prior quality performance.

3.5   The processes and deliverables of Deployment

The Deployment process is usually organised as a programme or project whose mandate is to develop, deliver and roll out an ICT solution.

3.5.1   Design phase

After the project has been kicked off, the actual work in deploying ICT solutions can start. On most occasions, this begins with the creation of a design. In the design phase, the ICT solution must be created and worked out on the drawing board with the current ICT infrastructure in mind. The new ICT solution's components must coexist with current ICT infrastructure components and must cooperate with current common ICT infrastructure services.

The current common ICT infrastructure services that are relevant for the ICT solution must be part of the design. Examples of these common services can be the naming service, directory service, communication service, network service, etc. These common services should be well defined and documented because they are vital for the functioning of the current ICT infrastructure.

The common ICT infrastructure services are part of the ICT infrastructure standards used within the organisation. They should rely on international or *de facto* standards that have broad recognition in the market. It is the responsibility of the Design and Planning process to recognise if changes in these common services are necessary.

Next to the common ICT infrastructure services, there may also be specific ICT infrastructure services that need to be taken into account during the design phase. These specific services are part of specific ICT solutions that are already in place, and mostly rely on products or product lines from an external supplier that have been adopted by the organisation as a company standard.

It can be advantageous for the project to have knowledge of specific services already available within the organisation, as training may not be necessary in that particular area. Examples of specific Infrastructure services can be a database service, a specific piece of middle-ware or an application service using a specific set of Application Program Interfaces (APIs). Staff involved with the Design and Planning process should be consulted when a design, for whatever reason, is not going to use a currently available specific Infrastructure Service.

Functional design

The functional design starts with the specifications that form the functional requirements for the proposed ICT solution. Together with the acceptance criteria, these form the basis for the functional design phase. The functional requirements are derived from the business requirements of the ICT solution. The acceptance criteria are primarily derived from business, the current standards and architecture documents on deployment, as well as criteria from ICT departments that will become concerned with operating and managing the ICT solution when it gets to a production status.

Often the functional requirements and acceptance criteria are 'high-level'. This means that the first step that needs to be done is to get a detailed set of requirements and criteria that should be met. This should be done in consultation with the business and should result in a document containing the functional requirements specifications, the acceptance criteria, and details of the different parties involved. This document should be approved by the Project Board.

It is also important that, at this early stage in the project, interested parties within ICT Management, including those responsible within Operations, are involved, and that they sign off the functional design document. This will eliminate the risk that an ICT solution will not be accepted because it fails to fit into the existing production environment.

> **Tip**
>
> **Have the person responsible for acceptance involved at an early stage.**

It is possible that the functional requirements from the business conflict with the acceptance criteria, or that the detailed functional design cannot meet the functional requirements of the ICT solution. In such cases, the functional requirements should be reviewed, a different product or platform should be chosen or the project should be stopped.

Processes and organisation

It is important that the project team pays attention in the design phase to the processes and organisational aspects relating to the introduction of the ICT solution. Often such aspects are not taken into account sufficiently, causing difficulties for the project or in the Operations phase.

In the functional design document, the processes that are involved in the roll-out of the ICT solution, and in the Operations phase, should be specified. Responsibilities should be identified and work instructions must be provided for when the ICT solution is being rolled out.

For example, it must be specified whether the ICT solution needs to be monitored under the responsibility of the Availability Management process. The parameters, thresholds and values should be specified for the various parts of the ICT solution. It is also necessary to ensure that the escalation procedures and work instructions are made available at the end of the project. Indeed, the design phase should specify all these parameters and, during the test and acceptance phase, these parameters should be tested and accepted as part of the ICT solution acceptance.

Technical design

It is in the technical design phase that the design is finalised. Technical design deals with technical aspects such as network protocol usage, systems configurations, versions, platform specific issues, etc. A technical design should specify the implications of introducing the ICT solution into the existing ICT infrastructure. An important part is how the ICT solution uses the common ICT infrastructure services like the Name Service, the Communication and Network Services, etc.

The technical design will use information from the CMBD, the current ICT infrastructure standards, architectures and information on existing software, hardware and network configuration standards and practices.

The technical design document will specify how the ICT solution fits into the current architecture, which common infrastructure services are used and what the configuration of the ICT solution should be. Naming conventions and standards are important in this stage.

3.5.2   Working environments

An ICT solution is being developed according to the underlying requirements from business and ICT infrastructure standards and must finally be part of the current ICT infrastructure in the production environment. To prevent interruption of the 'live environment', it is advisable that one or more separate but similar environments be created. In these separate environments, the project team can build and test the new ICT solution without impacting the live environment. The following environments are often found in practice:

- development environment
- test environment
- acceptance environment
- production environment.

These environments, and the relationships between them, are depicted in Figure 3.3.

These environments can exist in a number of different ways, depending upon the business, organisational, and technical context and constraints. There is always the production environment because the ICT solution is built to be part of this environment. However, depending upon the

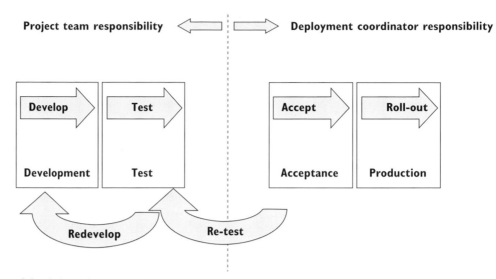

Figure 3.3 – Relationship between the various working environments

type of organisation, the importance of ICT for the business process and the complexity of the ICT infrastructure, the organisation needs to decide which environments are necessary. It may also be necessary to recognise that different technical domains may utilise specific methods or use certain environments for building new ICT solutions.

It is important for these environments to be built so that:

- the responsibility for the different environments is not in the hands of the users of these environments

- there is a clear separation between environments – it should not be possible for occurrences in one environment to have impact on another

- there is a clear, and preferably automated, procedure in place to renew the environment to its standard settings – including the procedures to migrate the ICT solution from one environment to the next one

- the environment has a similar set of services with the same configuration as in the production environment – these services must include at least all the common ICT infrastructure services and preferably all the specific ICT infrastructure services

- the environments have the same architecture and use the same standards and methods as the production environment.

In many organisations, a combined development and test environment is in place where new ICT solutions are built and tested. There are also other combinations possible, and sometimes there is a difference in environments between the technical domains. It is, for example, much more expensive to have an additional environment for mainframe compared to an additional environment for distributed systems. The business needs to consider the case for, and the justification of which environments are necessary.

In principle, it is no problem to consolidate certain ICT resources. This is, however, only possible in a highly standardised environment, for example, when there is standardisation on the version of the operating system or Relational Database Management System (RDBMS).

3.5.3   Build phase

The Deployment process generally involves the building of the ICT solution itself as it is developed and tested. The business requirements, described in the project-planning and project-initiation documentation, together with the design documents, facilitate the verification of the deliverables.

Building the ICT infrastructure solution

Creating the actual ICT infrastructure solution is part of the build phase. If possible, the ICT solution should be built and initially tested in a development environment, thus safeguarding the live operational environment.

As developments may take many different forms, and indeed embrace a number of technical domains (e.g., Network, Distributed and/or Central Systems, Mobile, Database and Application) as part of the ICT solution, it may not be possible to keep the solution separate from the production infrastructure. Indeed, the ICT solution may be part of an already existing ICT infrastructure, and is using existing ICT components; it therefore must fit in such a manner that it does not have an adverse impact on other business or ICT solutions.

When building an ICT solution within an existing ICT infrastructure, it is important that all ICT components (hardware, OS, software, network protocols and configurations, etc.) of the new solution do not conflict with each other. Sometimes incompatibilities exist between different versions of ICT components; for example, a database management system may require version yy of the OS, while an existing application is using the current version xx.

For this reason, it is essential to specify the version of the ICT components used within the ICT infrastructure. Plans for upgrading ICT components should be maintained and reviewed, providing visibility of, for example, situations in which an ICT solution working with version yy of the OS can only be implemented on a different and separate system. In the acceptance testing phase, tests should be conducted to check for potential version conflicts between new ICT components and existing components.

During the build phase, the focus lies on the build of the solution in a specific technical domain, primarily due to the technical specialisms of the different parties involved. Occasionally, work has to be done in several locations at the same time. This may be of benefit in that the different specialist groups can build and test their own product without being disturbed by other groups. For example, a network solution can be performed separately from a database or application solution.

It is important that Project Management guides this development process carefully. Everything has to work together in the later stages, so it is necessary to check at regular intervals to ensure that the acceptance criteria for the product as a whole are being met. The interpretation of design documents within the different technical development groups requires particular attention, since the meaning of technical terms in one domain can differ from the meaning of the terms in another domain. Communication and a common understanding are both vital here.

During the build phase, the role of common infrastructure services should not be overlooked. These services can significantly affect the development of an ICT infrastructure solution. For example, the configuration of a naming service at the network level can affect the development of systems, databases or applications; specific security settings at the application level can influence the security settings of systems.

If the development teams are unaware of these common infrastructure services and guidelines, the project or programme can get into trouble at a later stage. Deployment team members need to be aware that functional and technical design documents can lack this kind of information. Technical reviews and the raising of awareness, organised by Project Management, is a way to handle these issues during the process.

It should also be recognised during the build phase of an ICT solution that other aspects might need attention. Examples of these are:

- planning the usage of the development and/or test environments
- version control during the development process
- controlling the way to hand over new versions for acceptance testing
- controlling the setting of parameters and access rights to ICT components
- environmental issues, e.g., space, cooling, power, fire precautions, etc.
- accessibility and security measures
- safety measures.

Standardisation and integration aspects

An ICT solution is, on most occasions, built from a number of ICT resources or managed objects (MOs) as described above. They are the building blocks for current ICT infrastructures. In the build phase, these different blocks, often from different suppliers, are installed and configured together to create the ICT solution as designed. Standardisation can facilitate the integration of the different building blocks to provide a working ICT solution that is functioning according to the business requirements and acceptance criteria set by the organisation.

Standardisation within ICT infrastructures is an absolute necessity for the appropriate ICT processes to link up and communicate with each other.

ICTIM

During the build phase, it is important that Operations staff are kept fully informed and are involved as the ICTIM solution is built. The requirements from the Design and Planning process regarding ICTIM are used as a basis for providing Operations with an overall business and service perspective. This involvement ensures that the approach of 'Throw it over the wall when finished…' is avoided, and Operations can ensure that their operability requirements are part of solution design.

Cooperation with Operations will guarantee a structured transfer from the project to the responsible department(s). The chances for a successful project roll-out will be much higher, and those of an operational disaster minimised.

The development project should also be cognisant of ICTIM requirements, as the ICTIM practices must be part of the build process. For example, if there are requirements from the business regarding Availability Management for one or more of the MOs of the ICT solution, the project needs to deliver the necessary support mechanisms and documentation for monitoring these objects.

In most cases, one of the requirements will be that the ICTIM tools and processes must be applicable and provide adequate coverage of the ICT solution. Sometimes it may be necessary to enhance the existing tools and processes, or make other changes, in order to support the new ICT solution.

Open standards provide the basis on which it may be possible to integrate ICT solutions with each other. Such standards can facilitate integration at several levels. For example:

- event integration (messaging systems) – the ability to send information between ICT solutions

- data integration – the ability to share a common set of data between different ICT solutions

- functional integration – the ability of different ICT solutions to cooperate, interact and align their functional behaviour with each other.

Documentation

It is essential that the ICT solution is fully documented. This will ensure that the knowledge gathered during the development and test phases of the project can be passed over to both the user organisation, and retained for future developments. The documentation should provide information on all aspects of the expanded model of the three Ps (Business, People, Processes, Tools and Technology).

It is also important for reference purposes at a later stage that the information is ordered and maintained in a systematic manner. Typically, such documentation includes:

- business context and related business functions of the ICT solution
- roles and responsibilities in Operations and Management
- process descriptions related to the ICT solution
- Operations manual
- user manuals with work instructions
- hardware and software information
- logical and physical architectural overview
- detailed technical descriptions and references
- ICTIM description
- business continuity planning details
- summary and overview document for all the documentation.

The writing of documentation is difficult and time-consuming and should not be underestimated. It is important that it is done with the reader of the documentation in mind. In time, when the people who were involved in the project are no longer available, the documentation may be the only source of information for those that will become concerned with the ICT solution. A thorough quality review process, to include technical people not previously involved in the project, will help ensure that the documentation can achieve its objectives.

Ownership of the documentation is also an important issue. The owner is concerned with the documentation after the project is finished, including all updates to the documentation. It is important to manage the document versions, the document storage and the availability of the last version of the documentation, within the organisation. Controlled documents should be uniquely numbered, subject to version control, and their details stored in the Configuration Management system.

Training

On most occasions, the introduction of an ICT solution requires training of users, support staff, and the system engineers from the departments that are concerned with the live operation of the solution. The training needs of these groups is at different levels. Where system engineers need in-depth knowledge, users only need to know how to use certain functionality. Training issues should be considered as an integral part of the project from the Feasibility phase onwards.

Recognition of the different skill sets, capabilities and competencies within the various groups is a useful prerequisite in identifying the necessary training. In specifying the training programme, the number of people that require training needs to be determined, and the way the knowledge can be provided needs to be considered. While the need for training differs from project to project, the impact of training on the project can be significant. For example, if thousands of users need specific training, automated mechanisms, such as computer based training (CBT) solutions over the Internet or intranet, may become an attractive proposition to describe the use of a new ICT solution, and provide basic training and help.

The development of training material and the execution of the training activities is part of the build phase of the project.

3.5.4 Acceptance testing

The acceptance-testing phase is used to verify whether the requirements from the business are met. Acceptance testing involves a joint execution of an acceptance test plan. This plan will have been agreed by the different parties involved and must be approved by the Project Board.

It is important that an acceptance team is identified and available. Members of the acceptance team can be:

- representatives of the department(s) that will have some responsibility for or be directly involved with the ICT solution once it is deployed – these can be several people from different departments
- users
- support personnel
- those concerned with the functional behaviour of the ICT solution (i.e., Application Management).

For acceptance testing, an acceptance environment has to be created according to the installation and configuration documents associated with the ICT solution. The responsibility to set up this environment should be assigned to people who are not part of the project team. Project team members, however, will be involved in the process.

To ensure that issues are not overlooked, and that the solution can be effectively tested, it is important that the acceptance test environment is similar to the production environment. The information necessary to set up the acceptance test environment according to the production environment is derived from the CMDB and the DSL.

Part of the acceptance testing is also to test the replication of the ICT solution from one environment to another. This gives a better guarantee that the roll-out to the production environment will be successful.

Within the acceptance-testing phase, attention should be paid to backup and restoration procedures in case it ever becomes necessary to invoke Service Continuity Plans.

Testing methodologies

Acceptance testing needs to be taken seriously. The test script that has been developed must be followed throughout acceptance testing. Ideally, the acceptance tests are performed without help from the project team; however, in practice some assistance (in an advisory or guidance capacity) may be necessary. This should, however, only be done to get them up to speed, not to start looking for the solution to a problem.

Acceptance team members must write down their findings during the tests – when a test is failing, the reasons must be fully documented and they should continue with the next part of the acceptance test. The whole acceptance test script should be finished and the conclusions sent to the project team. When part of the acceptance test fails, the problem must be resolved and the appropriate acceptance tests should then be executed again by the same test team.

It is a good idea to automate the acceptance testing process up to a certain level. Specifically within large-scale ICT infrastructures or for business critical applications, a set of automated test procedures may become vital to guarantee the quality of the testing process within a reasonable time-frame. A number of tools are available to perform these actions.

Functionality tests

Functionality testing is performed primarily to verify that the ICT solution meets the functional requirements of the business. The behaviour of the ICT solution needs to be tested also, thus verifying that:

- the behaviour of a particular field within an application is as required
- a network interface is communicating with the right settings
- the user is satisfied with the result
- the ICT solution works with other ICT components
- there are no conflicts in versions of software, hardware or network components
- the common infrastructure services are used according to the way they should be
- the ICT Management solutions work according to the way they are designed
- access rights are set correctly.

Performance and volume tests

As part of the acceptance-testing phase, performance and volume tests should also be considered. As these tests can take significant effort, the importance to the business will dictate how detailed these tests will be. However, some attention to performance testing in this phase is a necessity.

The use of tools to generate a situation that is similar to the live environment is the best way to execute these tests. These tools range from simple scripts that are scheduled to run, up to a professional set of simulation hardware and software tools that are capable of simulating situations that profile thousands of users.

Documentation

Part of the acceptance testing is the documentation. In the acceptance phase, all documents regarding the ICT solution that is being delivered should be available and usable. It should be treated in the same way as the ICT solution in production. Acceptance criteria should be mentioned in the Acceptance Testing Plan.

Points of attention regarding documentation are:

- use of the organisation's standards and templates
- user manuals should be written with the users of these manuals in mind
- an overview document is necessary when there is a large number of documents, specifying what can be found and where
- documentation should give a complete, adequate and in-depth view on the ICT solution, so that it can be of value in the future when those that wrote the documentation are no longer available
- inclusion of figures and drawings are often 'worth more than a thousand words'
- descriptions of processes, procedures and work instructions – responsibilities should be specified in relation to the organisation
- important information should be placed towards the front of the documents and, where possible, supporting documents and details should be migrated to appendices to avoid information clutter and reader fatigue
- hyperlinks should be used where possible to reduce document volume.

Reporting

It is important that the results of the acceptance-testing phase should be reported. All aspects and results during the acceptance-testing period should be entered into a report that contains information on what was tested, when, by whom, how it was done, and what the results were. This information can be used as input for situations where additional testing is required or in situations when a problem occurs.

These acceptance test reports can give the Problem Management process the necessary information on how the ICT solution responded to a number of acceptance tests, without the need for rebuilding the whole test environment. The reports should be made bearing in mind that others will need to understand them later, when the current project team members are no longer available.

3.5.5   Roll-out phase

The roll-out phase is responsible for rolling out the accepted ICT solution to the 'live environment' or 'production environment'. This means that the ICT solution is rolled out, usually accompanied by a migration. The roll-out phase can make up a significant part of the total project and therefore its planning should start during the initiation phase, especially when a migration is part of the roll-out phase.

The roll-out phase should be executed through a roll-out or implementation plan that is created using a roll-out strategy. The creation of this plan falls under the responsibility of the project. The plan itself must be made in cooperation between the project organisation and the internal and/or external parties involved.

Define a roll-out strategy

This phase is used to identify the different roll-out scenarios that are possible in a particular situation and work them out at a high level of abstraction. From each of the options, the feasibility must be examined carefully. Depending on the requirements, it is possible to perform a quick shift to a few preferred scenarios that can be worked out in more detail.

In principle, there are two extreme scenarios:

- the 'big bang' scenario
- a staged transition scenario.

The 'big bang' scenario is a roll-out that is executed without interruption in time, whereas the staged transition scenario can contain many interruptions over time. In a 'big bang' scenario a number of steps are combined into one action. The staged transition scenario has a number of different steps that might be combined to finish the roll-out phase.

The choice of scenario can be made based on:

- which scenario reduces the risks that something may go wrong – small steps are more manageable
- business drivers that may force a 'big bang' scenario.

Roll-out plan

After the roll-out strategy is defined, a roll-out – or implementation – plan must be created to describe the roll-out in more detail and add additional information that enables the project organisation to execute the roll-out in a proper way. The roll-out plan needs to be approved by all parties involved.

The roll-out plan should contain at least the following information:

- overview of the parties involved
- description of the ICT solution to be rolled out
- roll-out strategy
- migration strategy
- back-out scenarios and procedures
- risks and Risk Management
- decision tree
- necessary changes managed by Change Management
- migration plan
- overview of necessary resources
- roll-out schedule
- site surveys
- provision for feedback of early roll-out experience.

Particularly in large, complex roll-outs, it is often best to start with a few selected sites which reflect the range of cases, and to amend the roll-out plans based on the experience gained on these. Any departure whatever from the planned infrastructure configuration MUST be fully evaluated on the reference system before it is committed to live roll-out. Any such changes made after roll-out has started must be subject to full regression testing.

Where a migration is included, it is essential to check that the data to be used during the migration is up to date and accurate. In practice, data can be obsolete, and a migration exercise provides an ideal opportunity to clean up the data before it is being used for migration, in order to save time and capacity during and after migration.

Testing

Testing in the roll-out and migration scenario is at least as important as testing the ICT solution itself. This is the case because the roll-out phase will affect the production environment directly. For this reason, it is advisable for the roll-out and migration to be automated as much as possible, for example, by the use of scripts to perform certain repetitive actions. NB: the scripts should become Configuration Items (CIs).

The migration test results are reported in the same way as for the acceptance-testing phase. The test report is, together with the migration plan, subject to the Change Management process. The request is processed and, if there are no objections, the change is accepted and planned.

Execute the roll-out plan

The roll-out plan specifies all the steps necessary to roll out the ICT solution. A schedule is drawn up identifying the different tasks involved, and when and by whom they will be completed. Resources are then allocated to be made available at the right moment(s) so that it is clear to everyone involved in the roll-out process who needs to do what and when, and also that the responsibilities regarding go/no-go decisions are clear.

It is necessary to ensure that there is adequate stakeholder involvement in Release Management activities and that the business ICT operational and support areas have achieved the necessary state of awareness and readiness in order to accommodate the roll-out of a new ICT solution.

The first considerations in a roll-out process must be those related to back-out. An additional backup may be necessary, specific hardware may be made available in stand-by mode, or there may be plans to switch over to a fall-back provision.

When all the necessary preparation has been undertaken and checked, the roll-out plan can be executed. However, for the plan to be successful, careful consideration of the resource schedule and, indeed, resource availability needs to be monitored and tracked. Human and technical ICT resources may fluctuate in their status and availability during the roll-out and this may affect the plan. Furthermore, in complex roll-out situations management needs to make sure that there is adequate communication between participants for task coordination and role interactions, in order to ensure the effectiveness of the process. Task coordination can be particularly significant if there are many activities being carried out concurrently.

The way things have to be organised will depend on the complexity of the roll-out. In the case of a distributed ICT solution, communications are of high importance and time zone differences may have to be taken into account. In situations where there is a business-critical service being rolled out, the down period is crucial. The more complex the situation, the more detail the roll-out plan should provide about what is done, and when. Also, some tests may be necessary during the execution of the roll-out plan; formal checkpoints will also need to be set up.

After the ICT solution has been configured and tested, a migration of existing data may be necessary. This process can be very time-consuming, especially in large migrations. The use of properly tested migration scripts is crucial. Manual activities should be avoided as much as possible, as they leave the migration open to human error.

> **Tip**
>
> **Automate the migration process as much as possible to avoid the introduction of human error.**

After-care period

A time period is usually specified during which some of the project team provide assistance to those involved in the management of the new ICT solution. This period is called the after-care period, and is used to help introduce people to the new ICT solution. During this period, knowledge is transferred, questions are answered and people are familiarised with the new solution. This is done on site.

To ensure expectations are met and to enable the effective handling of issues during this period, it is important that the roles and responsibilities of all parties involved, the levels of support, and issue escalation procedures are clearly defined in advance.

The time period for after-care is dependent on the complexity of the ICT solution and the ICT infrastructure it has become part of. This period can last from a few hours up to a period of several weeks, but as time progresses, the participation of the project team members should decrease and should be limited to just looking over the shoulder of the person that has become responsible. The after-care period should end when the organisation is familiar and confident with the new situation. At this time, everyone must be informed that normal incident reporting procedures are to be applied.

3.5.6 Handover

The handover is a phase where all the documentation and work instructions are finalised and carried over to the organisational units that are concerned with the technical domains that the ICT solution is covering. When all information is carried over, the project is evaluated and signed off. The last step is to disband the project team.

The information that is being carried over is specified in the project plan and should contain at least project documentation, work instructions and procedures. The information should cover at least the three Ps: People, Processes and Products (tools and technology).

Post-project evaluation

It is important to conduct post-project evaluation as it systematically ensures that the organisation will learn from project experiences and mistakes, and thus the Deployment and other ICTIM processes can be improved. Typically, this is the first thing that project organisations will forgo in an attempt to save time or money. However, such attempts at savings are short-sighted, as they prevent savings in future projects due to the mistakes made twice. These savings are, on most occasions, significantly higher than the execution of a post-project evaluation.

The post-project report serves several purposes, namely:

- it documents the results of the post-project evaluation meeting
- it provides a comparison of project results with project objectives
- it provides an evaluation of the project deliverables
- it documents best practices and lessons learned from the project
- it details the project handover and shutdown activities
- it documents project participants throughout the life of the project.

Project sign-off

The last steps in the Deployment process are the project sign-off and the decommissioning of the project team. The project manager will compose the post-project report and other reports to the Project Board. When the Project Board (with the business representative as part of it) shares the conclusion that the deliverables are delivered according to the requirements of the project plan, the project is signed off and the project team is disbanded.

The moment of project sign-off needs specific attention within the organisation and by project team members. The sign-off of a project can be used for promotional activities, internal and external marketing and motivation of people within the organisation. It can sometimes be seen as a milestone or can be a point where new business and initiatives can start. For these reasons organisations should be aware that they can use a project sign-off to their advantage and for profile building. Clearly, however, this assumes that the project has been demonstrably successful.

3.6   Tools

During the Deployment process, tools can be useful to automate certain tasks. Which tools to use very much depends on the type of project or programme, and on the requirements of the business. This section is intended to give an indication of the generic tool-set available for use during the Deployment process. It does not consider specific tools but rather gives an indication of the processes required during the tools selection.

3.6.1   Project Management tools

Project Management tools are important for managing the Deployment process itself. The choice of such tools is highly dependent on the required functionality, and the existing organisation's habits and skills. Some tools are better for project initiation and planning while others are better suited for the execution phase of a project.

Data import/export capabilities of Project Management tools are important. For example, if one tool is used for project planning purposes, it is useful to be able to export the information to a different tool that is capable of administering and reporting on the working hours of project employees in the execution phase.

The use of tools within an organisation should be specified in the Deployment standards. These standards can contain guidelines in using a tool within the organisation, reporting methods and templates.

3.6.2 Development tools

Development tools are useful during the execution phase of a project. In the case of software solutions development, such tools are indispensable; it is hardly possible to conceive of performing development without such tools. In other cases, such as infrastructure capability development, the use of tools can significantly reduce development time.

In many cases, when building the technology, the supplier of the technology also provides the development tools. It is important that these tools are capable of importing information from, and exporting information to, other technical domains. Because ICT solutions are developed for heterogeneous environments, it may also be necessary to combine the results from different development tools, using, possibly, yet another development tool.

3.6.3 Test tools

In large projects or programmes it is vitally important that tests can be automated as much as possible, because of the complex nature of large ICT infrastructure solutions and/or the large business impact of the solution.

Specific tools are used for regression or stress tests. In these tests, the ICT infrastructure solution is tested for capacity capabilities. This can be done by testing an environment that is similar to production or by using simulation tools that use certain knowledge bases.

In complex infrastructures it is hardly possible to have adequate acceptance testing done without the use of a number of standardised and automated test scripts. These automated procedures can help guarantee that minimum testing requirements are met, in spite of the complexity of the solution under test.

Reporting capabilities are important here because, in a later stage, results must be available for problem analysis.

3.7 Examples and best practices

There are numerous ways to improve the Deployment process, including self-developed tools or methodologies. In this section, examples are given of how different organisations have improved the deployment of their ICT solutions or components.

Best practice is usually derived from a combination of systems thinking, subject experience and an approach to business excellence by staff. They are hardly ever found solely through product training or technical libraries. The reason for this is that best practices have to be developed in the business context and environment, taking into account the mix of ICT components within the ICT infrastructure of the organisation.

Because the mix of ICT components differs from organisation to organisation, it is difficult to transfer a particular set of self-developed tools and methodologies between organisations. Secondly, such tools are often developed and maintained by technical specialists working on particular projects. It is often the case that project constraints result in little, if any, time being available to spend on knowledge transfer and documenting such tools, for other projects to benefit.

A fundamental principle behind the development of tools and methods to facilitate Deployment is that they should be derived from the architecture of the ICT infrastructure and business services and the requirements on which it is based. The architecture specifies all the different ICT components that co-exist within the ICT infrastructure, and the relations between the ICT components and the ICT solutions.

It is important to be aware of both the architecture and the business requirements when developing deployment-enabling methodologies and tools. For example, when developing a script to add an Operating System to a piece of hardware, it is necessary to ensure that there is no conflict with other common infrastructure services specified within the architecture. In addition, the business requirements on, for example, opening hours, may influence the way in which the script is built.

3.7.1   Building deployment-enabling tools

There are a number of factors that should be considered during the design and development of deployment-enabling methodologies and tools, including:

- standardisation
- automation
- data driven capability
- manageability
- reusability
- maintainability.

The standardisation of deployment methodologies and tools can help organisations to lower development time, and hence cost. Standardisation generally leads to benefits in deployment, for instance, the deployment of a new Operating System (OS) version the standard specifying all the services and parameters that are affected within the organisation.

When a standard has been established within the organisation, the procedure to deploy a new ICT component can be automated. This is often achieved through scripting; the script will specify all the services and configuration parameter settings and the order in which they need to be done. By using scripts, the creation of a new system with the same settings of the Operating System is easily performed.

A good deployment methodology should be data driven. This means that scripts will make use of one data table that will facilitate the import of values to all the variables. Such a table has to be set up in a way that is easy to use, and which can accommodate a new ICT component. Documentation should also be provided that gives examples and describes the structure of the table, so that it is clear to everyone how to use it.

Manageability of deployment tools is an important consideration for their usage. For example, logging and reporting during the execution of scripts is vital for situations when something is not working properly. It should be easy to determine where and why something went wrong.

Reusability should be considered on the basis that it is perhaps easier to reuse an already developed methodology for an ICT solution that has been deployed successfully, than to develop a new one.

Maintainability considerations focus on the documentation for the tools. For example, a flow diagram and comments in scripts are of major importance when an existing deployment tool has to be amended or updated.

3.7.2   Improvement examples

A number of examples are presented below, covering hardware, middle-ware, operating systems and Application Management.

A new desktop environment

A company had to develop an ICT solution to replace the Operating System (OS) for its desktops with a new version. The business had thousands of desktops to support the range of services it offered. One of the goals of the company was to get a more stable and manageable desktop environment for their workforce.

This was considered a major project due to the impact on the business and the large number of users involved. The new OS added a number of different functions on Security and ICT Management to the architecture of the ICT infrastructure. It also used current common infrastructure services, like name resolution, in a different way.

The company decided to hire subject matter expertise to help them with the project. The OS manufacturer was also involved in the feasibility and initiation phases of the project, and this provided useful insights into possible risks and likely impacts of the project.

It was decided that a pilot project would be undertaken to implement the new OS on a small number of desktops within one department, in order to get some useful experience of the new OS. The active participation by users at this early stage provided the project team with a greater understanding of the business, and enabled users to gain early experience of the new OS.

Following the success of the pilot, a larger project was defined to build the new ICT solution. The project consisted of several sub-teams, each developing a part of the ICT solution. These teams focused on the central and decentralised ICT infrastructure, ICT Management, migration and communications.

The central ICT infrastructure team had to deliver all the components for the new OS to work with the current ICT infrastructure. All the common infrastructure services, like file and print services, time service, security service, etc., were part of this sub-project. The decentralised ICT infrastructure team focused on the build of the new OS and the creation of an automated build procedure that was capable of rolling out the new OS to thousands of desktops in accordance with a fixed standard.

The ICT Management team had to deliver the ICT Management solution that fitted into the current ICT Management strategy, methodology and tools of the company. They were responsible also for the design of all the Service Management capabilities for the new desktop solution, including remote operations for Service Support personnel, monitoring and security services. The distribution of software was done under the guidance of this team.

The migration team was responsible for the logistics of the whole operation, and was responsible for the roll-out of approximately 80 desktop systems per day, during which the communications team played a major role in awareness for the user population.

A server environment

A company had chosen a particular OS type for all its servers. There were approximately 30 departmental servers used for a number of common infrastructure services such as: file, print, directory, and naming services. Other central servers were used for security, application, and database services.

The building process for these servers was standardised and automated by using a CD containing a number of scripts. This CD maintained all the software sets that were necessary for building the base of a new server, and the scripts took care of installation and configuration of the new server system.

It was capable of building the whole system and connecting it to the network, where information from a centrally located table was gathered to specify certain system parameters, for instance, the systems name, network configuration-IP addresses, sub-net mask, and also the management agents of a Systems Management tool.

After the generic server build process was completed, a number of software packages made the generic server a specific server, e.g., database, or application server. The packages were stored in a DSL on a Systems Management server. A technical specialist could create a specific server by sending one or more software packages to the new system.

When a new version of the OS of the server had to be implemented, tests were executed and a new CD was created for new server systems. The current servers were upgraded by using the upgrade routines provided by the OS manufacturer. This procedure was executed manually after a backup of the server data had been taken.

Application deployment

The application development takes place in a development environment. This is an environment with the same common infrastructure services as the production network, but is separated in such a way that other users are not influenced by the work of developers.

A new application or software release is tested in a separate test environment, particularly if it is likely to impact on the production environment. The test environment is used primarily by project team members and the environment is maintained under the responsibility of the project. The application remains in this environment until it is ready for acceptance testing.

The acceptance environment (in the production network) is used for acceptance testing by the user, or for bug fixing of the current production release. Once the development version is available for acceptance by the users, the release can be moved to the acceptance environment, so that the users can test the functionality at his/her regular workstation/environment.

The mechanism for transferring an application from the test to acceptance environments should be similar to that used in the Production environment. The acceptance and production environments should have minimal or no differences between them.

Network configuration

A company has a network infrastructure with a number of components like routers, switches and firewalls. It uses a network management software package for configuration of the network devices and for monitoring the status of the different ICT components. The network component status information is displayed on a central console, and when one of the network components is down, support personnel are alerted.

The configuration files of the network components are stored centrally. By doing so, new network components can be installed quickly. There are procedures in place for maintaining these configuration files, the whole process being performed under the guidance of the Configuration Management process.

Annex 3A   ICT Deployment roles

3A.1   Deployment process owner

It is the responsibility of the Deployment process owner to:

- review the Deployment process and the procedures for effectiveness, efficiency and compliance to own standards
- implement a continual process of improvement within Deployment
- produce Deployment process standards in consultation with the Deployment coordinator and Deployment Managers
- raise the awareness of the Deployment process
- ensure that appropriate Deployment tools are available and are automated and integrated, wherever possible.

3A.2   Deployment project manager

It is the responsibility of the Deployment project manager to:

- develop project plans for the deployment of ICT solutions
- manage the deployment of the ICT solution on a day-to-day basis
- utilise all the relevant standards, procedures and components that are used within the organisation
- maintain management reporting on a regular basis specified by the project plan.

3A.3   Deployment coordinator

It is the responsibility of the Deployment coordinator to:

- coordinate business development projects and programmes
- integrate the activities of the Deployment Management with those of associated business development teams
- ensure that all major business projects achieve project handover and acceptance criteria
- develop and implement business development standards
- perform post-implementation reviews of all major business development projects and all major deployment projects.

3A.4   Deployment Analyst

It is the responsibility of the Deployment Analyst to:

- develop project plans for the deployment of business solutions
- ensure that suitable environments exist within the designated locations
- manage and deploy the business solutions
- ensure that all management processes are followed

- ensure the use of only legal and authorised components, adhering to agreed, standard configurations, during testing and deployment
- perform RFC assessments and review the Forward Schedule of Changes (FSC).

3A.5   Deployment team member

It is the responsibility of the Deployment team member to:

- provide input to project planning processes
- communicate according to communication plan guidelines
- perform functional and technical design
- create the ICT solution working environment
- build the ICT solution
- support the acceptance testing process
- participate in the roll-out execution
- provide after-care support
- provide input to deployment project evaluation activities.

Annex 3B   Running a deployment project

3B.1   Project framework

Project Management methodologies are developed to make projects controllable and increase the chances of success. A methodology should be chosen to standardise the way the organisation deals with projects and facilitates in the development of professionalism.

There are different methodologies available for managing and controlling projects. When an organisation already makes use of such a methodology, it should be adopted for deployment projects. PRINCE2 (PRojects IN Controlled Environments) is one of the methodologies used in this perspective.

Communication

Communication is important in many ways. Because the deployment of ICT solutions is generally undertaken by a temporary organisational unit that is responsible for delivery within time and budget, communication is critical for the success of a project. This applies to the project team internally as well as externally to the steering committee, stakeholders, users and team members.

In most situations, communication is part of the Project Management methodology. The methodology specifies and formalises the way to communicate with the different parties at particular times and frequencies during the project. Examples of formalised ways of communication are meeting reports, brochures, intranet or a bulletin board.

Politics

Nearly every project will affect the functioning of the organisation. This can be the work of one particular person but it can also affect a division. Think of the implementation of an Enterprise Resource Planning (ERP) solution where the internal logistic process in the whole organisation is being automated.

On such an occasion, a number of parties with different interests regarding the project may be encountered. Specifically in larger organisations and/or where a project has a significant impact on different organisational units, these varying interests may result in opposing behaviour between the various hierarchical levels of the organisation. Such opposing views can present a risk for the success of the project, in terms of a lack of management commitment or project sponsorship from the senior levels within the organisation.

There are several ways to handle this kind of political situation, and the following guidelines are given:

- be sure that the business drivers for the project are well known and understood – the business is the part of the organisation that is likely to be paying for the ICT solution
- have a project sponsor from the appropriate level in the organisation – a project sponsor is ideally someone from the senior management
- be aware of the fact that commitment is needed from people or departments that have some stake in the ICT solution

- let 'People–Change Management' be a part of the project – while projects nearly always change the way people are used to working, attention to working practices must be part of the project
- ensure that there is effective communication with all stakeholders, and manage expectations.

Building a project team

Building a project team is not simply concerned with the hiring of a number of resources, putting them in a room, throwing a project plan on the table, and expecting a quality deliverable. It is important that a project team is balanced in terms of skill sets and personalities. A good project team has the right mix of both in relation to the project deliverables and the organisational environment in which the team has to work.

The first step in building a project team is choosing a project manager with the right skill set for the project. This person should be able to deliver the project deliverables to the budget and schedule on which the project is based. The project manager should have the appropriate communication skills and experience for the size of the project.

> **Key message**
>
> **The right project manager is critical for the success of the project.**

The project team members must also have the right skill sets to perform their actions within the project and make it successful.

3B.2   Project initiation and planning

A project always starts with an idea that should bring business advantages. However, ideas are very rarely suitable for direct execution. Before they reach a directly executable form, a great deal of work has to be done, especially when the impact on the business or ICT services and infrastructure is large. It should be recognised that sometimes a good idea does not develop as far as an execution phase primarily because of the lack of business advantages in relation to costs, or the lack of organisational sponsorship at an appropriate senior level, or because it was not possible for political reasons.

Project initiation and planning can be thought of in terms of three steps necessary to develop an idea up to the point at which the execution can start. Each of the steps provides a higher level of detail in specifying the objectives, necessary resources and the business benefits. The steps also provide suitable decision points to evaluate the idea and determine whether it still offers the advantages for the organisation that were promised.

Project feasibility phase

When an idea of interest to the business in launched, the first step is to investigate it from a high level.

The objectives of the project feasibility phase are to:

- gather sufficient information to assess the idea
- clarify and define the sponsor's business need
- understand the problem to be solved
- identify the desired approach to solve the problem.

The outcome of the project feasibility phase is a project charter document. This document contains the following information, and serves as input for the project initiation phase. It provides:

- a clear statement of the problem that needs to be solved
- an initial approach to solve the problem
- a definition of high-level expectations
- a statement of the project aims and intent
- a handoff between the sales/service design team and the delivery team
- a mandate in terms of the sponsor's authorisation to proceed to the initiation phase.

The project initiation phase

The project initiation phase is used to develop an outline of the project, gain commitment within the organisation and develop further the high-level description of the project to a level of detail that can be used in a project plan. This project plan distinguishes the stages of the project.

The objectives of the initiation phase are to.

- identify project objectives
- articulate business requirements and major deliverables
- develop high-level estimates of project scope, schedule, and resources.

In this phase, a project definition document is produced that specifies the project scope, schedule and necessary resources. These definitions still have a high-level signature but give a more detailed outline of the project as a whole. It provides details of the objectives and business drivers for the project, it identifies the major stakeholders, and gives an overview of the main deliverables that are necessary to build the ICT solution.

> **Tip**
>
> **Clear business requirements and acceptance criteria are the basis for a successful project.**

A project definition document is the basis for the project-planning phase.

The project-planning phase

Project planning is of major importance in achieving a successful project. Detailed project planning establishes the plans, processes, controls and tools that will be utilised during the execution phase of the project. As a result, there are relatively more activities in this phase. The amount of planning performed should be commensurate with the scope of the project.

The project planning process is subject to frequent iterations before completing the plan. The result is an agreement between project stakeholders regarding how the project will be executed, monitored and controlled.

The objectives of the project-planning phase are to:

- validate and refine business requirements
- drill-down the project scope to produce a detailed work breakdown structure
- finalise the project schedule, resource requirements and budget
- organise and finalise the project team
- establish project control procedures.

The start of the project-planning phase is on most occasions done through one or more workshops with the stakeholders and sponsor of the project. In these discussions, all the objectives have to be specified and agreed. The goal is to come to a level of detail where the project deliverables are specified with their necessary tasks and sub-tasks, as shown in Figure 3B.1. These tasks are the basis for the project plan and schedule. Based on these the amount of resources and the necessary skill sets can be specified.

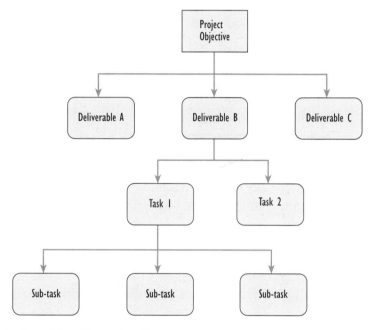

Figure 3B.1 – From deliverable to sub-tasks

Attached to the project plan, all the other organisational aspects have to be specified. The following items are the output of the project-planning phase:

- project plan
- project schedule (resource loaded)
- Risk Management plan
- quality plan
- change control process
- communications plan
- status reporting format
- project plan approval.

Project plan and schedule

The project plan is a formal and approved document used to manage and control project execution. It uses outputs of other planning activities to create a consistent, coherent document to form the project baseline.

Risk Management plan

Risk Management is a continual process by which risks are identified, quantified, responded to, and controlled. Within a project, it is the method for minimising the consequences of adverse events. Risk Management does not seek to make a business or a project stop taking risks ('risk averse'). Rather, it recognises that within any project there will be inherent risks. It seeks to make everyone associated with the project fully aware of all the risks and to ensure that the project is in a position to understand and manage the risks it is taking. The Risk Management plan identifies risks and the actions that will be taken to monitor and control them.

Quality plan

Quality planning ensures an active effort to monitor and control project quality in order to meet the required quality in ICT solutions. The Quality Management process within organisations specifies the level of quality, the quality standards and practices that have to be used in the Deployment process. The quality plan translates these high-level requirements regarding quality into responsibilities, tasks and actions within the programme or project.

The quality plan serves several purposes, namely, it:

- translates high-level quality requirements into responsibilities, tasks and actions
- provides an overall quality approach customised for the project
- establishes quality roles to be performed
- establishes project reviews and inspections
- establishes project metrics and checkpoints.

It is the responsibility of the project manager to manage project quality. These responsibilities include:

- quality planning – developing and implementing the project quality plan
- quality assurance – evaluating overall project performance
- quality control – monitoring specific project results against objectives (checkpoints, metrics, reviews).

The project team must be familiar with the quality plan and support the data collection and reporting processes.

Change control process

Change control involves the management of all proposed changes to the cost, schedule or scope for the programme. The change control process begins on the date of approval of the baseline project plan, budget and scope. Changes addressed in the change control process include changes to hardware, software, network, and any other changes which could potentially affect the schedule, cost or deliverables (scope) for any given approved projects. Examples include application specification changes, change in functionality, PC specifications, etc.

There are six main objectives of change control:

- document and justify a desired change to the project baseline
- provide appropriate data for desired changes
- inform all project participants of the desired change and accommodate feedback
- assess and document impact to cost, schedule and deliverables
- acquire the appropriate approval for the change as agreed with the business
- notify the appropriate stakeholders that the change is approved or rejected.

While the ICT solution is being developed within the Deployment process, project or programme changes are not handled by the Change Management process.

Communications plan

The objective of communications in any project is to keep people informed, to create an environment of trust, and to provide an opportunity for feedback. Each participant or group of people involved in or affected by the project has differing needs in the communications they receive or initiate. The objective of communications planning is to assist the project team in creating focused and efficient communications, through appropriate media, to and from the identified audience.

The communications plan specifies the way the project team should communicate with everyone involved with, or with an interest or stake in the project. These people include members of the project team as well as potential users of the ICT solution. There can be internal as well as external parties involved and communications planning should take into account the impact of the project in deciding how best to handle communications. When the impact is large, it is a good idea to have the marketing and communications department involved in the project. These people specialise in communications and can help the project to be successful.

When setting up a communications plan, consider:

- the message that has to be communicated
- the reasons for communicating the message
- the audience for the message
- the method(s) to be used to send the message
- the owner of the task to send the message to the audience, and the timing.

Communications during the Deployment process can be formalised or structured, for instance, in terms of a communications schedule for those people that are directly involved with the project. An example of a communications schedule is provided in Figure 3B.2. It should be noted that status reporting is an integral part of the communications.

Status reporting

Status reporting is one of the most important management methods within the Deployment process. Project status reports are created and used at several levels, and they provide a way to communicate and record decisions during the lifetime of the process. The status report can be seen as a diary and is important for evaluation afterwards.

	Client meeting	Steering group meeting	Project team meeting
Client	Monthly ✍		
Steering group	Monthly	Weekly ✍	
Project Manager	On request	Weekly ✍	Weekly ✍
Project team		On request	Daily

Figure 3B.2 – Example of a project communications schedule

Status reporting can contain the following information:

- an overall indicator of the status of the project
- an overview of what is accomplished in this period
- an overview of what is going to be accomplished in the next period
- points of attention for management, for example, potential risks
- projected and completed milestones and checkpoints
- variances in scope, schedule or resources, for example, budget overrun
- Change request status.

Project approval

To start a project or programme, approval from the business representative is necessary. Each project phase may only begin after approval has been provided in writing. There must be an approval for the execution of the project plan, the attached schedule and the required resources. The project organisation should also be approved. This accounts for the quality measures, an acknowledgement of the risks involved and the way of communicating and reporting.

Project kick-off

The project kick-off is the official starting point for the project. The project manager will be responsible for the execution of the project plan.

Annex 3C   Example of a communication plan

Audience	Month A	Month B	Month C	Month D
Identify all potential audiences in this column	Date Brief Descriptions (Include both recurring and one-off meetings, reviews, report distributions, key milestones and events)	Date Brief Description Date Brief Description Date Brief Description	Date Brief Description	
Examples				
Sponsor	1/1/xx Standing meeting with sponsor— review sponsor contract 17/1/xx Meeting to inform sponsor on recommendations	1/2/xx Standing meeting with sponsor	1/3/xx Standing meeting with sponsor	
Project team	Standing meeting every Tuesday and Thursday, 1-5 in Conf. Room C	Standing meeting every Tuesday and Thursday, 1-5 in Conf. Room C	Standing meeting every Tuesday and Thursday, 1-5 in Conf. Room C	Standing meeting every Tuesday and Thursday, 1-5 in Conf. Room C
Users	20/1/xx Product Roadshow for Users at Location X			
Change Advisory Board	18/1/xx Project Executive Summary due			

Table 3C.1 – Example of a communication plan

4 OPERATIONS

4.1 Introduction

An Operations process is required to ensure a stable and secure foundation on which to provide ICT services. The Operations process has a strong technology focus with an emphasis on 'monitor and control'. It is of an observing, serving and operational nature, ensuring the stability of the ICT infrastructure.

> **Definition – Operations process**
>
> **The Operations process comprises all activities and measures necessary to enable and/or maintain the intended use of ICT services and infrastructure in order to meet Service Level Agreements and business targets.**

Although Operations underpins and facilitates all other ICTIM processes and IT Service Management (ITSM) processes in their ever-changing needs and wants, it is conservative and inclined to preserve the status quo. Operations is perceived to be in the 'back office' of most ICT organisations and the activities and roles are often undervalued with a low profile. However, effective Operations people, processes and products are critical to the provision of quality ICT services. It is impossible to provide resilient, highly available services without good operational procedures. It is common for Operations to be a continuous process, often 24 hours a day, seven days a week, 365 days a year.

In order to deliver the results required by the business, service and performance measurement must operate top-down. The emphasis must be on overall service and business-related performance, not on individual component performance.

> **Example**
>
> A nationwide retail organisation measured operational performance against targets based on data centre responses and availability, which were excellent and exceeded their SLA targets. However, the business complained that the quality of their ICT services was poor and unacceptable. The business perception was based upon the quality of service delivered to the desktop NOT the service delivered by the data centre. Unfortunately, there were no operational targets measured or reported on for either the desktop or network infrastructure, although the targets within the SLAs implied that there were.

Key messages

1   It does not matter if components of the infrastructure are exceeding their
    operational targets – it is the quality of the overall service delivered to the
    users and the business that is critical.

2   The emphasis on measurement and operational targets should be from the
    service and business perspective.

3   All operational targets should be agreed and documented within SLAs and
    OLAs, and should be measurable, reported and reviewed.

If the overall end-to-end service is not performing to levels agreed within the SLAs and OLAs, no amount of demonstration that the infrastructure components are fine will make the users, customers or the business satisfied. It is essential, therefore, that Operations personnel are aware of the overall service targets and contents of the SLAs, and indeed of the appropriate OLAs, and that they constantly strive to ensure that ICT services and all elements of the infrastructure meet, or exceed their targets.

In today's high-tech world, questions often arise, such as:

■   'Do we really need people operating these computers for us?'

■   'Surely someone has come up with a way to automate that!'

■   'Do we need people for that particular task?'

The answer to all these questions is one of balance. The selective and appropriate use of automated processes is vital. However, it is also essential that people maintain control of these automated processes. The reasons are many and varied, and often poorly understood, so perhaps an analogy might be helpful.

The car, which most of us use on a regular basis, has over a century of development behind it. In some respects, its history is remarkably similar to that of ICT. When first introduced its possibilities were recognised by only a handful of visionaries – today it is pervasive in every sense. Its evolution is an amalgamation of incremental improvements and adaptations, mostly small steps, but some of them big leaps forward:

■   its usage is as diverse as ICT's – from simple point-to-point travel to highly
    technical Formula-1 racing

■   its limitations are also similar: when something goes wrong it can only correct
    itself up to a point – it cannot heal itself when damaged

■   it cannot perform any work on its own – there is always a conscious decision
    about what kind of work needs to be performed and there is always human
    oversight and 'control' when carrying out a particular task.

The human oversight and 'control' of ICT is the subject of this chapter. It is as necessary in ICTIM as it is in using a car, and it will be necessary for the foreseeable future. It is essential that this human oversight and control takes an end-to-end view covering all aspects of the services and does not simply focus on individual components and elements of the infrastructure.

The quality of service delivered to the business will be dependent upon the quality, availability, reliability and performance of the poorest component within the overall service. Often the hard work and dedication of many ICT staff can be destroyed by the neglect of areas of infrastructure or of other personnel.

'The chain is only as strong as the weakest link.'

4.1.1 Basic concepts

The basic concept of Operations is that of the 'monitor-control loop'. This is shown schematically in Figure 4.1.

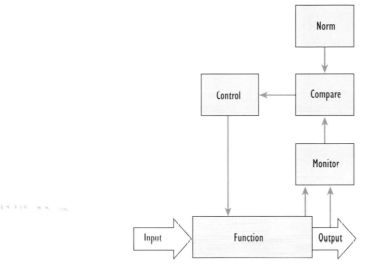

Figure 4.1 — The monitor control loop

This diagram simplifies Operations Management. The reality of any ICT infrastructure, from the smallest family owned and operated business to the largest global enterprise, is more complex, made up of a number of these diagrams, although the monitor and control loop is fundamental to all Operations.

Two additional concepts that are fundamental to operational management and the management of ICT systems in general are those of managed objects (MOs) and management domains.

Managed objects

Definition – Managed object

A managed object (MO) is the Open Systems Interconnection (OSI) management view of a resource that is subject to management. An MO is the representation of a technical infrastructure resource as seen by (and for the purposes of) management. An MO is defined in terms of the attributes it possesses, operations that may be performed upon it, notifications that it may issue and its relationships with other MOs.

Management domains

> ### Definition – Management domain
>
> A management domain is a set of MOs, to which a common Systems Management policy applies. A management domain possesses at least two of the following properties:
>
> - a unique name
>
> - identification of a collection of MOs which are members of the domain
>
> - identification of the inter-domain relationships applicable to the domain's relationship with other domains (rules, practices, procedures).

These concepts are illustrated in Figure 4.2.

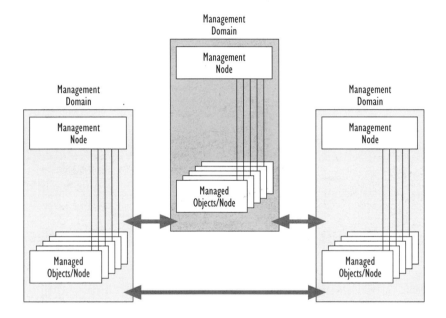

Figure 4.2 – Management domains and managed objects (MOs)

International and national standards relating to the management of ICT infrastructures (ISO, CCITT and ITU) refer to these concepts and the management areas that need to be addressed in order to manage an operational environment. These areas are referred to as Systems Management Functional Areas (SMFAs) and are explained in detail in Annex 4B, together with an explanation of how they map across to the ICTIM and ITSM processes.

With the introduction of the Configuration Item (CI) in the first edition of ITIL *Service Management*, a generic term for the physical elements of the IT Infrastructure became available. Generally speaking, the major difference is that a CI would be a static item and an MO would be a dynamic item. These differences are illustrated in Figure 4.3.

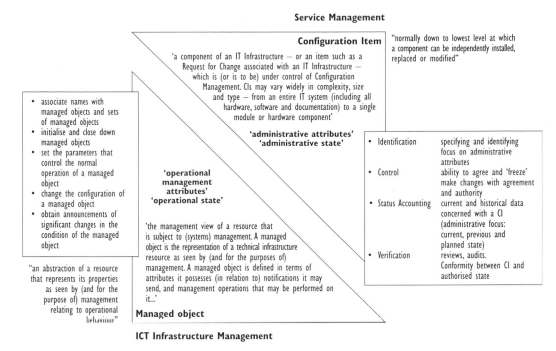

Figure 4.3 – Managed objects

A CI is defined as follows:

> **'A CI is a component of an infrastructure – or an item, such as a Request for Change, associated with an infrastructure component – that is (or is to be) under the control of Configuration Management.'**

In Operations, many of the basic elements of the ICT infrastructure are dynamic. For example, a file download service, which is provided by an FTP server, can either be accessible or not. This is because the status of the FTP server is constantly changing, second by second. The status of the FTP server can be any one of:

- running
- closed
- shutting down
- initialising
- dead
- off-line.

Within the construct of a CI, this would be impossible to achieve. The MO view of an FTP server would be live, with constantly changing (dynamic) status and data, whereas the concept of Configuration Management is more towards managing a database of CIs with relatively static data under control of the Change Management process. The script defining the FTP parameters could be a CI, as could the script defining the parameters of the SVC, or they could both be included in the build script for the operating system. However, it is more likely that either the physical network link or the range of SVCs would be controlled as a CI rather than the SVC itself. The SVC would appear on some management systems as an MO. Alternatively, the FTP server could be defined as a CI with a status of 'live' within the Configuration Management Database (CMDB); its actual, detailed operating status or instantaneous status could then be determined from interrogation of a network or Systems Management tool, as could the current status of the SVC.

In Operations, there is a need for a dynamic construct defining any object within the ICT infrastructure and reflecting the control that Operations can exert over that object. This construct is the MO. First introduced by ISO in late 1980s it has become the object of management in network and Systems Management products and tools. In everyday speech people refer to objects such as servers, print queues, files, etc., but when they perform management operations on those objects they perform them on MOs. These concepts of MOs and management domains are expanded in Annex 4B.

4.1.2   The goals

The main goals of the ICT Operations process are:

- to operate, manage and maintain an end-to-end ICT infrastructure that facilitates the delivery of the ICT services to the business, and that meets all its agreed requirements and targets

- to ensure that the ICT infrastructure is reliable, robust, secure, consistent and facilitates the efficient and effective business processes of the organisation.

4.1.3   The scope

The operational processes within an ICT organisation should include the management and control of all the operational components within the ICT infrastructure. However, this should include not only the control of each individual component but also the interaction between all these elements and their role in the provision of a quality ICT service. Operations have a critical role to play in assisting the other ICT and Service Management processes achieve their individual process objectives. An effective Operations unit within an ICT organisation can be the difference between overall success or failure of the ICT services. One of the major roles that Operations plays is within the event and incident handling processes. This role is indicated in Figure 4.4.

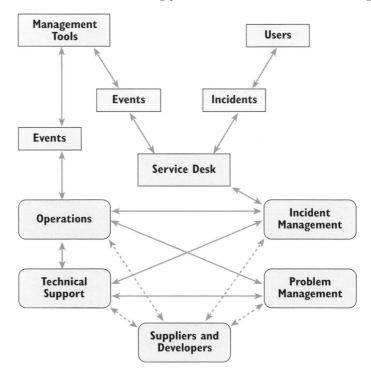

Figure 4.4 – The operational incident workflow

The Operations section often acts as the 24x7 'eyes and ears' of the ICT organisation, providing a round-the-clock presence and early warning system for all other areas of ICT and ITSM. This enables the early detection, correction and prevention of service failure. With effective processes, automated wherever possible, Operations can greatly reduce the business disruption caused by issues within the ICT services. In order to ensure an efficient and effective operational incident workflow, the Operations and Incident Management processes are often co-located and integrated into an 'Operations bridge'. The Operations bridge provides the combined functionality of a Service Desk and an Operational Control Centre for the initial control and escalation of all ICT issues.

Inputs

- the current ICT infrastructure
- OLAs that are negotiated and produced by SLM. These agree and document the operational targets and requirements for the ICT infrastructure. It is crucial that these targets within the OLAs are consistent and supportive of the SLA targets and are relevant to the ICT infrastructure and its method of operation
- Underpinning Contracts (UCs) should also be consistent and support the SLA targets
- operational processes and procedures
- strategies, plans, policies, standards and architectures.

Processes

- event, warning, alert and alarm processing and management:
  - progression and resolution of all event, warning, alert and alarm messages
  - liaison with Incident and Problem Management
  - liaison with Availability, Security and Capacity Management

- end to end management of the operational ICT infrastructure:
  - performance and configuration tuning of the operational infrastructure in conjunction with Capacity Management and Change Management
  - configuration and reconfiguration of MOs
  - system tuning and performance

- workload scheduling:
  - batch processing schedule management and maintenance
  - output scheduling and print management

- housekeeping and maintenance:
  - backup and restore
  - ICT infrastructure configuration maintenance
  - database administration
  - documentation maintenance
  - availability, resilience and recovery testing
  - health checking of the infrastructure
  - log and journal housekeeping

- storage management:
  - file and file systems maintenance

- database management and administration
- media management
- journal and log file maintenance
- backup scheduling and management
- usage reporting

■ liaison with all other areas of ICT, especially Technical Support, third party support and maintenance engineers and technicians

■ instigation of improvement or remedial activities in operational processes under the control of Change Management.

Deliverables

■ a stable and secure ICT infrastructure

■ a secure Operational Document Library (ODL) containing details of all operational processes, especially shift handover procedures

■ a log or database of all operational events, alerts and alarms. The majority of these should be fed into the Incident Management process and be recorded as incidents themselves

■ a set of operational scripts

■ a set of operational work schedules for all batch work, print schedules and system and data backups

■ a resilience and fail-over testing schedule

■ a set of operational tools that provide views and information on the operational state of the ICT infrastructure and its services, including all media movements and locations

■ management reports and information

■ exception reviews and reports

■ audit reports for effectiveness, efficiency and compliance.

Depending on why other ICT and Service Management processes require this data they might process it further to fit their needs. This requires an agreement on both sides on the format, channel and moment of delivery of the data.

It is, of course, possible to share data and define a view of the data that fits the needs of the particular process. The great advantage of using a single data source (even a single data instance) is that the basis of the information for any process is the same. This will result in minimal mismatches in the way the state or operation of the ICT infrastructure is viewed at any moment.

4.1.4   Objectives

The main objectives of Operations are:

■ to provide a stable and secure ICT infrastructure ready and able to be used as the foundation for the provision of ICT services for business benefit

■ to maintain and operate effective and efficient operational procedures, ensuring that all ICT services and components meet their operational targets and requirements

■ to ensure that all the operational requirements of other ICT and Service Management processes are satisfied and to assist them in delivering operational services that meet their agreed SLA targets.

4.2 Benefits, costs and problems

The benefits, costs and possible problems associated with establishing a successful Operations function are outlined below.

4.2.1 Benefits

It is anticipated that organisations that wish to develop or improve the professionalism of their operational practices in line with the guidance provided on ICTIM, and specifically in the area of Operations, can expect the following benefits:

■ improved management and control of all ICT infrastructure events, alerts and alarms

■ faster detection, response and resolution of incidents and problems, with clear definition of responsibilities

■ more resilient infrastructure with improved service availability with prevention of incident and problem recurrences

■ a framework for financial management and long-term cost reduction

■ help with the provision and maintenance of quality IT services

■ clear definition of the roles and responsibilities of individuals within Operations

■ a systematic approach to the assessment of staff performance and promotion

■ a platform for the development of automation in Operations and the use of an operational bridge, offering productivity and service quality improvements

■ improved supplier relationships

■ a climate within which procedures are accepted as being the norm, so that reliance on individual inherited skills diminishes

■ the generation of a professional environment where the performance of everybody can rise to the level of the best.

4.2.2 Costs

The main costs incurred in adopting the guidance in this module are likely to be:

■ adoption, tailoring and production of the procedures described within this section

■ the selection and purchase of operational management tools in conjunction with all other areas of ICT and Service Management

■ the configuration and integration of operational management tools and processes with all other ICT and Service Management tools and processes

■ customising of management tools and the development of operational scripts

■ additional software or management tools and packages required

■ any additional equipment requirements, e.g., network backup devices and solutions

■ the establishment and maintenance of the Operational environments

■ education and training for all operational staff.

123

The development of Operations professionalism should be viewed as an investment, which in the long run pays for itself both with automation, which reduces cost and improves quality, and with a move away from a dependence on inherited skills and local undocumented knowledge.

4.2.3 Possible problems

In most organisations the professional practices described in this module are seen as the correct way to operate. There may, however, be some resistance to changes in working practices. Operations staff have traditionally relied on historical knowledge, and often see themselves as essential to the efficient running of the organisation. The trend towards systematic procedures with more clearly defined roles and responsibilities and, above all, the move towards automation are, however, eliminating the 'craft' tradition.

In this climate, changes to bring operational working practices into line with the guidance in this module cannot necessarily be introduced rapidly. These changes should be handled as far as possible by the existing Operations staff to ensure committed knowledgeable change, at measured pace, to modern professional practices.

To avoid staff morale problems and to ensure staff take ownership of changes, it is recommended that any consultancy, brought in to modernise practices, is used in support of the people on site rather than in place of them. This approach will reduce the risks and the costs of achieving professionalism.

Many organisations use the argument that 'we are too busy fighting the fire to build a new house'. However, it must be realised that if things are to get better, at some time the organisation needs to take decisive action. In general, the more the fire-fighting activity, the greater the need for radical change. Additional possible problem areas are:

- a lack of awareness and knowledge of service and business targets and requirements
- the establishment of effective end-to-end operational management tools and processes
- a lack of focus on service and business availability
- lack of awareness and adherence to the operational aspects of security policies and procedures
- poor recognition of the need and importance of operational tools and processes by senior ICT Management
- resistance to change
- creating service- and business-focused operational staff
- documentation and adherence to agreed practices and processes
- maintenance of operational systems and services while implementing process improvements
- staff motivation and focus on repetitive operational processes.

4.3 The roles, responsibilities and interfaces

The functional discrimination of Operations personnel could possibly hinder the effective operation of the ICT infrastructure and the end-to-end performance of the Operations process. A process-oriented approach is an effective way towards reaching the end result of adherence to

SLAs, OLAs and UCs. The Operations process is often underpinned by a number of tools, and it is essential that the tools underpin the automation of the processes and support the staff in their roles and discharge of their responsibilities.

4.3.1   The roles and responsibilities

Adopting a process approach ensures that end-to-end management is achieved across the complete infrastructure, removing barriers and weak areas within the operational infrastructure, the tools, and people's roles. Within this end-to-end view of the Operations process, the following roles can be identified:

- **Production Services Manager/Operations Management/Shift Leader:** 24x7 management of the operational people, process and technology, facilitating teamwork throughout ICT Operations
- **Operations Analyst:** the day-to-day control of the complete ICT operational infrastructure, working directly with MO and all the operational ICT infrastructure components and services
- **Storage and Backup Management:** management and control of all information storage devices and space, and the scheduling, testing and storage of all backups and their subsequent recovery
- **Scheduling Analyst:** management and control of all aspects of the scheduling or operational workloads, including printers and output
- **Database Administration:** the management and administration of all operational databases.

In many organisations these roles are combined into individual or team functions. The scope and responsibilities of each of these individual roles is expanded in Annex 4A.

Skills

Skills are being eroded all the time because of the increasing number of changes and developments. This calls for continual education and development of new skills for staff to maintain the rapidly evolving ICT infrastructure. The demands that are being placed on the ICT infrastructure by new or expanded ICT services further increases the pressure to 'keep up'. People who are naturally attracted to new developments (early adopters), who are eager to find out how things work, while still being able to maintain the current infrastructure in a stable state, will thrive in a fast moving Operations environment.

There is always a need to have an understanding of programming techniques (3GL, 4GL, for scripting – see Annex 4C.1) within a multifunctional architecture of applications, networks, operating systems and databases. This needs to be developed together with training in operating, configuring and troubleshooting of the ICT services and infrastructure.

The externalisation of ICT infrastructure requires communication skills as well. An increasing number of consumers of IT services are 'foreign' to the organisation, because they are outside the organisation, and may seem remote to operational staff. The need for communication skills is, of course, not limited to the operational staff but extends to the whole of the ICT organisation.

Tasks

It is important to identify whether the ICT infrastructure deviates from what it is expected to be or do. The expectation is laid down in the OLAs and UCs, but it also comes from what is considered to be 'normal'. The definition of what is 'normal' will depend on the organisation (type, culture, products, maturity). It is also quite common that the definition of what is 'normal' is provided by the supplier, sometimes in the form of 'undocumented features' or by peer groups. The observations may be supported by measurement, followed by a comparison being made between the observed state and the accepted state, the norm. In technical terms, this is called a 'measurement control loop'.

The 'measurement control loop' is fundamental to operational management control and is often engaged when a change to the ICT infrastructure results in MOs being added, removed or changed.

Example

Changes to an MO may impact on other MOs, because they are tightly intertwined with, fully dependent upon, or form a chain with, the MO being changed. It is, therefore, possible that MOs, other than the one being changed, have to be temporarily inactive or even changed themselves, because somewhere in the ICT infrastructure a related MO is being changed.

Of course, there are many changes being implemented within an ICT infrastructure. These changes will often be effected through the Continuous Service Improvement Programme (CSIP), which provides overall coordination and continual improvement support to all ICTIM and ITSM processes. Whenever new or modified MOs are brought into the operational infrastructure, their normal operating profiles and thresholds must be established so that any processes or tools will be able to recognise and alert any abnormal behaviour.

The initiatives for these improvements originate in many places within the organisation, firstly, in the Operations process itself. Other examples of originators are:

- the other ICTIM processes due to changed information or output demand
- new or grown ICT services which require new or modified working procedures, methods or tools and techniques
- Service Management processes that cooperate closely with Operations or require data from Operations.

Responsibilities

The first responsibility is to provide an ICT infrastructure that functions in the way it is expected to function. The expected function is laid down in OLAs and, for suppliers, in Underpinning Contracts (UCs). These can be viewed as the technical consequences of the SLAs. In order to asses and accommodate the consequences of an SLA on the operation of an ICT infrastructure, it is vital that there is a 'translation' of the terms and conditions of the SLA as far as operators are concerned. An example might clarify this:

Example

*** SLA states service availability from 08.00 until 20:00 with specified performance, etc.***

*** OLA should state that the backup of the database cannot be scheduled before 20:00 and needs to be finished by 08:00.***

The targets within the OLAs and UCs must not contravene the targets within the SLA and must 'add up' to consistently deliver on service commitments made in SLAs.

4.3.2 External interfaces

The Operations processes provide essential information and services to all the ITSM processes. The ITSM processes negotiate and set the operational targets that the Operations procedures should continually strive to achieve, especially the Service Level, Availability, Capacity and IT Service Continuity Management processes. The Operations processes provide:

- a resilient and conformant ICT infrastructure to meet all its current and future operational targets
- operational information, data and reports if and when necessary to all the ITSM processes
- the day-to-day interface between ITSM processes and the MOs and ICT infrastructure components and resources
- the operational levels, standards and targets agreed within OLAs
- the coordination of third party support technicians and engineers and the control and recording of their access to all operational environments.

There are also a number of additional interfaces to various other areas of the organisation:

- **Application Management** is concerned with all aspects of the design and development, justification and procurement of applications for use within the organisation. Application Management should provide Operations with details of the operational requirements of all operational applications, information and databases
- **Human Resources** – on skill sets, personal development plans, training plans and approved training service suppliers
- **Security Management** – on all aspects of security including security policies, procedures and plans
- **Supplier Management** – on contract details and supplier performance.

4.3.3 Internal interfaces

The Operations processes underpin all the other ICTIM processes by providing:

- a resilient and conformant ICT infrastructure to meet all their current and future operational targets
- operational information, data and reports, when necessary, to all other ICTIM processes.

127

The ICTIM processes interface with Operations in the following ways:

- the management scope, methods and systems employed by Operations processes are designed by the Design and Planning process

- the Design and Planning process provides strategies, plans, policies, standards and architectures for Operations processes, especially ICT infrastructure architectures and ICT Management architectures

- incremental adaptations and improvements of these strategies, plans and policies are often performed by the Technical Support process

- advice and guidance on event correlation, categorisation and classification is obtained from Technical Support, together with assistance in the analysis, diagnosis and resolution of complex operational issues.

4.4 The management processes involved

The management processes of Operations are many and varied. The main processes and activities involved in the operational management of an ICT infrastructure are:

- operational control and management of the services, components and their configurations

- management of all ICT infrastructure events

- workload and output management and scheduling

- storage management, backup and recovery

- management and control of all aspects of ICT operational security

- management of the supporting operational process

- proactive operational management processes.

Wherever possible, these processes should be automated with minimal manual intervention. This can be achieved using management tools and scripting languages to pre-empt events and script predefined responses to the management of those events. Each of these process areas is considered in detail in the following sections.

4.4.1 Management of all ICT infrastructure events

The event management process is the main process of Operations. It is the hub around which all other operational, ICTIM and ITSM processes are built. It is essential that the process is effective, efficient and integrated both with the other processes within Operations and all other ICTIM and ITSM processes. The Fault Management (ISO) area (see Annex 4B) is a crucial element of this process. The essential elements of the ICT event management process are:

- **Event monitoring:** this is the process of 'observing' the ICT services and infrastructure for abnormal situations and conditions, preferably predicting and pre-empting situations and conditions and thereby avoiding possible service and component failures.

- **Event detection:** this process is triggered by 'warning' and 'alarm' events occurring within MOs, which indicate an abnormal state of the MOs or of a component within an MO.

- **Event logging:** this is the process of gathering and recording 'state change notification' information of MOs related to events.

- **Event examination and filtering:** requires analysis of the detected condition to see whether any action is required and determine the time-scale required for that action.

- **Event processing, correlation and escalation:** once the event has been deemed significant and requiring some action, further analysis should take place to identify if any other similar or related events have occurred that can be actioned at the same time. The criticality and impact of the event needs to be assessed, reported and escalated to the appropriate processes and personnel. This should involve the automated creation of incidents of the appropriate category, severity, urgency and priority.

- **Event resolution:** correction of the abnormal condition and restoration of normal operations, ideally by scripting an automating corrective action.

- **Event closure:** clearance and closure of the event and any associated incidents.

- **Management of the event lifecycle:** this ensures that all stages of the event lifecycle above are efficient, effective and continually improved. Wherever possible, automated scripting and integration of management tools should be used to speed up all stages of the event management lifecycle. For example, an event may be detected by one management tool that could automatically detect it, log it, examine it, process it, correlate it, escalate it, raise an incident on the central Service Desk/Incident Management tool and generate an alert to either an Operations or Technical Support pager or mobile phone, for immediate attention. It could also escalate the event for senior management attention if appropriate. Alternatively, it might be possible to avoid all this by taking some predefined, scripted action to resolve and recover the event automatically.

- **Event grouping:** consists of the definition and agreement of procedures for the categorisation, classification and correlation of events. This activity needs to be closely coordinated with the activities and classifications of incidents and problems within their owning processes.

- **Event reporting:** needs to include the logging, analysis and reporting of all infrastructure-related events.

4.4.2 Operational control and management of the services, components and their configurations

This process consists of all the activities essential to maintaining control and management of a resilient operational infrastructure, and includes the installation of new or changed components and the removal of old or obsolete ones.

All major changes to existing ICT services and components should be assessed against the checklist of acceptance criteria contained within Appendix M. The major activities are:

- **Installation:** the introduction of new or changed MOs into the technical infrastructure. This would not only include the activities for doing this but also the specification and completion of acceptance criteria for any new ICT infrastructure components prior to installation into the operational environment. This would include their operational profiles and thresholds.

■ **De-installation:** the removal of old or obsolete MOs from the technical infrastructure including disposal.

■ **Distribution:** the process of distributing MOs for the purpose of installation. This activity can also consist of the distribution of amended or new MO configurations. Uploading and downloading facilities within management tools and systems are required in order to support these distribution activities. These activities should be performed in conjunction with the Deployment process.

■ **Operation control:** ensures successful installation and initialisation of MOs, setting operating parameters and MO attributes that control the routine operation, monitoring, 'close-down' and deactivation of MOs according to defined standards and procedures. It should also support the interrogation and resetting of the transient state of any MO or MO component or attribute.

■ **Development and maintenance of an operational management tool-set:** the operational tool-set needs to be developed in line with the overall management architecture defined by D and P. Operations has responsibility for the operational management tool-set and must ensure that it covers all the required operational functionality and integrates with all other ICTIM and ITSM management tools.

■ **Configuration and reconfiguration:** is the ability to reset or adjust the status or operating parameters of any MO, or MO component.

■ **Housekeeping and preventative maintenance processes:** consist of all the regular and routine processes necessary to support and maintain a resilient ICT infrastructure, and includes activities such as:

- clearing or deletion of log files and journals
- deletion of temporary files or workspace
- cleaning of operational environments
- support and maintenance of management tools and systems
- management of operational users, files and passwords
- preventative maintenance
- shift handover and reporting
- equipment maintenance and cleaning
- operational reporting.

■ **Inventory and Asset Management:** is the identification, registration and verification of operational MOs and the collection of information relating to changes in the configuration of the MOs. This ensures that all the information required within the CMDB is accurately maintained. Ideally, integrated processes should ensure that information on asset changes detected by management systems and tools is used to automatically update the information within the CMDB, under the control of Configuration Management processes.

4.4.3 Workload, output, resilience testing management and scheduling

This process includes the development, maintenance and management of all operational schedules covering workloads, output and printer queues, and the scheduled testing of all resilience and recovery options. There are very close relationships with Capacity Management, Availability Management and IT Service Continuity Management processes. This process is responsible for implementing the operational aspects of each of these Service Management processes. Its constituent components are:

- **Workload scheduling and management:**
  - development, maintenance and management of all operational workload schedules
  - scheduling of all operational workloads and dependencies
  - scheduling of ad hoc and exceptional workloads with resolution of conflicts and dependencies
  - control and management of enterprise scheduling and inter-platform dependencies.

- **Output and printer scheduling and management:**
  - development, maintenance and management of all output schedules
  - control and management of printer queues and output.

- **Secure control and distribution of electronic and physical output and media:**
  - document and printer output
  - physical data and media transfers
  - electronic data and file transfers
  - movement of backup and recovery media off site under the direction of Storage, Availability and IT Service Continuity Management.

- **Resilience facilities and fail-over testing schedules:**
  - maintenance of testing schedules and production of test reports and exceptions
  - exercising of alternate or resilient environmental equipment and facilities
  - switching over to alternate routing and network circuits
  - conducting server fail-over testing
  - exercising of split and alternate site Operations
  - implementing the testing of all resilience equipment and options
  - Business Continuity, IT Service Continuity and disaster recovery testing.

4.4.4 Storage management, backup and recovery

This element of Operations is responsible for the control and management of all aspects of information storage and retrieval and includes all the processes and mechanisms necessary to ensure that the appropriate levels of storage, protection, access and retrieval are available and used for ICT information. A more comprehensive explanation of this area is contained in Annex 4D; it has close involvement with and underpins the operation of the Capacity, Availability and IT Service Continuity Management processes. It consists of:

- **Storage management and allocation**: this activity manages all aspects of the management, allocation and housekeeping of media and information storage. It involves aspects of policy making and implementation as well as the control and management of media movements.

- **System backup and recovery:** backup and recovery are complementary in the sense that backup is almost always scheduled in advance and recovery is usually reactive and unscheduled. This means that there is rarely a pressing need for a backup whereas there is nearly always a pressing reason for a restore. The more thought that is put into backup and recovery policies and strategies, in advance, the less disruption and damage the procedure will cause.

- **Information management:** would include the use of document and hierarchical information management systems. This process should ensure that the right information is stored in the appropriate media, with the right level of access and speed of retrieval.

- **Database management and administration:** is responsible for the regular management and administrative tasks necessary for support and maintenance of all operational databases.

4.4.5 Management and control of all aspects of ICT operational security

This process covers the control of all aspects of ICT operational security. It is one of the fundamental elements of any good Security Management process. All operational security processes should conform to security policies and guidelines and should be implemented under the direction of, and with the approval of, the Security Officer and the Security Manager. More comprehensive information can be found in the ITIL *Security Management* book. The key elements of operational security are:

- **Security monitoring:** monitors, verifies and tracks the level of security according to the organisational security policy and guidelines:
    - detection and containment of all intrusion attempts and attempts at unauthorised access to ICT information and systems
    - logging, management and reporting of all security events and exceptions.

- **Security control:** involves the control and management of access to all operational ICT services and infrastructure:
    - physical security: the element of Security Management that prevents unauthorised, unwanted and unnecessary physical access to ICT information and systems by using appropriate access control countermeasures
    - logical security: the component of Security Management that prevents unauthorised, unwanted and unnecessary logical access to ICT information and systems by using measures on classification, authentication and access controls pertaining to the ICT infrastructure.

4.4.6 Management of the supporting operational process

This involves the management of all the underpinning processes that are necessary for the support of effective and efficient operational processes. Many of these also provide invaluable support and information to other ICTIM and ITSM processes. It includes:

- **Operational document maintenance:** the development and maintenance of a central library containing all the documentation necessary for the support and smooth running of the operational ICT services and infrastructure. This is referred to as the Operational Document Library (ODL) and is often a combination of printed and electronic documentation. It is essential that a duplicate copy of all essential operational documents is also stored off site, ideally as a complete off-site copy of the ODL. This documentation should include all site maps, plans, room layouts, schematics and infrastructure topology diagrams.

- **Information logging and collection:** the process of gathering all types of information on the use of the operational ICT services and infrastructure. The array of information that may be needed is considerable. Appropriate and adequate levels of storage should be obtained from the storage management processes. The information should be regularly condensed and archived. The type of information required includes:

- performance-related data and logging information used for Capacity Management analysis and reporting purposes
- the combination and allocation of usage statistics and costs to defined sets of users and services for subsequent usage control or charging purposes by both Capacity and Financial Management
- the capture and collection of MO status and usage data for the purposes of subsequent analysis, control, allocation and reporting by Availability Management
- management and control of MOs, performance attributes, schedules, consolidations, historical utilisation, trends, business usage profiles, business transactions, business services, business user groups, business thresholds, business expected resource usage for use by Capacity and Financial Management.

■ **Information analysis:** the process of analysing operational measurement data in order to determine the cause of operational deviations and to formulate subsequent related improvement activities:

- analysis is, in many cases, a means to explain the observed performance of an MO or a set of MOs. Its regular and ad hoc usage comes about when there is an unacceptable operational degradation in the ICT infrastructure. The analysis activity needs to come up with answers on the cause of this operational deviation. Because of the ad hoc fashion, there will be little or no experience in analysing the data and there will be few or no tools to aid with this analysis. In order to take preventive measures before the operational degradation becomes noticeable, it is necessary to routinely analyse the recorded information as well as analysing it on an ad hoc basis
- analysis and development of trends in operational performance, both of the ICT infrastructure and the Operations personnel
- measurement, analysis and reporting of all operational OLA targets and achievements.

■ **Scripting:** the customising, configuration and automated scripting of procedures to aggregate and consolidate logging information or to control the actions and responses of management tools to detected events and conditions.

4.4.7   Proactive operational management processes

This includes the documentation and management of the actual operational processes themselves together with the implementation of a process of continual improvement, both within the ICT infrastructure itself and all the associated Operations processes:

■ **review of the Operations processes:** for efficiency, effectiveness and compliance

■ **internal or external audit of all operational processes:** or assessment and comparison with best practice guidelines on a regular basis

■ **instigation of remedial or improvement actions to the operational infrastructure:** this can be achieved using analysis of event logs, incident data and operational trend reports. By working with other ICTIM and ITSM processes, weak areas within ICT services and infrastructure can be identified and improved under the control of Change Management procedures

■ **instigation of remedial actions or improvements to the Operations processes:** again, by analysing operational information, reports, reviews and audits, remedial and improvement changes can be made to process weak spots

■ **operational tuning:** this is the process of determining the value of attributes and parameters of operational ICT services and MOs in order to optimise their performance. This can be achieved using analysis and trending of operational information and data. Again, these activities should only be completed in coordination and conjunction with all other ICTIM and ITSM processes, especially Capacity Management and Change Management.

4.5 The processes and deliverables of Operations

The Operations process is all about ensuring that the ICT infrastructure meets all its operational targets and objectives. Therefore, the major deliverables of the Operations process are:

■ **a stable, secure and resilient ICT infrastructure:** the provision of a stable foundation on which to base the delivery of a set of ICT services meeting their business needs and targets

■ **a secure Operational Document Library (ODL):** containing details of all operational documentation, processes and procedures, especially shift handover procedures. This should also contain all hardware and equipment manuals, application manuals and all site plans, office plans, equipment room layouts and major cable routes

■ **a log or database of all operational events, alerts and alarms:** this should be a complete record of all the events occurring within the operational infrastructure. The majority of these should also be fed into the Incident Management process and be recorded as incidents themselves. However, the event log can be analysed to identify trends and weaknesses within the infrastructure that can be discussed and rectified with other ICTIM or ITSM processes, such as Availability Management

■ **a set of operational scripts:** all the scripts required to run the operational workloads and to recover from all recoverable events and conditions

■ **a resilience and fail-over testing schedule:** the development, maintenance and implementation of a schedule for the regular testing of all resilience and fail-over components and techniques within the operational infrastructure

■ **a set of operational work schedules:** for all batch work, print schedules and system and data backups

■ **a set of operational management tools:** that provide views and information on the operational state of the ICT infrastructure and its services, including all media movements and locations

■ **management reports and information:** the collection of all the operational information and the production of all management reports

■ **exception reviews and reports:** ad hoc and one-off exception reports where thresholds, service targets or operational targets are exceeded

■ **review and audit reports:** reports from review and/or audit exercises on the effectiveness, efficiency and compliance of the Operations process, identifying areas of weakness and improvement.

4.6 The techniques, tools and technologies

The Operations process is very much 'the engine room' of ICT. It often lacks focus and profile. However, it is the foundation for the provision of quality ICT services to the business. In organisations where the Operations process does have focus and profile it is essential that they are both maintained.

> **Key message**
>
> *The better the Operations process is within an organisation the less perceived need there is for that process.*
>
> **This is because better Operations processes have fewer operational failures and meet more of their operational service targets. The temptation is therefore to remove focus, profile, resources and commitment from the process, often with devastating results for the organisation. Suddenly, operational failures start to occur and services once again fail to meet their operational targets. In these situations, Operations moves through a cycle of peaks and troughs of success and failure.**
>
> **It is essential, therefore, that even while things are going well operationally, focus and profile on the Operations process is maintained, even though this may be hard to justify to senior business and ICT Management.**

4.6.1 The techniques

The techniques used by organisations within the ICT Operations process are many and varied and are discussed in the following sections.

Operations bridge

This technique involves the co-location of the Service Desk and Operations staff in an 'Operations bridge' or a 'Network Operations Centre' or 'NOC'. This enables the Operations process and the Incident Management processes, people and products (tools and technology) to be closely integrated. This especially relates to the management of the event lifecycle and the incident lifecycle, which need to be closely linked to effect the rapid resolution of operational issues. This integration is illustrated in Figure 4.4. If the operational management tools and screens are clearly visible to both the Service Desk staff and the Operation staff, they can both see the effects of failures on the ICT infrastructure as they happen. Often this is achieved by having large screen displays or projected images on the walls of the Operations bridge area. The Service Desk then has all the information necessary to pass on to the users immediately they call, improving the quality of the service provided by the Service Desk to its customers.

Example

A financial organisation with a strategically important website continually failed to meet its operational targets, especially with regard to the quality of service delivered by the Internet site. The prime reason for this was their lack of focus on the monitoring of operational events and service availability and response. This situation was allowed to develop until senior Business Managers demanded action from the senior ICT Management. There were major repercussions, and reviews were undertaken to determine the underlying cause. After considerable pain and disruption, a trial Operations bridge was established with weekly reports on operational performance. Operational events were immediately investigated whenever they occurred and were individually reviewed after resolution. An improvement team was established, with representation from all areas, to implement the recommendations from the reviews and the feedback from the Operations bridge. This all resulted eventually in considerable improvement in the quality of service delivered to the business and its customers.

In some organisations, one or other of the Incident Management or event management processes is outsourced to a third party. If only one of them is outsourced, it becomes more difficult to create an Operations bridge unless one or other of the organisations locates members of their staff within the other organisation's offices. An alternative is to automate the interface between the tools of the two organisations in order to effect rapid exchange of information.

Some organisations outsource the Incident Management and event management processes in their entirety to a third party. This means that the Operations bridge is effectively run as a service. This situation has to be carefully managed to ensure that both processes function effectively and continue to deliver value for money.

There is another situation which is becoming increasingly popular within certain organisations where the Incident Management and event management processes are run in-house during prime shift and revert to an outsourced organisation to maintain 24x7 operation. This can be a more financially attractive situation for some organisations where 24x7 support of ICT services and infrastructure is required, but staff work only normal office hours.

Event analysis and trending

The analysis of Operational events and the trends in operational events can be used to drive the improvement of the Operations process. Two separate approaches can be used:

- Major operational event review:

  All major operational events occurring with the ICT infrastructure should be analysed to determine:

  - what went wrong?
  - what aspects of the resolution were done well?
  - what aspects of the resolution could be improved?
  - how can this event be prevented from reoccurring?

  These reviews should be completed in coordination with all other processes, especially Problem Management's major problem reviews and Availability Management's major outage analysis

■ Event trend analysis:

Events and event trends should be analysed to determine those areas causing the most pain and disruption to operational ICT services. The major areas should then be investigated and actions taken to reduce their impact or ideally prevent their reoccurrence.

Internal review and assessment

It is essential that, periodically, each organisation takes stock of its current situation so that reference points and baselines can be determined, against which future development and progress can be assessed. Industry, national and international standards exist or are being developed that facilitate this review process. SWOT analysis and Value Chain Analysis methods can also be used for internal review and assessment. These reviews and assessments can often be used to identify areas of weakness or non-compliance.

External benchmarking

Many organisations use external review and benchmarking as a means of assessing their effectiveness and efficiency. Several audit organisations provide methods of assessing and benchmarking ICT Operations processes. Some provide comparative details of other Operations organisations, industry averages and industry leaders' performance. The main advantage of external benchmarking is the objective point of view of an external organisation, not influenced by internal politics. It can also provide comparative figures with similar type organisations and market leaders. The only drawback is that the cost of a benchmarking service can be considerable. The majority of these benchmarking techniques can be based on either industry, national (e.g., BSI, NEN, DIN, the British, Dutch and German standards institutes, respectively) or international (e.g., ISO) standards. However, some organisations have their own proprietary evaluation and scoring methods.

In order to be of real value, external benchmarking exercises, like internal reviews, should be completed on a regular basis.

Continual process of improvement

As well as measuring and reviewing operational performance, mechanisms and attitudes for improving performance within Operations processes should be actively encouraged. This will ensure that, no matter how good the Operations processes are, they will continually improve. Aspects of this need to be incorporated into overall ICT, Operations team and individual performance assessments. In this way, they will become established as part of normal everyday operations.

4.6.2   The tools

The tools required for an efficient Operations process are many and varied. However, operational tools should not be selected in isolation. In order to ensure integration of Operations Management tools with all other management tools, it is essential that a management architecture and management standards are developed and adopted for the selection and implementation of all management tools. This architecture should be developed by the D and P processes and adopted and applied by all other ICTIM and ITSM processes.

The hub of any management tool architecture is event management. This is used to collect, correlate, distribute, progress and resolve events. This process is fundamental to the integration and operation of all other tools.

Systems Management or network management tools

The principal tool of the Operations process is the Systems Management tool or network management system. There are many different tools offering various facilities within this area, so it is essential that a system with the required functionality is selected. These tools are, by design, either proprietary or non-proprietary in their operation and support, although hybrid systems do exist. It is vital that they provide end-to-end management of the ICT infrastructure and not just elements within the infrastructure. These tools principally enable the availability, reliability configuration and operability of components within the ICT infrastructure to be controlled and managed. These are the fundamental tools of Operations and they support the day-to-day operation and management of the ICT infrastructure by providing:

- categorisation, interpretation, recording and management of ICT infrastructure events, warnings and alarms, leading to possible incident recording and problem determination and control

- monitoring and interrogation of ICT component status and condition and all aspects of ICT infrastructure operation and control

- ICT infrastructure equipment reload, reset and recovery

- monitoring, control and management of ICT infrastructure security

- traffic monitoring, collection and storage of data on service and performance levels of all aspects of the operational ICT infrastructure

- ICT infrastructure component configuration maintenance, including download and upload facilities

- activation/deactivation of ICT infrastructure components

- proactive preventative maintenance

- diagnostic monitoring, tracing and analysis facilities

- ICT infrastructure testing and monitoring

- automation of operational procedures.

Environmental management tools

Several tools exist for the monitoring of environmental equipment and conditions. Generally speaking, they should be able to react to particular events or thresholds and indicate by means of a warning or alarm that action is needed, either on a local or a remote alarm system. Indeed, if the situation is critical enough then in extremes the environmental monitor should be capable of initiating a tidy equipment shutdown to limit the damage to the operational environment.

Service, application and database management tools

Tools are required by Operations for the management and control of all aspects of operation, availability and performance of the services, application and databases. Again, the tools are many and varied but generally provide:

- user concurrency levels
- service, application and database transaction statistics, volumes and response times
- transaction control, management, processing, queuing times, tracing and diagnosis
- service, application and database security, access control and management
- logging of all events, warnings, alarms and failures
- resource utilisation levels
- audit trail facilities.

Diagnostic tools

Diagnostic and testing tools of many different types and sophistication exist, and can be used for a multitude of purposes from problem diagnosis to traffic simulation and planning. These tools can often facilitate rapid identification and resolution of complex ICT infrastructure failure conditions and vary in their complexity, functionality and cost. They may vary from simple log analysers or cable testers to sophisticated network protocol analysers or hybrid analysers with dual functionality. However, they often require detailed knowledge of both the ICT infrastructure and of the tools themselves. These tools are more than pure test and diagnostic aids. They can form an integral part of the Capacity Management function, because of their ability to record and analyse performance information. These purpose-built devices can remain permanently connected to the ICT infrastructure at strategic points, and be left to accumulate status, statistics and performance information. They provide useful information to the Capacity Management function. However, if left connected, appropriate security measures will be necessary in order to avoid disclosure of passwords and other sensitive information.

Scheduling tools

Large ICT organisations may have many different centralised and distributed server platforms. The task of scheduling and managing the workload across such a diverse infrastructure is a complex and challenging one. It is impossible to perform this manually, so most organisations turn to the use of an enterprise scheduling tool to coordinate and control the scheduling of job execution, data flows, file transfer and output and printer management. The selection of the appropriate tool is crucial to the success of an effective Operations process. However, the Operations process, again, cannot be considered in isolation. The needs of processes such as Capacity, Financial and IT Service Continuity Management are paramount in the consideration of an appropriate enterprise scheduling tool.

Storage management tools

Most ICT organisations are moving or have moved to the use of indirectly attached storage solutions. This involves the use of Storage Area Networks (SANs) or Network Attached Storage (NAS) solutions. This means that most storage management processes are responsible for the control, allocation and management of both directly attached storage and indirectly attached storage (NAS and SAN). In order to perform this function effectively tools are required that allow:

- setting and implementing space allocation, hierarchical management, copying and backup policies
- mirroring, raid sets and 'hot swapping' of failed components with in-flight recovery

- monitoring, setting thresholds and reporting on media storage usage
- security and access control facilities
- easy housekeeping and maintenance of the storage media
- support of the efficient and effective use of databases and file systems.

Performance tools

These tools may be required by Operations, but some or all of them may already be in use within the Capacity Management function. It is preferential that the tools used by Operations are the same or similar tools as those used by the Capacity Management process if one exists. If a separate Capacity Management function does not exist, the tools may have to be obtained by cost justifying the advantages to Operations. The types of facilities required within these sorts of tools are similar to those of Capacity Management and are:

- real-time monitoring of ICT service response, component response and client and customer response times
- real-time monitoring of ICT service and component usage and traffic volumes
- support of a database for recording past statistical information and performance history
- statistical analysis facilities
- import and export facilities with other Capacity Management tools
- trending and modelling facilities.

Service Management tools

Tools to assist with the implementation of all the Service Management disciplines will be required within the organisation. Some tools may already exist within the current Service Management processes. Where they already exist, Operations tools will need to inter-operate with their existing functionality. These aspects should be addressed within the overall management tool architecture produced by the D and P processes.

Some existing Service Management tools have options for interfacing to ICT infrastructure and other management tools. Ideally, products will provide assistance on all the Service Management disciplines together with the Operations process in a fully integrated and modular system.

Other techniques

A set of additional methods and techniques that are sometimes used within operational environments have also been included in Annex 4C. These include:

- scripting techniques
- set theory
- queuing theory
- performance management.

4.6.3   The technologies

The ICT infrastructure in use within an organisation must support and enable the business processes of the organisation itself. However, they must also facilitate and underpin the operation of effective operation and support processes. If the ICT infrastructure fails to do this effectively, it will be impossible for the Operations process to meet the operational needs and targets defined within SLAs and OLAs. Operations needs to be closely involved with all other areas of ICTIM in selection and implementation of new ICT technologies to ensure that effective operational management facilities are supported by any new ICT technologies. Operations facilities should be one of the basic mandatory requirements for the selection of any major new ICT technology. These requirements should be specified by the Operations process and included by D and P in the ITT/SOR of the new technology.

Once new ICT technology has been selected and purchased, Operations should work closely with the Deployment process during the testing stages:

- to ensure that any new systems pass their operational acceptance criteria, meeting or exceeding their operational requirements
- to develop any new operational support or management processes or procedures before or during the deployment
- to develop any new skills or knowledge required either by formal, workshop or on-the-job training.

This will mean that the new technologies can be supported and managed once they are deployed to the operational environment.

Annex 4A   ICT operational roles

4A.1   Production Services Manager/Operations Manager/Shift Leader

A Production Services Manager/Operations Manager/Shift Leader is responsible for the coordination, control and management of a team of operational staff. An appropriate mission statement could be:

> **To set up and manage an efficient computer operation that is capable of delivering, with support from other ICTIM functions, IT services to the quality required in the Service Level Agreements, whilst absorbing change at a rate consistent with business needs.**

The main objectives of such a role are to:

- motivate and develop the operational staff under their control to ensure that all ICT services meet their SLA targets, within the agreed financial budget; ensure that these staff have up-to-date job descriptions, are regularly appraised, and have a current training plan for personal development; arrange for the recruitment of staff as necessary

- develop and maintain controls and procedures to ensure that the operational processes run efficiently; ensure that in the event of failure Operations can recover services in accordance with a predefined and tested recovery or continuity plan, to agreed fallback levels of service within the agreed targeted recovery time

- ensure that the physical environment is maintained and secure, according to contractual requirements and business needs

- ensure that any new ICT infrastructure meets the agreed operability and manageability criteria for live running prior to accepting them for operational use

- plan and oversee the installation of ICT infrastructure and liaise regularly with vendor staff, to ensure adequate support is provided

- ensure that all operational management reports and information are produced in a timely fashion for all other ICT, Service and Business Management processes

- ensure that all contractual documentation relevant to maintenance contracts is complete

- ensure that operational processes are continually developed and improved

- ensure that all operational staff are aware of and comply with all operational, ICT and Service Management processes.

Responsibilities

- be the owner of all of the ICT Operations process

- manage operational activities on a day-to-day shift basis, ensuring that all the agreed operational targets are met

- direct Operations staff to run the ICT production cycle in line with the controls and processes established to meet production deadlines and ensure that there is an effective handover with other shifts in order to maintain the level of ICT services across shift boundaries

- develop, maintain and enforce acceptance criteria and procedures for the implementation of new ICT infrastructure into the operational environment

- ensuring that all operational ICT infrastructure is operated in accordance with security, environmental and all other organisational policies

- ensure, with Problem Management/specialist support/vendor assistance as required, that incidents arising from or affecting the production cycle have minimum effect and are resolved within the target time-frame; ensure that all such incidents are recorded according to the defined Incident Management procedures and that any ICT infrastructure changes proposed to resolve incidents and problems are subject to Change Management control

- provide regular feedback on operational performance to the ICT Management recommending any improvements required

- handling all exceptions within scope and escalating where necessary those matters beyond the appropriate level of authority

- ensure that ICT infrastructure and environmental housekeeping procedures and system backups are performed to the prescribed standard

- look after Operations personnel matters, including staff development, training, education, performance reviews, appraisals, disciplinary issues and counselling; ensure that all operational staff are aware of and comply with all operational and organisational policies and processes

- train Operations staff in new services, applications and equipment, and arrange and run any necessary training, ensuring that appropriate operational documentation is produced

- check the completion of acceptance criteria for all new and changed services

- be responsible for quality assurance, validation and acceptance of all ICT infrastructure component deliveries

- ensure that all third party personnel are appropriately supervised within all ICT operational environments

- manage the operational budget ensuring that actual expenditure is within the forecasted level

- regularly review ICT operational processes for efficiency, effectiveness and compliance with a view to instigating a continuous process of improvement within all ICT operational areas

- develop a service-, customer- and business-focused culture within ICT operational areas and processes

- ensure that Operations continuity and recovery plans are maintained in line with overall IT Service Continuity Plans and Business Continuity Plans.

4A.2   Operations Analyst

An Operations Analyst is responsible for performing all operational processes and procedures, ensuring that all ICT services and infrastructure meet their operational targets. An appropriate mission statement would be:

To ensure that all ICT services and infrastructure meet all their operational targets.

The main objectives of such a role are to:

- ensure that all ICT services meet their SLA targets and that the operational infrastructure meets all its operational targets
- provide second-line support to the Service Desk and Incident Management on operational incidents
- operate and implement all operational ICT infrastructure and procedures
- ensure that the physical ICT environment is maintained and secure according to security and contractual requirements and business needs
- provide day-to-day contact and coordination of third party engineers and support staff
- ensure that the operational requirements of all other ICT, Service and Business Management processes are satisfied
- perform the day-to-day management and operation of all ICT infrastructure processes
- maintain all operational documentation.

Responsibilities

- efficiently and effectively investigate, diagnose, progress and action all operational events, alarms and incidents to the agreed quality and targets, ensuring that issues are escalated where appropriate and all records are updated in a timely fashion; develop and maintain effective interfaces with the Service Desk, Incident and Problem Management, ensuring that they have the appropriate documentation
- monitor, analyse, review and report on all ICT Operations, services, service levels and service quality on a daily basis
- maintain operational logs and journals on all events, warnings, alerts and alarms, recording and classifying all messages; maintain all operational data collection procedures, mechanisms and tools
- maintain all operational documentation, processes, management and diagnostic tools and spares, ensuring that spares are maintained at the agreed levels
- ensure that all routine housekeeping tasks are completed on all operational infrastructure and be aware of, check and test all availability, resilience, emergency and security test procedures and processes
- gather and record all required service level information and produce statistics for use in measuring operational Key Performance Indicators (KPIs)
- monitor suppliers and Service Providers for service quality, health and safety standards, ensuring that they meet the terms and conditions of their contracts
- use standard management tools and processes to carry out all defined housekeeping, system backup, and restoration procedures where necessary
- use management systems tools to determine loads, collect routine performance statistics and create routine reports as required
- implement operational changes in accordance with Change, Release and Configuration Management procedures, utilising the appropriate tools and test equipment
- select appropriate standard procedures and tools, and carry out defined tasks associated

with the planning, installation, upgrade, operation, control and maintenance of the operational infrastructure

- ensure that all operational security policies, processes and procedures are complied with

- design and maintain the production schedules and methods, setting up scheduling guides to ensure that workloads are run correctly and on schedule, with the minimum of supervision

- ensure (within the bounds of Operations' overall responsibility) that the ICT infrastructure supports efficient ICT Operations, and failing this:

  - identify and analyse any faults and take corrective action
  - ensure that correct incident reporting is completed
  - use Problem Management processes where appropriate

- supervise junior staff in the operation of ICT equipment and train them in the use of such equipment

- ensure that all computer equipment is maintained according to policies and recommendations and perform regular checks on environmental equipment and conditions

- develop the appropriate skills in writing and supporting all operational scripts and control language, being able to make minor amendments using appropriate Change Management processes and ensuring that file and control language standards are used where relevant

- ensure that standards for files and for job control are set up and maintained

- participate in the evaluation of all new services and systems ensuring that new ICT infrastructure adheres to operability and acceptance standards, liaise with development and project teams throughout the development lifecycle and conduct pre-live checks highlighting any significant events with recommended solutions

- carry out any necessary system tuning to maintain optimum performance levels in conjunction with Capacity Management

- maintain a catalogue of operational equipment types, consumables, cable types and default configurations

- replace any old or faulty equipment in conjunction with Availability, Change and Configuration Management.

4A.3 Storage and Backup Management

The Storage Management role is responsible for the management and control of all aspects of backup and recovery schedules, and the testing and storage and all aspects of storage planning, allocation, monitoring and decommissioning. In some organisations, these responsibilities may be divided into separate roles. An appropriate mission statement would be:

> **To supply and control all appropriate media necessary for the running of the ICT services in line with current and future operational targets, and to ensure that all ICT services and infrastructure are backed up and can be recovered in line with their operational and business requirements, as documented within SLAs and OLAs.**

The main objectives of such a role are to:

- ensure that all operational schedules meet
- ensure that appropriate backup and recovery strategies and policies are produced and maintained in conjunction with D and P
- ensure that all existing backup and recovery operational procedures are adhered to and are compliant with the backup and recovery policies.

Responsibilities

- liaise with Security Management and IT Service Continuity Management to ensure that all their requirements are met by the current backup and recovery policies
- specify, select and manage the use of backup and recovery packages and tools
- specify, select and manage the use of operational support packages, e.g., tape/disk management
- order magnetic tapes, diskettes, cartridges, paper, microfiche and all other media and devices when required
- develop and maintain a log system for recording the use of all ICT media, to ensure adequate, but not wasteful, levels of stock are kept
- issue media as directed or authorised by senior staff or in line with the production or test schedules
- set up and maintain a clear physical identification system for magnetic tapes, cartridges, etc., for easy identification
- perform security backups and associated rotation of media, ensuring that the correct backup tapes are in the correct secure environment (e.g., 'father' on site, 'grandfather' and copy of 'father' off site)
- maintain an out-of-hours media-control log that clearly shows usage and authorisation.

4A.4   Scheduling Analyst

The Scheduling Analyst is responsible for the management and control of all aspects of the scheduling, monitoring and reporting of the organisation's operational workload, including the management and control of all aspects of the scheduling and administration of printers and output. An appropriate mission statement would be:

> **To ensure that all operational workloads are scheduled and run in accordance with the schedules and targets agreed within SLAs and OLAs.**

The main objectives of such a role are to:

- ensure that the day-to-day ICT workload schedules are prepared in line with the scheduling guidelines
- ensure that operational workloads are run according to their defined schedules
- ensure that changes to normal schedules and all ad hoc workloads are subject to Change Management procedures.

Responsibilities

- document operational schedules and maintain them under strict Change Management
- run all agreed ad hoc workload requests provided the appropriate changes have been raised
- to present output in decollated, collated, or other form as appropriate
- to distribute output, data and media to the users in an efficient manner, to ensure the correct data is available in line with the agreed SLAs
- operate and maintain all equipment and management tools in an operational state
- liaise with the Service Desk staff with regard to specific user requirements for workload and output and, where necessary, alter schedules or output routines as a result, provided the appropriate Change Management procedures have been followed
- develop and maintain all the necessary operational scheduling documentation
- ensure that the scheduling staff are aware of all operational schedules and procedures
- ensure that all printers and other equipment are maintained appropriately
- ensure that all workload scheduling reports are produced in a timely fashion.

4A.5   Database Administrator

The characteristics of data structures need to be maintained to the levels as specified in the governing OLAs and UCs. Database Administration is the management and preservation of data as an information system component, according to the requirements and provisions posed by both the use and the characteristics of the data infrastructure. The object of management in the database domain is the data infrastructure. Part of this data infrastructure will be managed by processes in the ICTIM domain. Other parts will be managed by processes in either the Service Management domain or the Application Management domain.

The data infrastructure consists of the data carriers, the data structures, the data definitions and the actual content that together form part of one or more information systems. A data infrastructure employs means from the ICT infrastructure whose primary function is the storage of, and the access to, data, such as the database management systems, file systems and storage systems. The data infrastructure adds standard data models and data definitions as well as standard data structures, Operations and access mechanisms. The application-specific programs are built on top of that, adding other data and Operations.

Database Administration is an essential part of delivering quality IT services, utilising data that is employed across the organisation. It involves the management and administration of all operational databases. Since different users will be using different technologies, formats and access mechanisms, connection to the data infrastructure may be far from easy and therefore requires extensive knowledge. A large diversity of connections with both data-supplying and data-consuming systems has to be realised and maintained.

Looking at the exploitation of the data infrastructure, it can be seen that data is characterised by its syntax and its empiry. The syntax of data concerns its format and structure for storage and retrieval. The empiry of data is the signal or medium used to fix the data. An appropriate mission statement would be:

> **To ensure that all operational databases meet or exceed the targets agreed within SLAs and OLAs.**

The main objectives of such a role are to:

■ ensure that all operational databases meet their availability, reliability and performance targets as documented in SLAs and OLAs

■ ensure that all operational workloads are run according to their defined schedules

■ ensure that all changes to normal schedules and all ad hoc workloads are subject to Change Management procedures.

Responsibilities

■ the logical and physical design, layout, sizing and placement of all operational databases

■ the administration of database objects such as indexes, tables, views, constraints, sequences, snapshots and stored procedures

■ the archiving, backup and recovery of databases, in conjunction with storage management

■ the administration of users and profiles

■ the administration of files and devices

■ defining the standards for testing of databases

■ recommendations on the tuning and adjustment of databases when optimisation is deemed necessary, in conjunction with Capacity and Change Management

■ the administration of system repositories and archive files

■ liaise with Storage Management on the allocation of database storage space

■ liaise with D and P on the development of database standards and policies

■ the housekeeping on all databases:
  – database roll-back and roll-forward routines and scripts
  – backup and recovery routines and scripts

■ the production of reports on all the operational aspects of databases.

Annex 4B International Standards Organisation Management and Systems Management Functional Areas (SMFAs)

The International Standards Organisation's (ISO) Open Systems Interconnection (OSI) management framework defines five specific Systems Management Functional Areas (SMFAs) for the management of ICT systems, often referred to as FCAPS from the initial letter of each management area:

- Fault Management (ISO)
- Configuration Management (ISO)
- Accounting Management (ISO)
- Performance Management (ISO)
- Security Management (ISO)

These areas are expanded and explained within this annex.

4B.1   Fault Management (ISO)

Fault Management (ISO) is the process within Operations that is concerned with the detection of (potential) faults, the isolation of the fault and its correction and resolution. The core of Fault Management (ISO) is its direct relationship with the MOs and ensuring the correct operation of these MOs.

A fault is a deviation from the expected operation of an MO. This does not necessarily mean that there is something wrong or broken, but can often mean that an MO or MOs could be failing to meet their operational objectives. It can also mean that there is something out of the ordinary, or the MO is behaving abnormally and therefore needs attention. Attention of operational staff will normally be gained by a management tool raising an event, warning or alarm and will involve the appropriate activities necessary to restore the normal operation of the MO or MOs involved.

Fault Management (ISO) does not exist within Service Management as a separate process but is an essential part of Incident Management. Incident Management relies on rapid detection, identification, diagnosis, resolution and restoration of normal operation for all incident situations. Fault Management (ISO) facilitates many of these parts of the Incident Management process and includes the:

- maintenance and examination of error logs and journals
- acceptance and progression of fault notifications, events, warnings and alarms
- isolation of the affected MO(s) and identification and tracing of faults
- completion of diagnostic tests
- diagnosis, resolution and rectification of faults.

Good automated Incident Management and indeed Problem Management processes are heavily dependent upon effective and efficient Fault Management (ISO) processes and tools. The better organisations implement automated interfaces and processes between Fault Management (ISO) and processes and tools and their corresponding components within Incident Management and Problem Management. These interfaces to Service Management processes can be taken more broadly in some organisations to also include other processes such as Service Level, Availability, Capacity and even IT service continuity.

4B.2   Configuration Management (ISO)

Configuration Management (ISO) provides facilities for identifying, associating names, controlling, collecting data from, the continuous operation of and the termination of connections of MOs within a management domain. The area of Configuration Management (ISO) allows the detection of new MOs, the changing of the status of MOs and the detection of status changes in MOs. This means that the Configuration Management (ISO) process not only facilitates the operational management of MOs and sets of MOs but can also be used to underpin many of the Service Management processes, particularly the Change, Release and Configuration Management processes.

Configuration Management (ISO) includes the:

- setting and resetting of parameters for the routine operation of MOs
- association of names with MOs and sets of MOs
- initialisation, reset and close-down of MOs
- collection of information on demand about the current state of MOs
- receiving and obtaining announcements of significant changes in the state or condition of MOs
- changing of the configuration of MOs or sets of MOs.

4B.3   Accounting Management (ISO)

Accounting Management (ISO) is the process of identifying and determining resource usage for accountable MOs and sets of MOs in relation to service transactions (users and user recognised services). It enables resource usage data to be collected, combined and allocated for subsequent analysis, reporting, usage control and charging purposes.

Not every MO or the use of an MO is accountable. The Accounting Management (ISO) process can provide invaluable information to the Service Management IT Financial Management process as well as giving useful information to the Capacity Management process. Accounting Management (ISO) includes the:

- calculation of the users' resource consumption and the costs incurred
- setting of accounting limits and tariffs to be associated with the use of resources.

4B.4   Performance Management (ISO)

Performance Management (ISO) allows the behaviour of MOs, sets of MOs and the effectiveness of activities to be evaluated. It involves the collection, analysis and tuning of parameters of MOs and sets of MOs in order to maximise the 'potential use' of these MOs, the management domain and the end-to-end service. Performance Management (ISO) is an essential and invaluable element of the Service Management and Capacity Management processes.

Performance Management (ISO) includes the:

- gathering of statistical information
- maintenance and examination of logs, journals and system state histories
- determination of system performance under natural and artificial conditions
- alteration of the mode of operation of MOs for conducting Performance Management (ISO) activities.

4B.5   Security Management (ISO)

Security Management is the process of managing the level of confidentiality, integrity, availability and verifiability related to the business use of the ICT infrastructure. The purpose of Security Management (ISO) is to support the application and operation of security policies. As such, Security Management (ISO) is one aspect of logical security within the ITIL Security Management process. Security Management (ISO) includes the:

- creation, deletion and control of security services and mechanisms
- the distribution of security-related information
- the detection, recording, analysis and reporting of security-related events.

Annex 4C   Additional Operations techniques

This annex contains details of some additional techniques that may be used in some Operations processes. The techniques included are:

■ scripting techniques

■ set theory

■ queuing theory

■ performance management.

These are covered in detail in the following sections.

4C.1   Scripting techniques

Minimising the impact of events, alarms, alerts and warnings is a fundamental element of the provision of quality ICT services. This activity often relies heavily on the scripting and configuration of management tools in event analysis, control, escalation and management. Therefore, the capability of developing, testing and implementing robust scripts is an invaluable asset within an Operations organisation.

Almost every control language has the ability to support the writing of scripts. Scripts are commands strung together in a simple text file and then executed by the Operating System or the management software as if the commands were typed in one after another. Almost every command language will evolve into some sort of programming language. With each new version, 'improvements' will add functionality and this new functionality will be used. Adapting an attitude of 'structured programming' instead of 'scripting on the fly' will prove beneficial in the long term. Script files will be CIs just like any other asset and should be subject to Change Management.

The need for comment and explanation within these scripts is evident, but the main reasons are:

■ The writer will not always be the main user or owner of the script file. Therefore, it is essential that all scripts are commented on and documented so that other people can support and develop them.

■ It is common sense. What seemed a great script when it was originally written can easily appear confusing and complex when returned to some time later. Therefore it is useful to detail:

   – what the script is supposed to do
   – what is it supposed to process
   – why it is doing it
   – what the main constraints are
   – when it was written, including any updates
   – who wrote it.

Here is an example of how to make a script readable. It is written by NASA as part of a program listing for the Apollo, steering computers that put the Apollo safely on the Moon and then brought its crew home again. In those days, scripting was not an issue; everything was done by programming languages that were created for specific machines.

Figure 4C.1 is an example of a piece of coding ready to be assembled to a bit-stream for the processor to execute. Note how the listing shows clearly:

1 program code

2 comment

3 date of production

4 version

5 explanatory introduction

6 program file name.

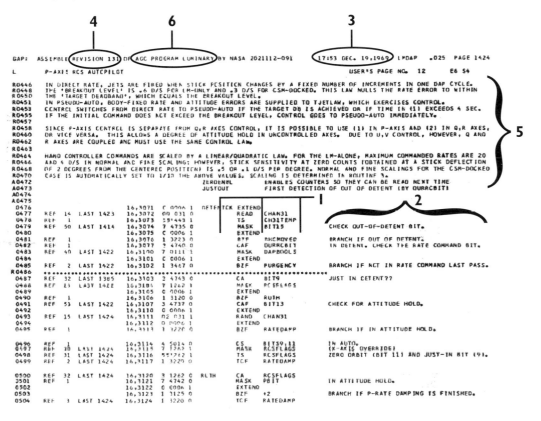

Figure 4C.1 – NASA Program listing

4C.2   Set theory

When dealing with domains, MOs and sets of MOs, it is helpful to have a little background knowledge of set theory, the mathematical description of set characteristics. Since this is not a publication on mathematics, only the essential understanding of set theory will be described here.

A set is a collection of elements. The elements in a set are said to be 'members' of the set and are also called objects – in this case MOs. The elements in the set can be defined in any way one chooses. For example, all servers are members of the 'server set'. All elements or objects are said to be members of the 'universal set'. This set contains all elements and objects and all sets of elements.

It is important to define the Universal Set with much care, as elements outside the Universal Set cannot be addressed. The definition of sets and the possibilities that are a consequence of those sets should all work towards the objective of exerting control and management over the complete ICT infrastructure.

A subset is a set in its own right but with an additional specified attribute. It would, therefore, have fewer elements than the full set. For example, all Unix servers are members of the subset 'Unix Server Set'. The null set or empty set is the set that contains no elements. A set loses this title once an element with all the attributes required for the set is found and hence becomes a member of the set.

A union is the addition of two or more sets. Members added to any of the sets will become a member of the union.

An intersection is the enumeration of element(s) satisfying the rules of membership for two or more sets.

When defining sets it is necessary to determine the Universal Set. This might be, for example:

- all the infrastructure equipment
- anything the 'sniffer' can detect
- all CIs in the CMDB.

Some of the most commonly used determinants for sets are:

- **location:** in some situations it can be useful to group MOs into sets based on locations – this can help determine which operator is concerned with which MO
- **function:** real-time, batch or interactive, web servers, database servers, file servers
- **instrumentation:** when tools are used to instrument the ICT infrastructure this can be used as a determinant in deciding which MO is member of what set
- **technology type:** PCs, mid-range, mainframe – sometimes based on the Operating System, such as Windows, Unix, OS/390, etc.

Although it is often very tempting to have the name of an MO reflect something or everything about its function, location or set membership, it is inadvisable to do so. Sets can be used for many different types of operational activity, for example:

- recycling Unix servers
- distributing a new anti-virus data-file to file servers
- suspending batch activity on all Unix machines that are not database servers.

4C.3   Performance Management

ICT infrastructure components have different performance properties and characteristics and therefore behave differently within the operational environment. The analysis of their performance and the subsequent tuning of their operation must recognise and account for these differences. The Capacity Management process is ultimately responsible for performance management. Therefore, any actions taken by Operations within this area should always be in conjunction with, if not under the direction of, Capacity Management.

When different elements near their saturation point, they each behave in a different way. A processor, for instance, cannot run at half throttle. When a system resource monitor tool indicates a 50% load on a processor, this means that half of the instructions that are being processed are program instructions, either from applications or from the operating system itself, and the other half are so-called NOP instructions (No Operation or null instruction). Putting these program instructions and NOP instructions together, one arrives at 100% processor load or full throttle – the CPU is always fully on or fully off, never half on.

The reason that a system monitor tool will indicate the percentage of program instructions being processed by the processor is that 100% often means that *more than 100% is required*. In this case, there will be a queue of program instructions waiting for the processor to process, which means a shortage of processing power. Depending on the specific situation appropriate measures must be taken. A processor load of 90% may be nothing to worry about: every instruction will be executed with the same speed as when the processor load is 5%.

The most common cause for 100% processor load, and thus very likely a more than 100% processor load, is a poorly written application. An application might enter what is known as a loop, the continuous processing of a small number of program instructions, which can only be interrupted if a specific condition is met. The application code, however, specifies this condition in such a manner that it can never be met. The constant execution of the instructions in the loop will cause the system monitor tool to display a processor load of 100% because all the NOP instructions now make way for the loop instructions. Depending on the processor-sharing mechanism this could also adversely affect other programs executing concurrently on the same processor: they will slow down or come to a halt. This, of course, requires action from the Operations staff. The course of action is to 'kill' the process that is running the program with the loop instruction and try and force that process to print out a listing of the contents of the memory space, so it can be analysed to pinpoint the offending instructions.

There are a large number of tools and techniques to aid writing applications to prevent these errors, but the deciding factor is still human and that is how many of these logical errors originate.

When memory nears it saturation point, all activity on the system will experience delays. The reason for this delay is the fact that most of the memory available is in the form of virtual memory. This is an imitation of internal memory on a slower and cheaper medium, often hard disk, transparent to the system, but an imitation nonetheless. The more demand there is for memory, the more apparent the drawbacks of the virtual memory becomes. The drawback is often speed: the difference in speed between solid state memory and a hard disk is in the range of one or two orders of magnitude.

There are a number of techniques to be used to lessen the speed penalty:

- **configuration tuning:** often major improvements in memory performance can be obtained from the configuration or configurational tuning of the virtual memory set up
- **caching:** reserving a region of memory for frequently accessed data – this cache can also be situated between the processor and the internal memory to speed up the fetching of data from internal memory
- **striping hard disks:** combining hard disks into a logical unit and distributing read and write actions between them simultaneously will speed up data transfer and thus improve the speed of the virtual memory – striping is one of the techniques used in RAID arrays
- **compression:** if CPU power is available, the time lost in decompressing the data can prove to be much less than the time it takes to transfer.

The law of diminishing returns

Consider a configuration that is running at 80% of its maximum performance. The first tuning effort may gain half of the unused performance potential. In turn, the second tuning effort may gain half of the unused performance potential and the third tuning effort may gain half of the unused performance potential.

Example

Assume that the tuning efforts carry the same cost. This translates for the first tuning effort in a gain of 10% (half of 20%). The second tuning effort will gain 5% (half of the remaining 10%). The third and last tuning effort will gain 2.5% (half of the remaining 5%).

In economic terms this means that the second tuning effort is twice as expensive as the first and the third tuning effort is four times as expensive as the first!

Simply put

The more a configuration is tuned, the less benefit is received. The law of diminishing returns is proved in practice yet again.

Component functionality

Providing the design, manufacture and deployment of any configuration within the ICT infrastructure is properly carried out, most out-of-the box configurations are reasonable. If there are, however, specific requirements or demands, the parameter set of the MOs involved will need to be adapted. It is imperative that a solid understanding of the workings and required functionality of the MO and the way the parameter settings influence their functionality is established, before any changes to the parameter set are implemented. The same type of MO will be configured quite differently depending on its required function.

Every component of the ICT infrastructure is to a certain extent general purpose. The supplier or manufacturer does not exactly know in which situation the component is to perform in what way. It is the responsibility of Operations to know exactly what function each component is there to perform. Therefore, each and every component needs to be tuned to perform its required function effectively. Initially this will involve setting the parameters of the MO to values that satisfy the requests made on its functionality. This will be satisfactory for most of the time.

However, there often remains 'room for improvement'. This opportunity occurs because of the experience gained over time with a particular MO, because of changes in other parts of the infrastructure, or because of changes in the way this MO is utilised.

The 'need for improvement' is often a consequence of volume growth, although it could also be the result of poor design or poorly controlled changes.

Tuning

Tuning is the activity undertaken to progress from using a resource, to using a resource optimally. This is where performance tuning comes in. By setting parameter values, it is often possible to improve the performance of an MO. Note that an improvement does not necessarily mean more of this or more of that (or even less of this or less of that for that matter). Tuning an MO or set of MOs from 'it's okay' to 'its optimum' is just as much an improvement as any other.

Improvements, essentially, are either quantitative or qualitative. For example, enlarging the buffers for a network interface card can result in higher throughput and thus a quantitative improvement. Limiting the number of virtual circuits running over a data link can decrease 'packet drops', which means a steadier connection and thus a quality improvement.

There are a number of manufacturers offering 'tuning' or 'performance' tools. These tools are often platform specific and are sometimes provided by the platform manufacturer.

Infrastructure bottlenecks

A well-known pitfall of tuning is the 'sub-optimisation pitfall'. All attention and effort is put into the ultimate performance of one or two MOs. Apart from being uneconomical in the usage of time and resources it is also often counterproductive. Alleviating one bottleneck only exposes the next bottleneck in the sequence. Bottlenecks are an inherent part of any ICT infrastructure. A complex ICT infrastructure can be considered to consist of a series of bottlenecks as illustrated in Figure 4C.2.

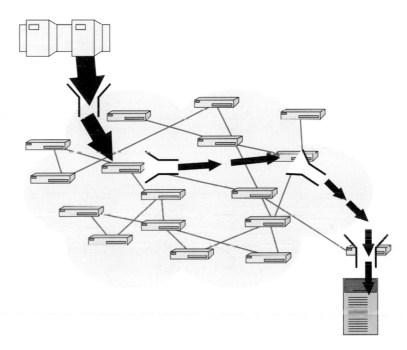

Figure 4C.2 – The bottleneck effect

The way in which these bottlenecks hinder the normal operation of the ICT infrastructure is of course dependent on the demand placed on the infrastructure by the ICT services that use it. It is also dependent upon the speed and throughput of the 'narrowest' bottleneck. Even though subsequent bottlenecks may be wider, the end-to-end performance will still be constrained by the effects of the slowest link. Also, even though the speed and throughput of the constraining bottleneck may be doubled, this benefit may not be fully realised because of the effect of another slow bottleneck on the end-to-end route of the service traffic may now become a limiting factor. The effects of 'sub-optimisation' can only be overcome by considering the end-to-end picture of the overall infrastructure.

Causes of poor performance

Poor performance can have many causes; the most common are listed below:

- **Lack of resources:** insufficient processor power, slow or insufficient memory (including memory leakage), slow or insufficient input/output (I/O) components.

- **Lack of tuning:** incorrect parameter settings for MOs results in mismatches between capability and utilisation. Either an absence of tuning or the wrong tuning are the most common causes.

- **I/O fragmentation:** storing files in separate fragments or chunks instead of a contiguous range, often results in a great number of seek operations that increases overall I/O response times.

- **Data transfer:** is in most cases very configurable: packet length, window size, etc. – all of these can contribute to overall performance issues. A mismatch between any of these parameters can often cause severe performance degradation.

- **Poor programming:** the potential pitfalls in designing, programming and implementing an application or script are too many to list. One of the most common causes of application or script-induced performance degradation is the incorrect use of the application or script platform's capabilities and internals.

- **Poor database design:** database designs are often 'cast in concrete'. Redesigning and implementing a database requires great knowledge, insight and effort. The major restructuring of a database can be a costly and disruptive activity. The internal controls of database systems often allow adjustments to enhance the performance.

- **Malicious code:** viruses, worms, Trojans, hacker's tools and the like can all be causes of poor performance, either intentionally or unintentionally.

- **Bugs:** most, if not all, applications, scripts, programs – indeed, every piece of code – will carry bugs (programming mistakes of some kind). Programmers, compilers, code-generators, linkers, interpreters, and Operating Systems all carry a certain numbers of errors within them. This can result in unwanted behaviour of an application.

- **Faulty hardware:** most people involved in ICT have had an experience along the lines of: 'and when I wiggled the cable it suddenly worked'. Hardware has a tendency not to break immediately but to die slowly, resulting in an increased demand on internal error correction mechanisms, resulting in poor perceived performance because of the 'alternative' use of the resources.

- **External causes:** users are often a cause of poor performance because they make naïve errors. This means that they make an inefficient or obvious wrong use of the application. This can usually be overcome with more comprehensive education and training.

- **Architectural mismatch:** an application system may be limited architecturally to run on a limited number of threads (say, for example, two). When the application is migrated to a multi-processor (say five-processor) server, this may cause extensive bottlenecks within the application architecture that are not apparent to the casual viewer, i.e., the system may show 40% CPU, 30% memory utilisation and a clean I/O system, yet will not handle any more load because it is limited to two concurrent threads.

Annex 4D   Backups and storage

Information systems' main objective is the processing of data. This data is processed into information to help an organisation realise its goals. The rules that govern the behaviour of an organisation are encoded into programs that govern the processing of the data. The data is kept in a data storage facility, in the form of databases or files.

The true value of any information system is in the data that it holds and the interpretation and analysis of that data. Information is one of the most valuable assets of any organisation. Very few, if any, organisations would be able to function without their information or data. To prevent damage to the organisation in the event of the data becoming lost or unavailable, copies are made and stored in secure, off-site locations as contingency. This is known as making backups.

4D.1   Backup and restore

Backup is the part of Security and Availability Management that guarantees the duplication of data for recovery usage in abnormal circumstances or for long time retention (archiving). Restore is the element of Security and Availability Management that guarantees the successful recovery of previously backed-up data for normal use.

> **Hint**
>
> **Checking whether something has indeed been written onto the backup media is always necessary. Apart from this relatively simple check, it is necessary to determine whether the backup media does contain the data that was meant to be backed up. Last but not least, after each backup is taken a check should be performed in order to determine if it is possible to recover the system contents from the backup media. If all three checks are positive, a successful backup has been performed. If any one of these three checks fails, investigate, repair and retry until they are all successful.**

Backup media does not live forever – it ages and is subject to wear and tear. The main causes of ageing and wear and tear are electromagnetic fields, temperature, humidity, light and mechanical stresses (read/writes). Some are manageable in such a way that the effects can be dampened and thus the life of the backup media can be extended. There is, however, always a definite point at which backup media becomes 'no longer fit for use' and has to be discarded. The determination of this point should be approached in a 'better safe than sorry' manner, given the importance of data stored on the backup media. Not spending money for new backup media is as good as not making a backup.

The determination of the fitness of any backup media can be approached in various ways. The simplest form is to note the date of purchase and the number of uses of particular backup media and discard it after either it has been used x times or it is y months old, whichever comes first. Sophisticated systems for the tracking, tracing and controlling of backup media use more elaborate algorithms to determine the viability of backup media including the number of errors in read/write actions. The 'fit for use' determination, in such a case, is often part of a larger management construction that (pro)actively manages all media including backup media. In the case where backup media is being discarded, its contents should be transferred to alternative media first if it is still required and the obsolete media should be physically destroyed.

> **Hint**
>
> **If the material on a backup media is likely to be sensitive, it is important that the data is safely removed before it is scrapped.**

One observation to keep in mind is that all media contains and produces errors. When selecting backup media it is helpful to translate error rates to real world items. One error in ten billion is only meaningful to the initiated. One wrong figure in five thousand insurance policies is meaningful to a larger group.

Justification

There are two main reasons why backups are taken:

1 data is so valuable to any organisation it is natural to protect it, thereby protecting the organisation's interests

2 there could be legal obligations that force the organisation to protect and store its data by making backups. Organisations that have a vital role in the community are often obliged by law to make and retain copies of crucial data.

Timing

Deciding on the timing and the frequency of backups depends on how much data an organisation can stand to lose without suffering serious disruption or loss.

Compare, for example, a stock market with a translation agency. The prices on the stock market will change almost every few seconds. If the data containing the prices of the stock for the last few minutes is lost, it will be impossible to determine who bought or sold what against what price. The stock market itself will be severely damaged if this was the case. It is quite different for the translation agency. If *it* loses a couple of minute's worth of data, it will be a nuisance but that is all.

Therefore, the deciding factor in determining when to make a backup is the timeliness requirement for the data. As a rule of thumb, this is often the data concerning clients and the data concerning transactions. The first source in determining which data is crucial to an organisation is the SLA. It will contain the description of the critical ICT services for the organisation and it will provide pointers to which data it uses and thus which data is crucial.

The importance of the data is not the only criteria in determining when to make a backup – the opportunity to make a backup is also a factor to consider. All too often, backup jobs are configured to ignore files with any kind of lock on them. Locked files are more likely to be used for the most important data because they are more often accessed and changed. It is these important files that are ignored by the backup job, contrary to the goal of making a safe copy of important data.

Determining the right moment to make a backup is thus not a simple task but has to be done in consultation with customers, users, Service Managers and Operations.

Checking the backup

The following points should be considered when checking the backup:

- A backup has been made

  The fact that the backup job has finished without errors or warnings does not necessarily mean that an actual backup is produced. The above-mentioned lock issues could, in extreme cases, result in no copy of a particular file being produced.

- The correct data has been backed-up

  If a backup has been produced and files have indeed been copied to the backup media, it is still not certain whether these files are the files that were meant to be copied. A check on the actual target files for the backup and the copy on the backup media needs to be made. This check might include file name, file size, creation date or amended date, depending on how the data and the generations of data are denoted.

- When it was required

  Many organisations choose to run backup jobs outside normal hours. This is an attempt to limit the 'burden' of the backup job as much as possible. The burden is caused by the resources that are consumed by the backup job and the exclusive read-lock that is often demanded by backup jobs in order to make a consistent copy of the data. Starting a backup job after normal hours does not guarantee that the backup job will finish before the start of the normal day. Assessing the total run time and taking appropriate measures for worst-case possibilities and special activities like end-of-period work will prevent the backup overrun.

- Where it is required

  Even though it may seem easy to define where the backup job needs to write the data to, this can go wrong and remain undetected. With sequential media like tapes, it is possible to put one backup set after the other until the tape is full and the backup job asks for a new tape. It is necessary to define how long a backup set needs to be saved so that tapes can be overwritten when appropriate. With network backup solutions, the problem is even more complex.

- Backing up non-flat file systems (databases)

  Making backup copies of non-flat file systems can prove to be quite complex. Databases may need to be put into a special state in order to ensure that a restorable backup is taken. There are a number of tools available that can help achieve this reliably and easily.

- Testing the recovery

  Periodically, recovery tests should be completed on backups to ensure that the information is recoverable in a usable manner. This is a vital aspect of backup and recovery.

Media

The appropriate media should be used to ensure that the information can be retained for the period necessary and can be recovered within the required time-frame.

- slow-fast read
- slow-fast write

- long-short retention, e.g., shelving and storage pyramid
- alternating sets
- rotating sets
- naming conventions (including versions and distinguishing)
- duplication
- ageing of media
- storage
- general care (including transportation)
- sufficient spare media
- legal aspects, how long the media must be stored.

Restoring

The different recovery methods and requirements will also need to be considered:

- single file (access time best, worst, most likely)
- single record
- number of files (also within different folders)
- entire disk (or any medium)
- file system
- scratch data
- intermediate data (short lifecycle, say a day)
- crucial data.

Usage

The usage of data concerns the medium or signal with which the data is stored. The bits are stored as a physical representation of the data by modulating a signal on a medium.

Database management disciplines can be broken down into:

- **data structure management:** concerned with the data structures and their technical translation from the logical description
- **physical data management:** manages the physical data as it is laid down on the media within the infrastructure
- **technical data management:** supplies the support for the usage of the data by other infrastructure components and maximises its efficiency.

4D.2   Storage Management

Storage Management contains all aspects of the management of the physical data stored on media. The data has to be maintained at the level of the medium or signal with which the data is represented. Storage Management will translate the terms and conditions stemming from the intended use to characteristics of the data media. The terms and conditions should be documented within SLAs, OLAs and UCs and should include:

- reliability

- retention time
- reparability
- storage capacity
- storage cost
- transfer rate
- access time
- access pattern
- security.

Characteristics of data media need to be managed in order to adhere to the determinations laid down in OLAs and UCs. This is achieved through a number of activities undertaken by Storage Management:

- **managing storage:**
  - controlling of and reporting on the adherence to the terms and conditions
  - the granting of storage space on any medium
  - the moving of data between media (staging)
  - the removal of obsolete data (scratching)
  - the (re)organising of the storage space (de-fragmentation) for efficient access

- **safeguarding data:** producing copies of data for storage in a safe location to be used in case of the unavailability or mutilation of the operational data

- **reparation of data:** when operational data is damaged, the copy that was made as a safeguard is used to restore the data

- **destruction of data:** when operational data is no longer required or when the medium on which it is stored is past its technical life span, the data needs to be destroyed before disposing of the medium – depending on the medium, this may require special techniques and/or equipment.

Storage Management in reality

In reality, there is often a very loose connection between the trends, changes and decisions about the usage of the infrastructure and the management of storage media. This is often caused by complex (or perceived complex) relations between data characteristics on one side and the services on the other side. Storage Management is all too often 'the last to know and the first to be blamed'.

During the development of applications and services, the terms and conditions of the characteristics are estimated. Changes in the utilisation of the infrastructure, the nature of the ICT services or even the business processes themselves can have a profound effect on the ability of Storage Management to adhere to OLAs and UCs.

Current 24x7 availability demands make it nearly impossible to de-fragment, reallocate and scratch media off-line. The design, implementation and operational procedures will have to cater for this 'always on' demand requirement. Furthermore, databases and file stores have a tendency to outgrow any other phenomenon in the ICT domain. For example, if the number of users doubles, the amount of data from those users could triple. Some media have, because of their design, a maximum acceptable fill factor, and this becomes an accelerator for storage management. Hard disks, for example, will show a performance degradation above 70% full. This figure is subsequently used as a threshold value in the policies for the monitoring of those hard disks.

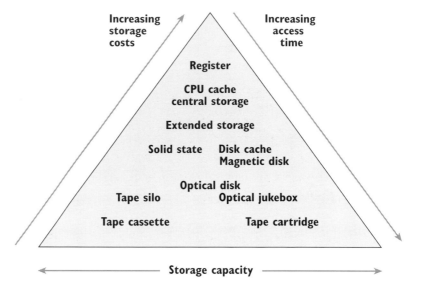

Figure 4D.1 – The pyramid of storage solutions

The advent of storage systems, like RAID and SAN, has provided an increase in performance and reliability. Due to the construction of these systems they can easily be repaired, maintained and serviced without disruption of their primary function. This comes at a price, however. The software needed to manage these systems is often quite complex and 'hides' the bare essentials that can make it a 'black box'. Complex and complicated configuration tools are necessary to make these systems present themselves as a 'virtual' disk that is usable for other components within the infrastructure. As shown in Figure 4D.1, there are also trade-offs between costs and speed of access.

Performance of the total background memory is directly influenced by the distribution of data over file stores and interfaces. This applies to on-line transaction processing as well as to batch processing. It is still wise to spread out frequently accessed files, for example, by placing database journal files on different spindles to those for the live data.

Magnetic tape is still being used as a medium for data storage and probably will be for the foreseeable future. It normally comes in the form of cassettes or cartridges. Their use is often that of 'near-line' storage as a backup medium in combination with tape-robots.

5 TECHNICAL SUPPORT

'There is a time in the life of every problem when it is big enough to see, yet small enough to solve.'
… Mike Levitt

5.1 Introduction

The Technical Support process and functions within an ICT organisation ensure that the necessary support and expertise is available to underpin the overall service delivered by ICTIM. Technical Support should maintain an in-depth pool of technical advice and expertise to provide information, guidance and actual resources, for example, for deployment activities and for the support and maintenance of all aspects of the ICT infrastructure.

Technical Support can be defined as:

> **Definition – Technical Support process**
>
> **The development of knowledge for the evaluation, support and proofing of all current and future ICT infrastructure solutions.**

To carry out their role effectively, Technical Support staff need to know about, or be able to obtain information regarding, the organisation's technology, technical processes and documentation. This knowledge is primarily used to achieve the main objective of the Technical Support processes, i.e., to provide a 'centre of excellence' to assist and underpin all areas of ICT and Service Management in the provision of end-to-end, business focused, ICT services.

The range of activities undertaken by Technical Support is both broad and diverse and includes:

- Research and Development associated with new technologies; this role may be undertaken in terms of technology market awareness or vendor discussions, and may be undertaken jointly with Capacity and/or Infrastructure Planners.

- Third-line Technical Support, generally in relation to incidents reported to the Service Desk and overall Problem Management.

- Supplier Management – Technical Support may have not only developed an in-depth understanding and knowledge of the technology deployed within the ICT infrastructure, but also built strong relationships with technology suppliers and support organisations. They may therefore play an active role in Supplier Management and provide specialist advice and expertise in relation to the procurement of ICT components.

- Liaison with Design and Planning, particularly in terms of support and documentation, e.g., in preparing Statement Of Requirements and Invitation To Tender documents.

- Liaison with Deployment during release and operational acceptance; Technical Support may provide assistance to both Deployment and Operations in relation to methodologies, procedures and mechanisms for migration across environments and into production.

- Analysis, interpretation and distribution of information from ICT Management tools. This information may form the basis of regular management reports on all aspects of the ICT infrastructure.

- Tactical implementation of overall improvements to the quality of ICT service provision.

Some of the relationships between Technical Support, Capacity Management, Design and Planning, Deployment, and Operations are mentioned above. Technical Support not only provides a support role, in terms of business and technology changes, for instance, to ensure the smooth technical running of the supported systems. It also provides advice and guidance on systems tuning to Operations and Availability Management to enable continual improvement of the availability and performance of development and production services to the business.

5.1.1   Basic concepts

The concept of the Technical Support function and processes revolves around the underpinning technical knowledge and communication to facilitate an effective and responsive ICT infrastructure that delivers business critical services.

Most people who utilise or are concerned with ICT will be familiar with seeking assistance when faced with increasingly complex and unfamiliar technologies. Users of Information Systems may also be perplexed and require support when familiar interfaces that supply their need for information are changed. The requirement to have a responsive and effective support process is more critical now than it has ever been.

General enquiries are dealt with, and first-line support is usually provided by, Service Support and, in particular, the Service Desk. For the Service Desk to be effective, it needs to have up-to-date and relevant support information and scripts, and this documentation and guidance may often be developed with the help and assistance of Technical Support. Indeed, it is in the interest of Technical Support to ensure that first-line support is effective and that as few 'trivial' incidents as possible get referred as far as Technical Support.

Technical Support is likely to play a reactive, supporting role in relation to Incident and Problem Management. In the latter case, they may also be proactive in analysing trends, for instance, in relation to (say) the reoccurring failure of certain ICT components. They may also provide advice and recommendations to Change Management on the impact or risks associated with, for example, a proposed change to an ICT component or system.

Technical Support may make technical resources available to assist with Release Management and Configuration Management during deployment, as well as providing the necessary technical and physical resources and information in support of ICT and Service Management, Planning, Deployment and Operations. It also has an equally important liaison and support role in assisting Service Delivery, for example, Capacity Management, Availability Management, and IT Service Continuity Management.

It should also be recognised that to establish and retain an in-depth understanding and knowledge of the ICT infrastructure takes time and there is a 'learner curve' associated with new technology. It is therefore imperative that Technical Support is fully informed of changes or new infrastructure design proposals and policies. Therefore, Design and Planning has a particularly important role in providing the necessary information to Technical Support staff, in order for them to be fully prepared in advance of changes in ICT and thus facilitate their support role.

To meet business and organisational needs the Technical Support processes can be provided through a variety of organisational forms or information channels, including:

- dedicated in-house teams, supporting common or specialised areas of the infrastructure, such as networks or specific operating systems

- managed services from third parties providing the technical experience required

- combinations of both managed and in-house support, where the organisation buys in specialist functions, often to address cost or resource availability issues

- a growing number of high quality information resources, such as websites and context-sensitive search engines

- automated tool-sets that register and possibly deal with a problem using scripted scenarios.

The business should take a great deal of care in deciding the form of Technical Support process or agents that will perform a specific supporting role, and the organisational structure or function, to ensure that the overall service to the business is not jeopardised by the support arrangements.

5.1.2   The goals

The primary goal of Technical Support is to ensure that the business has highly available, cost-effective ICT services that underpin business objectives. To achieve this goal, Technical Support provides the necessary resources, skills and competencies to underpin the other ICTIM processes. Technical Support therefore needs to become a centre of technical excellence and assist Operations and Deployment in the provision of end-to-end services.

To utilise technical expertise effectively, Technical Support needs also to develop skills in resource scheduling and administration in order to deploy its limited resources cost-effectively and to greatest business advantage within financial constraints.

Technical Support should also aim to facilitate continual improvement of service provision to the business units, Service Management and ICT Management functions. Primarily, this is achieved by the implementation of active investigations into the suitability and sustainability of the organisation's infrastructure.

5.1.3   The scope

The scope of the function and processes will depend on the type, size and implemented or future infrastructure, such as voice, data, mobile telephony and wireless data communication. The complexity and critical business drivers (Service Level Agreements) of the environment to be supported will assist in the determination of the levels and type of support resource required. For example, a 24x7 business critical system such as a global e-commerce website might require a dedicated team of support staff to be readily available should there be a failure of infrastructure, batch processing or an on-line application. The support function will be required to underpin all implemented technologies.

Automation of monitoring, alerting, and escalation, in conjunction with Incident Management, set to predefined limits within Service Level Agreements, will be required to enable effective systems support. The Technical Support function will implement and maintain these automated tool-sets as well as analyse the output from the same systems.

Specific in-house technology resources may be used as part of the Technical Support function. The basic functionality will be the same whether using internal or external resources to underpin and provide the support of the technical environment.

Inputs

The inputs to Technical Support will be utilised in both reactive and proactive modes of operation. Events arising from the Service Support processes will normally be reactive, whereas Service Delivery requirements will normally be more considered and proactive in nature. Outputs from Service Support will be used as input to Technical Support. For example, automated alarms and alerts from operational system management units might raise a Service Desk incident. The incident may require the resources within Technical Support to intelligently analyse and act upon the outputs from automated and manual investigations to return to normal levels of service.

Problem Management, concerned with the identification, analysis and rectification of root causes of incidents, will work closely with Technical Support resources. The close relationship may extend to the secondment of technical resources to the Problem Management function. Problem Management provides the guidance and structure to produce and maintain known error logs, facilitate technical workarounds and produce permanent fixes; it also underpins the technical competencies of the support roles.

The implementation of the workaround or fix will involve the input from, and to, the Change Management processes, resulting in the delivery of a new RFC (Request for Change).

The ICTIM functions of Design and Planning, Deployment, Operations, and those of Service Delivery and Service Support, provide various inputs to the support function. The inputs include:

- current ICT infrastructure documentation such as network maps and content from the Technical Infrastructure Library

- quality assurance documentation provided as part of the handover to an operational environment

- commercial procurement policies and standards as part of the Supply Chain Management processes

- IT Service Continuity Plans that will define the level of technical activity required to safeguard and restore critical systems

- contracts, Operational Level Agreements and Service Level Agreements documenting third party support arrangements

- Release Management processes

- Deployment tactics

- operational requirements that are the basis of the need for skilled resources.

The proactive work of Technical Support is facilitated by data and other inputs from a variety of sources including Service Delivery. In a managed environment, the technical inputs may be actively monitored, including:

- technical bulletins from suppliers to either affect a fix or improve service availability and performance. Examples of these inputs may be exposed vulnerabilities or exploits identified within an infrastructure by CERT (originally known as the **C**omputer **E**mergency **R**esponse **T**eam), e-mail alerts or items posted on websites

- technical White Papers on specific technology domains, such as known problems or new facilities, that will improve the operation of specific infrastructure components
- technical advice and guidance from external consultancies to undertake a specific task or generic operation within the organisation's infrastructure
- site standards such as information security and ISO 17799/BS 7799 to assist the technical implementation of the security policies created using the guidelines contained within these public documents
- output from monitoring tools to enable the compilation of trend information.

Processes

The processes that will define the actions of Technical Support can be grouped into three main functional areas:

1 Research and evaluation

2 Projects

3 Business as Usual (BaU).

Technical Support underpins all technical functions within an organisation. Each functional area aligns itself to peer ICTIM functions. Research and evaluation will operate with the D and P function to provide the technical competencies to meet the required business-planned amendments to service provision within an organisation. The Projects area will benefit from the use of technical staff for the deployment of the solution provided by the D and P processes. Operations aligning with Business as Usual will aim to provide a stable, cost-effective and forward-looking environment on which the organisation's business will depend.

Analysis of the data output from tools could be used within three areas with a different emphasis for each process. For example, data output from a linked monitoring and trending tool might be used to evaluate the effectiveness of a new business solution and highlight line capacity to D and P, whilst providing real-time data during the deployment of a new product. The same tool may also be used to satisfy BaU requirements to monitor services and ensure that the operational parameters described within an SLA are not compromised, by the use of exception alerting mechanisms.

Research and Evaluation

Typical research and evaluation activities are likely to include:

- in-depth review and analysis of output from ICT Management tools (both historical and real-time) to verify or refute the expected results from the D and P function
- production of reports detailing infrastructure performance, assisting Capacity Management planning
- testing and verification of infrastructure designs prior to deployment activities
- technical liaison with suppliers and consultants to provide the 'best fit' in terms of cost and technical solution and success criteria for a particular technology domain.

Projects

Typical project activities are likely to include:

- creation and maintenance of operational, test and staging environments and their associated documentation
- provision of technical assistance along with Release Management to distribute and make live new, tested releases of infrastructure solutions
- specific in-depth technical investigations as proof of concept and deployment
- secondment to project teams to provide a technical solution to the business.

Business as Usual

BaU activities on a day-to-day basis are likely to include:

- specialist involvement in investigations of incidents and problems with the current infrastructure that require an in-depth technical understanding not usually found in the Operations area
- creation, maintenance and augmentation of the organisation's knowledge base and Technical Infrastructure Library
- verification of CIs ensuring that detailed information stored in a Configuration Management Database (CMDB) is correct and made available through the CMDB tool-set and access methods
- in-depth analysis of Operations data environment on behalf of Availability Management, for example, to assist in service outage investigations
- the identification of opportunities for continual improvement, through Knowledge Management and constant skill review
- training Service Support staff in the use of causal analysis tools and processes, where appropriate. Technical Support will have the detailed knowledge to maintain and utilise the tools effectively
- technical guidance during feasibility studies and pilots of new or amended ICT infrastructure components.

Deliverables

Technical Support outputs will include:

- analysis and recommendations on the performance of individual components and the infrastructure as a whole
- technical reports on problem and incident control
- SLA exception reports
- procedures for operational staff
- feedback to D and P function regarding planned system implementations
- technical project input to assist planning processes
- test results utilising test lab equipment and tools
- assistance with the Deployment process

- tools and infrastructure to support Release Management
- updated and verified CMDB CIs.

5.1.4   Objectives and terms of reference

The objective of the Technical Support and all ICT processes is to enable the organisation's ICT infrastructure to operate in a controlled and cost-efficient manner, bringing the benefits of ICT to the business.

The main objectives in bringing the benefits of ICT Technical Support to the business are to:

- provide cost-effective third-line support utilising detailed and integrated Configuration Management, Change Management and Financial Management processes
- implement Release Management processes for all infrastructure components and related equipment
- participate in detailed infrastructure analysis and site surveys covering installation and environmental standards
- manage supplier relationships and provide a technical interface for suppliers
- provide technical assistance and evaluation for disaster recovery testing
- develop and maintain a Technical Library
- develop centralised on-line operational and support procedures
- develop centralised on-line documentation and diagrams using automatic tools where appropriate
- maintain test facilities and assist with testing of new releases and hardware
- provide evaluations of new tools and technologies
- ensure that all infrastructure components are subject to Change Management and Configuration Management.

5.2   Benefits, costs and possible problems

The benefits, costs and possible problems associated with establishing a successful Technical Support process are outlined below.

5.2.1   Benefits

The benefits of good technical support processes manifest themselves in two ways:

I   Benefits to the business:

- increased service availability through better process management and control
- improved performance of supported services to enable business objectives to be met
- lower long-term costs through the efficient management of infrastructure resources, efficient maintenance of infrastructure fabric, and effective support for new and existing services.

2   Benefits to ICT:

- creation of a centre of excellence with local knowledge of system behaviour
- service availability trend information
- better performance through understanding of capabilities and deficiencies of installed equipment – 'the undocumented features' or 'bugs'
- better ICT process functionality through close communication with D and P, Deployment and Operations
- creation of test and verification facilities enabling systems to be benchmarked and tested prior to submission into a production environment.

5.2.2   Costs

The use of automated processes through tool-set integration may assist the organisation to utilise support staff in a more effective manner. Therefore, although an integrated tool-set may initially be more expensive, it is likely to reap considerable business benefits. An important consideration of an integrated tool-set is the IT Financial Management process within Service Delivery. It may be necessary for the Technical Support process to recognise cost types and codes that are standard throughout the organisation.

The costs associated with the creation of a sensible and effective Technical Support environment can be related to the three Ps: Processes, People, and Products.

Processes

The development of processes to enable the effective support of an organisation's ICT infrastructure will contribute to the overall cost of the function. The processes put into place will determine the resources required, and hence costs dependent on the complexity of the solution and organisational duties, such as:

- management of staff, creation of processes and procedures
- transfer of knowledge and skills from (say) partners to internal staff
- establishment of alerting mechanisms and monitoring – it should be noted that the costs of evaluation, purchase, configuration and set-up are likely to be incurred by Technical Support, but Operations are likely to incur costs associated with monitoring
- keeping infrastructure knowledge up to date; supplementary training may be required along with the certification of individual technical competencies
- testing and benchmarking new facilities prior to deployment to the live environment
- handover from an implementation project to a support environment completed to the satisfaction of the support group and client
- creation of handover documentation, training, diagnostic scripts and operational procedures
- automating support tasks such as an automated notification system that will read system events or other values, comparing against pre-set performance thresholds and taking appropriate action
- reporting to Change Management on the success or failure of a change process.

People (staff)

Staff costs will vary according to location, skill levels required and complexity of the environment. The Design and Planning process will identify the skill levels required to support a particular technology. Cost elements include:

- salary of specialist staff
- training for compliance with infrastructure and business requirements
- certification of competence with a particular technology or process
- membership of user groups/special interest groups
- travel costs incurred in supporting distributed environments
- accommodation at home site and for remote support environments
- meetings.

Products (tools)

The purchase and use of multidisciplinary tools enables the effective control of element reporting and analysis of installed infrastructure components, encompassing:

- integrated Service Management tools
- reporting
- capacity
- diagnostic and root cause analysis
- load stress tests
- configuration and logical connection schematics
- known error log (KEL) display
- security, including: vulnerability scanning, penetration testing and implementation
- test lab facilities (monitoring and support will be required as well as the test equipment itself).

5.2.3   Possible problems

The principal problems that may be associated with the establishment of ICT Technical Support processes are normally associated with some 'lacking' element. Typical aspects associated with Technical Support that are often found to be lacking in organisations, include:

- time
- staff resource
- senior management commitment
- adequate monitoring tools
- adequate documentation
- adequate handover processes from deployment and planning
- training
- integration of management software with released product
- service-based culture
- communication between support and other ICT functions.

The above points all contribute to problems within the support process itself. Other problems include:

- poor attitude, bypassing of established procedures and working practices – this is difficult to overcome and is often indicated by set responses such as: 'no one ever tells us'
- unrealistic targets and expectations
- OLAs that are not backed up with the reciprocal contracts with suppliers
- artificial 'walls' between support groups and the project and planning functions
- technical staff bypassing Change Management procedures because they think they know what they are doing when they do not.

5.3 The roles, responsibilities and interfaces

Technical support is concerned with structuring and underpinning other processes to guarantee the services delivered by Design and Planning, Deployment, and Operations, as well as other Service Management processes.

Technical Support aims to develop knowledge and understanding of Operations and Deployment, to assist in the provision of end-to-end services.

5.3.1 The roles and responsibilities

The Technical Support process is not an isolated island of knowledge. To be effective, the staff and functions must be aware of business drivers necessitating ICT solutions, and must coordinate their activities with those of other ICT infrastructure and Service Management processes.

A number of generic roles have been identified that are necessary for effective interaction with other processes and to manage the Technical Support process.

Technical Support can be achieved through the following roles:

- **Technical Support Manager** – managing a Technical Support function, consisting of people, process and technology
- **Technical Planner** – involved in the research and development of new ICT infrastructure, and the technical planning and configuration
- **Technical Support Analyst** – providing proof of all new ICT solutions required by the business, analysis of ICT infrastructure technical issues, liaison with Design and Planning on the production of new 'Operational Requirement' documents
- **Technical Support Specialist/Team member** – involved in the maintenance of test and evaluation facilities, providing assistance with the building and testing of all new solutions for deployment, and providing a technical reference point for all areas of ICT and external partners.

In many organisations, these roles are combined into individual or team functions. The scope and responsibilities of each these roles is expanded in Annex 5A.

Skills

Technical Support is dependent upon the specialist skills and expertise possessed by team members. It is necessary to recognise the core skills and competencies required by the organisation in relation to the current and future ICT infrastructure.

There is a continual need to appraise the skills and competencies of Technical Support in relation to the needs of the business and the demands of other ICT and Service Management functions.

Tasks

Technical Support is involved in a variety of planning, analytical, and other technical activities. It is therefore imperative that competencies in planning and resource scheduling are developed in order to plan and provide adequate support to other ICT processes.

Technical Support must be capable of analysing and interpreting the data from existing ICT Management tools, and be able to report effectively on the quality of ICT services to the Design and Planning function(s), in order to influence the overall business planning process.

Responsibilities

From the management perspective, Technical Support needs to undertake efficient and effective analyses of ICT performance data and provide timely performance reports and management summaries, including Service Level and exception reports.

Technical Support is involved in the tactical planning of all infrastructure changes and maintains the analytical and technical capabilities to help realise the tactical plans by providing:

- in-depth technical expertise
- quality assurance capabilities, in relation to technical standards.

5.3.2 External interfaces

There are several major interfaces with areas outside ICTIM, including:

- Facilities Management within the organisation of, for example, electrical contractors, building management, and security
- Service Management disciplines
- Application Management.

Technical Support needs to interface and establish working relationships with many organisations and groups in order to provide a comprehensive service. Some of the major interfaces are with areas outside ICTIM, and the frequency and types of communication are dependent upon the size, complexity and technology domains present. To provide in-house support arrangements, a range of technical competencies is required. However, managing external support arrangements requires staff with management skills able to communicate and verify the organisation's technical requirements to the external Service Provider, and to ensure that real business benefit is derived from the relationship.

The common services provided to the organisation will also be utilised by Technical Support. Services such as architectural services, building maintenance, water, gas and electrical provision will be among the frequent contacts. The Technical Support groups will have a close working relationship with Service Providers and will be involved with the maintenance and implementation of new and existing services.

The maintenance and monitoring of contracts with suppliers of technical services will be undertaken by Technical Support. Typical activities include in-depth technical discussions with suppliers over improvements to the infrastructure, services, and investigations into poorly performing equipment or software.

Technical Support may also have a liaison role with Security, for instance, with corporate security policy advisors to implement the techniques described within the policy. Technical Support will, in most instances, underpin the technical security infrastructure. Security of data, access to critical systems and physical resources are also included within the remit of most organisations' supporting processes.

Technical Support is not an entity that exists as a stand-alone service; team members liaise with all Service Management disciplines and with Application Management.

The nature of the interface with either an external organisation or other ITIL process is organisation-dependent. However, the most common interfaces with the ITIL processes and Technical Support will be initiated by:

- **Service Desk incidents** – either through customer reports or automated incidents raised by tools monitoring the infrastructure for abnormal behaviour
- **RFC (Request for Change)** – changes to the infrastructure as part of new service implementation, or maintenance activity, including those raised to resolve a particular problem
- **planning documents from Design and Planning** – facilitating the introduction of amendments to existing or new services. An example might be the review of an ITT (Invitation To Tender)
- **supplier review meetings** – meetings with suppliers to ensure that the service that is supplied to the organisation is fit for purpose and adhering to service levels agreed at the signing of the contracted service
- **operational documentation** – documents provided from Deployment processes or to Operations, such as handover details of new services
- **Service Level Management** – inclusion of SLA details to assist Technical Support to formulate a successful monitoring and alerting process.

5.3.3   Internal ICTIM Interfaces

The internal interfaces between the Technical Support processes and other ICT Management areas will need to be closely integrated. Technical Support needs to establish clear communication pathways to the areas and particular roles it intends to support. However, the implementation of a Technical Support process will be determined with a particular organisation, i.e., in terms of establishing the most effective way to communicate and to provide the necessary support services.

As a minimum requirement, Technical Support should hold regular review meetings with other ICTIM areas to ensure ongoing service improvement.

5.4 The Technical Support processes

Technical Support is the centre of excellence regarding all matters of a technical nature. Knowledge pertaining to the operational characteristics of equipment, the definition of performance thresholds, configuration and maintenance of supporting tool-sets, are all to be found within this influential function.

The relationship between Technical Support and the Service Desk, incident and problem control is paramount to the successful operation of the business and technical infrastructure. Technical Support will become involved with the Service Support functions and processes during establishment, handover and subsequent Business as Usual activities of infrastructure operation.

The support function should be the final point of technical escalation within the organisation. The function itself may be required to escalate the incident or problem outside the organisation to specialist consultancy partners, or liaise with suppliers on behalf of the organisation. Management of technical responses, including risk assessment and implementation of countermeasures to mitigate the identified risks as necessary, generally relies on the technical knowledge within the support function. Furthermore, amendment of systems to incorporate the change to achieve required service levels is normally the responsibility of this function in conjunction with Change Management processes.

Technical Support also provides proof of concept and solution to facilitate the development of new or enhanced infrastructure. Typical activities of Technical Support include:

- research and development of new technologies
- third-line Technical Support
- budget planning and control
- procurement
- Supplier Management
- liaison with Design and Planning on the preparation of Statement Of Requirements (SOR) and Invitations to Tender (ITT)
- tactical implementation of overall service improvements
- liaison with deployment on release methodologies, mechanisms and operational acceptance
- acting as a technical reference point for all areas of IT and third parties
- technical planning, scheduling and management for support, administration and Operations functions and tools
- provision of analysis and management reports on all aspects of the ICT infrastructure
- maintenance of documentation and procedures.

5.4.1 How to achieve a successful Technical Support function

A successful Technical Support function can be attributed to three key points, as follows:

1 establish a core group of technically competent resources
2 develop processes and procedures for service-related technical tasks
3 manage communications within Technical Support and with other processes.

Establish a core group of technically competent resources

An effective Technical Support function is based on establishing a core group of technical staff. The group may rely solely on internal resources or utilise the abilities of third parties, perhaps underpinned by a manufacturer's support contract, or a mixture of both. It may vary in size from one member to hundreds, depending upon the organisation and the technology domains supported.

The staff fulfilling the supporting roles must be made aware of where they fit into the scheme of the ICTIM functions. Senior management should ensure that there is broad awareness of the roles and responsibilities of Technical Support and be able to relate their activities to the overall organisational goals and business objectives. All too often, technical staff are left to their own devices and do not feel part of the business that they are employed to support.

Personal and team development is critical to the success of the processes, and integration with D and P, Deployment and Operations should be a priority issue.

Awareness campaigns and training are vital in developing the Technical Support roles and facilitating integration activities. Some of the issues are likely to be dealt with by the Human Resources function, but in-depth technical training necessitates specialist courses and skill acquisition.

Training of staff for personal and team building is facilitated by:

- formal courses (ITIL, proprietary by technology and manufacturer)
- skills transfer (from consultants and internal interfaces with competent staff within a specific technology)
- PDP (Professional Development Plan, working with an outside organisation such as the British Computer Society)
- co-working teams, ensuring skills are acquired as the technology is implemented
- realistic objectives and assessment (organisational)
- constructive testing, which should be used to reinforce theoretical training through test laboratory working
- regular updates augmenting existing skills.

Develop processes and procedures for service-related technical tasks

The organisation must be careful when dealing with technology-related issues so that the technology is not an end in itself. The technology is implemented to increase the potential of the business. Service issues must be paramount when working with underpinning technologies. SLAs will need to be understood and their contents adhered to.

Technical support staff will, in the main, respond to requests from D and P, Deployment and Operations. The requests will take the form of RFCs, incidents raised by the Service Desk or automated tools, root cause analyses of more taxing technical difficulties, evaluation and testing of new or modified equipment, or techniques dealing closely with the D and P process (this will normally be part of a project).

Responding to requests from peer processes should not be the only driver for Technical Support to begin a task. The support process must not view a successful day as one in which no requests from the Service Desk or Problem Management are received. Active investigations into improvements to services (Service Improvement Programme) will benefit the organisation and improve the effectiveness of ICTIM processes, Service Delivery and Service Support.

All tasks undertaken by Technical Support, in-house or outsourced, should be documented and submitted for review by the requesting process. The professionalism of Technical Support will need to ensure that the tasks for evaluation or change are received and acted upon. Too much resource in effort and time will be wasted if the results of the tasks are not communicated effectively. The lack of communication will result in wheel reinvention occurring on a regular basis leading to unnecessary costs for the organisation.

Manage communications within Technical Support and with other processes

Ideas, results of technical evaluations and investigations need to be communicated effectively between Technical Support, ITIL processes and the rest of the business. How effectively this is achieved will depend on the management, size, internal structure and complexity of the organisation.

The Technical Support processes and functions need to have a sufficiently high profile and be able to demonstrate their role in the provision of a quality service that is expected by the business from ICTIM functions. This goal can only be achieved by the successful communication of improvements, underpinned by appropriate technology and sustainable technical services.

Communication within the Technical Support process is just as critical between technology domains. This activity will entail co-working and skills transfer between diverse groups such as UNIX, Networks, Desktop and NT support. **NB: Team coordination is critical to success.**

Activities that will assist in the communication are:

- CAB (Change Advisory Board) attendance to represent technical details of a Request for Change
- Problem Management investigating root cause analysis to assist the creation and maintenance of a known error database
- Creation of technical white papers and implementation techniques for ICTIM processes
- Input to Capacity Planning by interpretation of output and maintenance of monitoring tools
- Input to Service Management by highlighting service disruptions
- Creation of a technical library, both on- and off-line, to assist the first- and second-line staff in the Service Desk areas
- Early involvement in the D and P processes (projects) to ensure that any solution has technical merit by the evaluation of new, or amendment to existing, techniques.

5.5   Impact of the Internet on Technical Support

The Internet provides a range of information resources and sources of 'Technical Support' to the ICT professional and end user alike. The ease of access and availability of such information sources and resources, for download by clients and support staff, provides a 'self fix' option to many organisations in which staff believe they can become proficient in self-support.

Due to the growth of ubiquitous support on the Internet and the growth of the home-grown technical 'experts', organisations need to be wary of, and ensure that they can control, the number of staff and management that can apply a 'fix' to a problem without adequate Change Management processing. This 'freedom' may be an attractive proposition to the end user, particularly if the supporting organisation is not responsive or does not provide what the customer wants.

There is no doubt that the availability of the technical resources on the Internet assists the qualified support professional who adheres to Service Delivery, Support and ICTIM processes and procedures. Known errors, fast searching by keyword, and support groups all help the reduction of incident and problem resolution times.

However, there are a number of serious repercussions in relation to Change and Configuration Management, which could inevitably lead to the demise or at least severely hamper the effectiveness of the Technical and Service Support processes.

Uncontrolled changes or fixes to problems may have significant impact on related ICT components and systems, and may lead to a significant amount of time wasted in problem diagnosis and service restoration. The use of the Internet by unqualified staff attempting to establish a 'fix' will be wasting time looking at tasks that are not their responsibility and may infringe licensing laws. This is likely to have implications for Service Support costs, and may also lead to instability in service provision with consequent business costs and losses.

To manage this situation, organisations need to develop a policy regarding support via websites and ensure that Internet resources are used in a structured and controlled manner by both Technical Support staff and the general population. Organisations are losing financial benefits of Technical Support processes by tampering, no matter how good the intentions of non-technical staff. However, control of risk and establishment of organisational security and download policies will enable a controlled environment to be established and maintained.

The implementation of an Internet usage policy will need to be backed up with processes and tools to manage effectively the expectations of the management and client population.

Annex 5A   Technical Support roles

5A.1   Technical Support Manager

A **Technical Support Manager** is responsible for the coordination, control and management of a team of Technical Support staff. The management role is responsible for agreeing the interface definition with other ICTIM processes, and for the establishment and maintenance of working practices and procedures.

A key function of a Technical Support Manager is to raise both awareness and the profile of the Technical Support process. This may be achieved through analysis and management reporting on all aspects of the ICT infrastructure by means of:

- management summaries
- performance reports
- Service Level reports
- ad hoc exception reports.

The Technical Support Manager also plays a key role in quality assurance of Technical Support activities.

The main objectives of such a role are to:

- motivate and develop the Technical Support staff under their control and ensure that the necessary levels of support are provided to other ICTIM functions and Service Management processes
- develop and maintain controls and procedures to ensure that the Technical Support processes are efficiently run and are effective
- ensure that all management reports and information is produced and disseminated in a timely fashion for all other ICT, Service and Business Management processes
- ensure that all Technical Support processes are continually developed and improved
- ensure that all Technical Support staff are aware of, and comply with, all Technical Support, ICT and Service Management processes.

5A.2   Technical Planner

A **Technical Planner** is involved in the research and development of new ICT infrastructure, and its technical planning and configuration.

Technical planning may provide valuable input to other planning processes, for example, in the planning and documentation of operational changes.

5A.3   Technical Support Analyst

A **Technical Support Analyst** provides proof of all new ICT solutions required by the business.

The main responsibilities include:

- analysis of ICT infrastructure technical issues

- liaison with Design and Planning on the production of new 'Operational Requirement' documents
- implementation of all tactical service improvements
- development and maintenance of documentation and procedures
- technical support and assistance with feasibility studies
- participation in pilot studies for new ICT infrastructure components
- production and explanation of management metrics and reports.

5A.4   Technical Support Specialist/Team Member

A **Technical Specialist/Team Member** provides assistance with the building and testing of all new solutions for deployment, and provides a technical reference point for all areas of ICT and external partners. They are also concerned with the maintenance of test and evaluation facilities.

Technical specialists are likely to be involved in the:

- analysis of ICT infrastructure technical issues
- diagnosis of technical problems that cannot be resolved elsewhere
- provision of technical advice and guidance for all other areas
- support, development, configuration and integration of all management tools and processes
- liaison with Deployment on release techniques and technology.

They play a key role in the:

- maintenance of the current infrastructure fabric
- documentation
- data analysis from monitoring tools and processes
- provision of technical expertise in the supported application areas, such as network interfaces within individual and diverse operating systems.

6 BIBLIOGRAPHY

6.1 Associated reference books and documents

The Balanced Scorecard: Translating Strategy into Action
Robert S. Kaplan, David P. Norton 1996
Harvard Business School Press, Boston, MA
ISBN 0-87584-651-3

Competitive Advantage: Creating and Sustaining Superior Performance
Michael E. Porter 1998
Simon & Schuster
ISBN 0684841460

Information Technology Changes the Way You Compete
F.W. McFarlan 1984
Harvard Business Review

Managing IT as a Strategic Resource
David F. Feeny, Gerd Islei, Leslie P. Willcocks (eds) 1997
McGraw-Hill
ISBN 0-07-709364-X

Managing Successful Projects with PRINCE2, Revised Edition
OGC 2002
Available from TSO (The Stationery Office), www.tso.co.uk
ISBN 0-11-330891-4

Strategic Management – Concepts and Cases
Arthur A. Thompson Jr, A.J. Strickland 2000
McGraw-Hill
ISBN 0-07-251875-8

The Strategy-Focused Organization
Robert S. Kaplan, David P. Norton 2000
Harvard Business School Press, Boston, MA
ISBN 1578512506

Structures in Fives: Designing Effective Organizations
Henry Mintzberg 1993
Prentice Hall, NJ
ISBN 0-13-855479-X

6.2 Appropriate guidelines and standards

BS 7799 – *Code of Practice for Information Security Management*

BS 15000 – *Specification for IT Service Management*

BSI – *Code of Practice for IT Service Management* (DISC PD 0005)

BSI – *IT Service Management. Self-assessment Workbook* (DISC PD 0015)
Ivor MacFarlane

Application Management
OGC
Available from TSO (The Stationery Office), www.tso.co.uk
ISBN 0-11-330866-3

How to Manage Service Provision
OGC 2002
Available from Format Publishing, www.formatpublishing.co.uk and TSO, www.tso.co.uk
ISBN 0-903091-12-8

Planning to Implement Service Management
OGC 2002
Available from TSO, www.tso.co.uk
ISBN 0-11-330877-9

Security Management
OGC
Available from TSO, www.tso.co.uk
ISBN 0-11-330014-X

Service Delivery
OGC 2001
Available from TSO, www.tso.co.uk
ISBN 0-11-330017-4

Service Support
OGC 2000
Available from TSO, www.tso.co.uk
ISBN 0-11-330015-8

APPENDIX A LIST OF ACRONYMS AND GLOSSARY

A.1   Acronyms

AMDB	Availability Management Database
AMS	Application Management Specification
API	Application Program Interface
ARCI	Accountability, Responsibility, Consulted, Informed
BIA	Business Impact Analysis
BIS	Bring Into Service
BPR	Business Process Re-engineering
BS	British Standard
BSC	Balanced Scorecard
BSI	British Standards Institute
CAB	Change Advisory Board
CAB/EC	Change Advisory Board Emergency Committee
CAD	Computer-Aided Design
CASE	Computer-Aided Systems Engineering
CBT	Computer Based Training
CCTV	Closed Circuit Television
CDB	Capacity Management Database
CEO	Chief Executive Officer
CFIA	Component Failure Impact Analysis
CI	Configuration Item
CIO	Chief ICT Officer
CMDB	Configuration Management Database
CMM	Capability Maturity Model
COBIT	Control Objectives for Information and Related Technology
CSF	Critical Success Factor
CSIP	Continuous Service Improvement Programme
CSS	Customer Satisfaction Survey

CTO	Chief Technology Officer
D and P	Design and Planning
DAS	Directly Attached Storage
DHS	Definitive Hardware Store
DMI	Desktop Management Instrumentation
DMTF	Distributed Management Task Force
DSA	Distributed Service Administrator
DSAC	Distributed Service Administration Coordination
DSL	Definitive Software Library
EFQM	European Foundation for Quality Management
EFT	Electronic Funds Transfer
EPOS	Electronic Point-Of-Sale
ERP	Enterprise Resource Planning
ESM	Enterprise Systems Management
EXIN	Examination Institute for Information Science
FCAPS	Fault, Configuration, Accounting, Performance, Security
FM	Facilities Managed/Management
FSC	Forward Schedule of Changes
FTP	File Transfer Protocol
ICT	Information and Communications Technology
ICTI	ICT Infrastructure
ICTIM	ICT Infrastructure Management
ICTSG	ICT Steering Group
IEE	Institution of Electrical Engineers
I/O	Input/Output
IS	Information Systems
ISEB	Information Systems Examination Board
ISG	IT Steering Group
ISO	International Standards Organisation
IT	Information Technology
ITBRM	IT Business Relationship Management
ITIL	IT Infrastructure Library
ITSC	IT Service Continuity

ITSM	IT Service Management
*it*SMF	IT Service Management Forum
ITT	Invitation To Tender
IVR	Interactive Voice Response
KEL	Known Error Log
KPI	Key Performance Indicator
KSI	Key Success Indicator
MAC	Movements, Additions and Changes
MBO	Management By Objectives
MO	Managed Object
MTBF	Mean Time Between Failures
MTBSI	Mean Time Between System Incidents
MTTR	Mean Time To Repair
NAS	Network Attached Storage
NOP	No Operation
NSM	Network Services Management
OGC	Office of Government Commerce
OLA	Operational Level Agreement
OR	Operational Requirement
OS	Operating System
OSI	Open Systems Interconnection
PAT	Portable Appliance Testing
PDU	Power Distribution Unit
PID	Project Initiation Document
PIN	Personal Identification Number
PIR	Post Implementation Review
PMF	Process Maturity Framework
PRINCE	PRojects IN Controlled Environments
QoS	Quality of Service
RAID	Redundant Array of Inexpensive Disks
R and D	Research and Development
RFC	Request For Change
RFP	Request For Proposal

ROI	Return on Investment
RSV	Reference Site Visit
SAN	Storage Area Networks
SEI	Software Engineering Institute
SLA	Service Level Agreement
SLM	Service Level Management
SLR	Service Level Requirement
SMART	Specific, Measurable, Achievable, Realistic, Time-related
SNMP	Simple Network Management Protocol
SOCITM	Society of Council IT Managers
SOR	Statement Of Requirements
SPI	Software Process Improvement
SPICE	Software Process Improvement and Capability dEtermination
SPMF	Service management Process Maturity Framework
SVC	Switched Virtual Circuit
SWOT	Strengths, Weaknesses, Opportunities and Threats
TCO	Total Cost of Ownership
TOR	Terms of Reference
TQM	Total Quality Management
TTO	Transfer To Operation
UC	Underpinning Contract
UPS	Uninterruptible Power Supply
VCA	Value Chain Analysis
VLAN	Virtual LAN
WMI	Windows Management Instrumentation
WORM	Write Once, Read Many (optical read-only disks)

A.2 Glossary

absorbed overhead

Overhead which, by means of absorption rates, is included in costs of specific products or saleable services, in a given period of time. Under- or over-absorbed overhead: the difference between overhead cost incurred and overhead cost absorbed: it may be split into its two constituent parts for control purposes.

absorption costing

A principle whereby fixed as well as variable costs are allotted to cost units and total overheads are absorbed according to activity level. The term may be applied where production costs only, or costs of all functions are so allotted.

action lists

Defined actions, allocated to recovery teams and individuals, within a phase of a plan. These are supported by reference data.

alert

Warning that an incident has occurred.

alert phase

The first phase of a Business Continuity Plan in which initial emergency procedures and damage assessments are activated.

allocated cost

A cost that can be directly identified with a business unit.

application portfolio

An information system containing key attributes of applications deployed in a company. Application portfolios are used as tools to manage the business value of an application throughout its lifecycle.

apportioned cost

A cost that is shared by a number of business units (an indirect cost). This cost must be shared out between these units on an equitable basis.

asset

Component of a business process. Assets can include people, accommodation, computer systems, networks, paper records, fax machines, etc.

asynchronous/synchronous

In a communications sense, the ability to transmit each character as a self-contained unit of information, without additional timing information. This method of transmitting data is sometimes called start/stop. Synchronous working involves the use of timing information to allow transmission of data, which is normally done in blocks. Synchronous transmission is usually more efficient than the asynchronous method.

availability

Ability of a component or service to perform its required function at a stated instant or over a stated period of time. It is usually expressed as the availability ratio, i.e., the proportion of time that the service is actually available for use by the customers within the agreed service hours.

Balanced Scorecard

An aid to organisational performance management. It helps to focus not only on the financial targets but also on the internal processes, customers and learning and growth issues.

baseline

A snapshot or a position which is recorded. Although the position may be updated later, the baseline remains unchanged and available as a reference of the original state and as a comparison against the current position (PRINCE2).

baseline security

> The security level adopted by the IT organisation for its own security and from the point of view of good 'due diligence'.

baselining

> Process by which the quality and cost-effectiveness of a service is assessed, usually in advance of a change to the service. Baselining usually includes comparison of the service before and after the change or analysis of trend information. The term benchmarking is usually used if the comparison is made against other enterprises.

bridge

> Equipment and techniques used to match circuits to each other ensuring minimum transmission impairment.

BS 7799

> The British standard for Information Security Management. This standard provides a comprehensive set of controls comprising best practices in information security.

budgeting

> Budgeting is the process of predicting and controlling the spending of money within the organisation and consists of a periodic negotiation cycle to set budgets (usually annual) and the day-to-day monitoring of current budgets.

build

> The final stage in producing a usable configuration. The process involves taking one of more input Configuration Items and processing them (building them) to create one or more output Configuration Items, e.g., software compile and load.

business function

> A business unit within an organisation, e.g., a department, division, branch.

business process

> A group of business activities undertaken by an organisation in pursuit of a common goal. Typical business processes include receiving orders, marketing services, selling products, delivering services, distributing products, invoicing for services, accounting for money received. A business process usually depends upon several business functions for support, e.g., IT, personnel, and accommodation. A business process rarely operates in isolation, i.e., other business processes will depend on it and it will depend on other processes.

business recovery objective

> The desired time within which business processes should be recovered, and the minimum staff, assets and services required within this time.

business recovery plan framework

> A template business recovery plan (or set of plans) produced to allow the structure and proposed contents to be agreed before the detailed business recovery plan is produced.

business recovery plans

> Documents describing the roles, responsibilities and actions necessary to resume business processes following a business disruption.

business recovery team

> A defined group of personnel with a defined role and subordinate range of actions to facilitate recovery of a business function or process.

business unit

> A segment of the business entity by which both revenues are received and expenditure is caused or controlled, such revenues and expenditure being used to evaluate segmental performance.

Capital Costs

> Typically, those costs applying to the physical (substantial) assets of the organisation. Traditionally this was the accommodation and machinery necessary to produce the enterprise's product. Capital Costs are the purchase or major enhancement of fixed assets, for example, computer equipment (building and plant) and are often also referred to as 'one-off' costs.

capital investment appraisal

> The process of evaluating proposed investment in specific fixed assets and the benefits to be obtained from their acquisition. The techniques used in the evaluation can be summarised as non-discounting methods (i.e., simple payback), return on capital employed and discounted cashflow methods (i.e., yield, net present value and discounted payback).

capitalisation

> The process of identifying major expenditure as Capital, whether there is a substantial asset or not, to reduce the impact on the current financial year of such expenditure. The most common item for this to be applied to is software, whether developed in-house or purchased.

category

> Classification of a group of Configuration Items, change documents or problems.

change

> The addition, modification or removal of approved, supported or baselined hardware, network, software, application, environment, system, desktop build or associated documentation.

Change Advisory Board (CAB)

> A group of people who can give expert advice to Change Management on the implementation of changes. This board is likely to be made up of representatives from all areas within IT and representatives from business units.

Change Authority

> A group that is given the authority to approve change, e.g., by the Project Board. Sometimes referred to as the Configuration Board.

change control

> The procedure to ensure that all changes are controlled, including the submission, analysis, decision-making, approval, implementation and post-implementation of the change.

change document

> Request for Change, change control form, change order, change record.

change history

Auditable information that records, for example, what was done, when it was done, by whom and why.

change log

A log of Requests For Change raised during the project, showing information on each change, its evaluation, what decisions have been made and its current status, e.g., Raised, Reviewed, Approved, Implemented, Closed.

Change Management

Process of controlling changes to the infrastructure or any aspect of services, in a controlled manner, enabling approved changes with minimum disruption.

change record

A record containing details of which CIs are affected by an authorised change (planned or implemented) and how.

charging

The process of establishing charges in respect of business units, and raising the relevant invoices for recovery from customers.

classification

Process of formally grouping Configuration Items by type, e.g., software, hardware, documentation, environment, application.

Process of formally identifying changes by type e.g., project scope change request, validation change request, infrastructure change request.

Process of formally identifying incidents, problems and known errors by origin, symptoms and cause.

closure

When the customer is satisfied that an incident has been resolved.

cold stand-by

See 'gradual recovery'.

command, control and communications

The processes by which an organisation retains overall coordination of its recovery effort during invocation of business recovery plans.

Computer-Aided Systems Engineering (CASE)

A software tool for programmers. It provides help in the planning, analysis, design and documentation of computer software.

Configuration baseline

Configuration of a product or system established at a specific point in time, which captures both the structure and details of the product or system, and enables that product or system to be rebuilt at a later date.

A snapshot or a position which is recorded. Although the position may be updated later, the baseline remains unchanged and available as a reference of the original state and as a comparison against the current position (PRINCE2).

See also 'baseline'.

Configuration control

Activities comprising the control of changes to Configuration Items after formally establishing its configuration documents. It includes the evaluation, coordination, approval or rejection of changes. The implementation of changes includes changes, deviations and waivers that impact on the configuration.

Configuration documentation

Documents that define requirements, system design, build, production, and verification for a Configuration Item.

Configuration identification

Activities that determine the product structure, the selection of Configuration Items, and the documentation of the Configuration Item's physical and functional characteristics including interfaces and subsequent changes. It includes the allocation of identification characters or numbers to the Configuration Items and their documents. It also includes the unique numbering of Configuration control forms associated with changes and problems.

Configuration Item (CI)

Component of an infrastructure – or an item, such as a Request for Change, associated with an infrastructure – which is (or is to be) under the control of Configuration Management. CIs may vary widely in complexity, size and type – from an entire system (including all hardware, software and documentation) to a single module or a minor hardware component.

Configuration Management

The process of identifying and defining the Configuration Items in a system, recording and reporting the status of Configuration Items and Requests For Change, and verifying the completeness and correctness of Configuration Items.

Configuration Management Database (CMDB)

A database which contains all relevant details of each CI and details of the important relationships between CIs.

Configuration Management plan

Document setting out the organisation and procedures for the Configuration Management of a specific product, project, system, support group or service.

Configuration Management Tool (CM Tool)

A software product providing automatic support for change, Configuration or version control.

Configuration Structure

A hierarchy of all the CIs that comprise a configuration.

Contingency Planning

Planning to address unwanted occurrences that may happen at a later time. Traditionally, the term has been used to refer to planning for the recovery of IT systems rather than entire business processes.

Continuous Service Improvement Programme

An ongoing formal programme undertaken within an organisation to identify and introduce measurable improvements within a specified work area or work process.

cost

The amount of expenditure (actual or notional) incurred on, or attributable to, a specific activity or business unit.

cost-effectiveness

Ensuring that there is a proper balance between the Quality of Service on the one side and expenditure on the other. Any investment that increases the costs of providing IT services should always result in enhancement to service quality or quantity.

cost management

All the procedures, tasks and deliverables that are needed to fulfil an organisation's costing and charging requirements.

cost of failure

A technique used to evaluate and measure the cost of failed actions and activities. It can be measured as a total within a period or an average per failure. An example would be 'the cost of failed changes per month' or 'the average cost of a failed change'.

cost unit

In the context of CSBC the cost unit is a functional cost unit which establishes standard cost per workload element of activity, based on calculated activity ratios converted to cost ratios.

costing

The process of identifying the costs of the business and of breaking them down and relating them to the various activities of the organisation.

countermeasure

A check or restraint on the service designed to enhance security by reducing the risk of an attack (by reducing either the threat or the vulnerability), reducing the impact of an attack, detecting the occurrence of an attack and/or assisting in the recovery from an attack.

CRAMM

The UK Government's Risk Analysis and Management Method. Further information is available from www.insight.co.uk/cramm/ or tel. 01932 241000.

crisis management

The processes by which an organisation manages the wider impact of a disaster, such as adverse media coverage.

Critical Success Factor (CSF)

A measure of success or maturity of a project or process. It can be a state, a deliverable or a milestone. An example of a CSF would be 'the production of an overall technology strategy'.

customer

Recipient of the service; usually the customer management has responsibility for the cost of the service, either directly through charging or indirectly in terms of demonstrable business need.

data transfer time

The length of time taken for a block or sector of data to be read from or written to an I/O device, such as a disk or tape.

Definitive Software Library (DSL)

The library in which the definitive authorised versions of all software CIs are stored and protected. It is a physical library or storage repository where master copies of software versions are placed. This one logical storage area may, in reality, consist of one or more physical software libraries or filestores. They should be separate from development and test filestore areas. The DSL may also include a physical store to hold master copies of bought-in software, e.g., fireproof safe. Only authorised software should be accepted into the DSL, strictly controlled by Change and Release Management.

The DSL exists not directly because of the needs of the Configuration Management process, but as a common base for the Release Management and Configuration Management processes.

Delta Release

A Delta, or partial, Release is one that includes only those CIs within the Release unit that have actually changed or are new since the last full or Delta Release. For example, if the Release unit is the program, a Delta Release contains only those modules that have changed, or are new, since the last Full Release of the program or the last Delta Release of the modules.

See also 'Full Release'.

dependency

The reliance, either direct or indirect, of one process or activity upon another.

depreciation

The loss in value of an asset due to its use and/or the passage of time. The annual depreciation charge in accounts represents the amount of capital assets used up in the accounting period. It is charged in the cost accounts to ensure that the cost of capital equipment is reflected in the unit costs of the services provided using the equipment. There are various methods of calculating depreciation for the period, but the Treasury usually recommends the use of current cost asset valuation as the basis for the depreciation charge.

differential charging

Charging business customers different rates for the same work, typically to dampen demand or to generate revenue for spare capacity. This can also be used to encourage off-peak or night-time running.

direct cost

A cost that is incurred for, and can be traced in full to a product, service, cost centre or department. This is an allocated cost. Direct costs are direct materials, direct wages and direct expenses.

See also 'indirect cost'.

disaster recovery planning

A series of processes that focus only upon the recovery processes, principally in response to physical disasters, that are contained within BCM.

discounted cashflow

An evaluation of the future net cashflows generated by a capital project by discounting them to their present-day value. The two methods most commonly used are:

> – yield method, for which the calculation determines the internal rate of return (IRR) in the form of a percentage
> – net present value (NPV) method, in which the discount rate is chosen and the answer is a sum of money.

discounting

The offering to business customers of reduced rates for the use of off-peak resources.

See also 'surcharging'.

disk cache controller

Memory that is used to store blocks of data that have been read from the disk devices connected to them. If a subsequent I/O requires a record that is still resident in the cache memory, it will be picked up from there, thus saving another physical I/O.

downtime

Total period that a service or component is not operational, within agreed service times.

duplex (full and half)

Full duplex line/channel allows simultaneous transmission in both directions. Half duplex line/channel is capable of transmitting in both directions, but only in one direction at a time.

echoing

A reflection of the transmitted signal from the receiving end; a visual method of error detection in which the signal from the originating device is looped back to that device so that it can be displayed.

elements of cost

The constituent parts of costs according to the factors upon which expenditure is incurred viz., materials, labour and expenses.

end user

See 'user'.

environment

A collection of hardware, software, network communications and procedures that work together to provide a discrete type of computer service. There may be one or more environments on a physical platform, e.g., test, production. An environment has unique features and characteristics that dictate how they are administered in similar, yet diverse manners.

expert user

See 'super user'.

external target

One of the measures against which a delivered IT service is compared, expressed in terms of the customer's business.

financial year

An accounting period covering 12 consecutive months. In the public sector, this financial year generally coincides with the fiscal year, which runs from 1 April to 31 March.

first-line support

Service Desk call logging and resolution (on agreed areas, for example, MS Word).

first time fix rate

Commonly used metric, used to define incidents resolved at the first point of contact between a customer and the Service Provider, without delay or referral, generally by a front line support group such as a help desk or Service Desk. First time fixes are a sub-set of remote fixes.

Forward Schedule of Changes (FSC)

Contains details of all the changes approved for implementation and their proposed implementation dates. It should be agreed with the customers and the business, Service Level Management, the Service Desk and Availability Management. Once agreed, the Service Desk should communicate to the user community at large any planned additional downtime arising from implementing the changes, using the most effective methods available.

full cost

The total cost of all the resources used in supplying a service, i.e., the sum of the direct costs of producing the output, a proportional share of overhead costs and any selling and distribution expenses. Both cash costs and notional (non-cash) costs should be included, including the cost of capital.

See also 'Total Cost of Ownership'.

Full Release

All components of the Release unit are built, tested, distributed and implemented together.

See also 'Delta Release'.

gateway

Equipment which is used to interface networks so that a terminal on one network can communicate with services or a terminal on another.

gradual recovery

Previously called 'cold stand-by', this is applicable to organisations that do not need immediate restoration of business processes and can function for a period of up to 72 hours, or longer, without a re-establishment of full IT facilities. This may include the provision of empty accommodation fully equipped with power, environmental controls and local network cabling infrastructure, telecommunications connections, and available in a disaster situation for an organisation to install its own computer equipment.

hard charging

Descriptive of a situation where, within an organisation, actual funds are transferred from the customer to the IT organisation in payment for the delivery of IT services.

hard fault

The situation in a virtual memory system when the required page of code or data that a program was using has been redeployed by the operating system for some other purpose. This means that another piece of memory must be found to accommodate the code or data, and will involve physical reading/writing of pages to the page file.

host

A host computer comprises the central hardware and software resources of a computer complex, e.g., CPU, memory, channels, disk and magnetic tape I/O subsystems plus operating and applications software. The term is used to denote all non-network items.

hot stand-by

See 'immediate recovery'.

ICT

The convergence of Information Technology, Telecommunications and Data Networking Technologies into a single technology.

immediate recovery

Previously called 'hot stand-by', provides for the immediate restoration of services following any irrecoverable incident. It is important to distinguish between the previous definition of 'hot stand-by' and 'immediate recovery'. Hot stand-by typically referred to availability of services within a short time-scale such as 2 or 4 hours whereas immediate recovery implies the instant availability of services.

impact

Measure of the business criticality of an incident. Often equal to the extent to which an incident leads to distortion of agreed or expected Service Levels.

impact analysis

The identification of critical business processes, and the potential damage or loss that may be caused to the organisation resulting from a disruption to those processes. Business impact analysis identifies:

– the form the loss or damage will take
– how that degree of damage or loss is likely to escalate with time following an incident
– the minimum staffing, facilities and services needed to enable business processes to continue to operate at a minimum acceptable level
– the time within which they should be recovered

The time within which full recovery of the business processes is to be achieved is also identified.

impact code

Simple code assigned to incidents and problems, reflecting the degree of impact upon the customer's business processes. It is the major means of assigning priority for dealing with incidents.

impact scenario

Description of the type of impact on the business that could follow a business disruption. Usually related to a business process and will always refer to a period of time, e.g., customer services will be unable to operate for two days.

incident

Any event which is not part of the standard operation of a service and which causes, or may cause, an interruption to, or a reduction in, the quality of that service.

incident control

> The process of identifying, recording, classifying and progressing incidents until affected services return to normal operation.

indirect cost

> A cost incurred in the course of making a product providing a service or running a cost centre or department, but which cannot be traced directly and in full to the product, service or department, because it has been incurred for a number of cost centres or cost units. These costs are apportioned to cost centres/cost units. Indirect costs are also referred to as overheads.
>
> See also 'direct cost'.

Information Systems (IS)

> The means of delivering information from one person to another; ICT is the technical apparatus for doing so.

informed customer

> An individual, team or group with functional responsibility within an organisation for ensuring that spend on IS/IT is directed to best effect, i.e., that the business is receiving value for money and continues to achieve the most beneficial outcome. In order to fulfil its role the 'Informed' customer function must gain clarity of vision in relation to the business plans and ensure that suitable strategies are devised and maintained for achieving business goals.
>
> The 'informed' customer function ensures that the needs of the business are effectively translated into a business requirements specification, that IT investment is both efficiently and economically directed, and that progress towards effective business solutions is monitored. The 'informed' customer should play an active role in the procurement process, e.g., in relation to business case development, and also in ensuring that the services and solutions obtained are used effectively within the organisation to achieve maximum business benefits. The term is often used in relation to the outsourcing of IT/IS. Sometimes also called 'intelligent customer'.

interface

> Physical or functional interaction at the boundary between Configuration Items.

intermediate recovery

> Previously called 'warm stand-by', typically involves the re-establishment of the critical systems and services within a 24 to 72 hour period, and is used by organisations that need to recover IT facilities within a predetermined time to prevent impacts to the business process.

internal target

> One of the measures against which supporting processes for the IT service are compared. Usually expressed in technical terms relating directly to the underpinning service being measured.

invocation (of business recovery plans)

> Putting business recovery plans into operation after a business disruption.

invocation (of stand-by arrangements)

> Putting stand-by arrangements into operation as part of business recovery activities.

invocation and recovery phase

> The second phase of a business recovery plan.

ISO 9001

> The internationally accepted set of standards concerning Quality Management Systems.

IT accounting

> The set of processes that enable the IT organisation to account fully for the way money is spent (particularly the ability to identify costs by customer, by service and by activity).

IT directorate

> The part of an organisation charged with developing and delivering the IT services.

IT Infrastructure

> The sum of an organisation's IT related hardware, software, data telecommunication facilities, procedures and documentation.

IT service

> A described set of facilities, IT and non-IT, supported by the IT Service Provider that fulfils one or more needs of the customer and that is perceived by the customer as a coherent whole.

IT Service Provider

> The role of IT Service Provider is performed by any organisational units, whether internal or external, that deliver and support IT services to a customer.

ITIL

> The OGC IT Infrastructure Library – a set of guides on the management and provision of operational IT services.

key business drivers

> The attributes of a business function that drive the behaviour and implementation of that business function in order to achieve the strategic business goals of the company.

Key Performance Indicator

> A measurable quantity against which specific Performance Criteria can be set when drawing up the SLA.

Key Success Indicator

> A measurement of success or maturity of a project or process.
>
> See also 'Critical Success Factor'.

Knowledge Management

> Discipline within an organisation that ensures that the intellectual capabilities of an organisation are shared, maintained and institutionalised.

known error

> An incident or problem for which the root cause is known and for which a temporary Work-around or a permanent alternative has been identified. If a business case exists, an RFC will be raised, but, in any event, it remains a known error unless it is permanently fixed by a change.

latency

> The elapsed time from the moment when a seek was completed on a disk device to the

point when the required data is positioned under the read/write heads. It is normally defined by manufacturers as being half the disk rotation time.

lifecycle

A series of states, connected by allowable transitions. The lifecycle represents an approval process for Configuration Items, problem reports and change documents.

logical I/O

A read or write request by a program. That request may, or may not, necessitate a physical I/O. For example, on a read request the required record may already be in a memory buffer and therefore a physical I/O is not necessary.

marginal cost

The cost of providing the service now, based upon the investment already made.

maturity level/milestone

The degree to which BCM activities and processes have become standard business practice within an organisation.

metric

Measurable element of a service process or function.

Operational Costs

Those costs resulting from the day-to-day running of the IT services section, e.g., staff costs, hardware maintenance and electricity, and relating to repeating payments whose effects can be measured within a short time frame, usually less than the 12-month financial year.

Operational Level Agreement (OLA)

An internal agreement covering the delivery of services which support the IT organisation in their delivery of services.

Operations

All activities and measures to enable and/or maintain the intended use of the ICT infrastructure.

opportunity cost (or true cost)

The value of a benefit sacrificed in favour of an alternative course of action. That is the cost of using resources in a particular operation expressed in terms of forgoing the benefit that could be derived from the best alternative use of those resources.

outsourcing

The process by which functions performed by the organisation are contracted out for operation, on the organisation's behalf, by third parties.

overheads

The total of indirect materials, wages and expenses.

Package Assembly/Disassembly Device (PAD)

A device that permits terminals, which do not have an interface suitable for direct connection to a packet switched network, to access such a network. A PAD converts data to/from packets and handles call set-up and addressing.

page fault

> A program interruption that occurs when a page that is marked 'not in real memory' is referred to by an active page.

Paging

> The I/O necessary to read and write to and from the paging disks: real (not virtual) memory is needed to process data. With insufficient real memory, the operating system writes old pages to disk, and reads new pages from disk, so that the required data and instructions are in real memory.

PD0005

> Alternative title for the BSI publication 'A Code of Practice for IT Service Management'.

percentage utilisation

> The amount of time that a hardware device is busy over a given period of time. For example, if the CPU is busy for 1800 seconds in a one-hour period, its utilisation is said to be 50%.

Performance Criteria

> The expected levels of achievement which are set within the SLA against specific Key Performance Indicators.

phantom line error

> A communications error reported by a computer system that is not detected by network monitoring equipment. It is often caused by changes to the circuits and network equipment (e.g., re-routeing circuits at the physical level on a backbone network) while data communications is in progress.

physical I/O

> A read or write request from a program has necessitated a physical read or write operation on an I/O device.

prime cost

> The total cost of direct materials, direct labour and direct expenses. The term prime cost is commonly restricted to direct production costs only and so does not customarily include direct costs of marketing or research and development.

PRINCE2

> The standard UK government method for Project Management.

priority

> Sequence in which an incident or problem needs to be resolved, based on impact and urgency.

problem

> Unknown underlying cause of one or more incidents.

Problem Management

> Process that minimises the effect on customer(s) of defects in services and within the infrastructure, human errors and external events.

process

> A connected series of actions, activities, changes, etc., performed by agents with the intent of satisfying a purpose or achieving a goal.

process control

> The process of planning and regulating, with the objective of performing the process in an effective and efficient way.

programme

> A collection of activities and projects that collectively implement a new corporate requirement or function.

provider

> The organisation concerned with the provision of IT services.

Quality of Service

> An agreed or contracted level of service between a service customer and a Service Provider.

queuing time

> Queuing time is incurred when the device, which a program wishes to use, is already busy. The program therefore has to wait in a queue to obtain service from that device.

RAID

> Redundant Array of Inexpensive Disks – a mechanism for providing data resilience for computer systems using mirrored arrays of magnetic disks.
>
> Different levels of RAID can be applied to provide for greater resilience.

reference data

> Information that supports the plans and action lists, such as names and addresses or inventories, which is indexed within the plan.

Release

> A collection of new and/or changed CIs which are tested and introduced into the live environment together.

remote fixes

> Incidents or problems resolved without a member of the support staff visiting the physical location of the problem. Note: Fixing incidents or problems remotely minimises the delay before the service is back to normal and are therefore usually cost-effective.

Request For Change (RFC)

> Form, or screen, used to record details of a request for a change to any CI within an infrastructure or to procedures and items associated with the infrastructure.

resolution

> Action which will resolve an incident. This may be a Work-around.

resource cost

> The amount of machine resource that a given task consumes. This resource is usually expressed in seconds for the CPU or the number of I/Os for a disk or tape device.

resource profile

> The total resource costs that are consumed by an individual on-line transaction, batch job or program. It is usually expressed in terms of CPU seconds, number of I/Os and memory usage.

resource unit costs

Resource units may be calculated on a standard cost basis to identify the expected (standard) cost for using a particular resource. Because computer resources come in many shapes and forms, units have to be established by logical groupings. Examples are:

- CPU time or instructions
- disk I/Os
- print lines
- communication transactions.

resources

The IT services section needs to provide the customers with the required services. The resources are typically computer and related equipment, software, facilities or organisational (people).

Return On Investment

The ratio of the cost of implementing a project, product or service and the savings as a result of completing the activity in terms of either internal savings, increased external revenue or a combination of the two. For instance, in simplistic terms if the internal cost of ICT cabling of office moves is £100,000 per annum and a structured cabling system can be installed for £300,000, then an ROI will be achieved after approximately three years.

return to normal phase

The phase within a business recovery plan which re-establishes normal operations.

Risk

A measure of the exposure to which an organisation may be subjected. This is a combination of the likelihood of a business disruption occurring and the possible loss that may result from such business disruption.

risk analysis

The identification and assessment of the level (measure) of the risks calculated from the assessed values of assets and the assessed levels of threats to, and vulnerabilities of, those assets.

Risk Management

The identification, selection and adoption of countermeasures justified by the identified risks to assets in terms of their potential impact upon services if failure occurs, and the reduction of those risks to an acceptable level.

Risk reduction measure

Measures taken to reduce the likelihood or consequences of a business disruption occurring (as opposed to planning to recover after a disruption).

role

A set of responsibilities, activities and authorisations.

roll in, roll out (RIRO)

Used on some systems to describe swapping.

Rotational Position Sensing

A facility which is employed on most mainframes and some minicomputers. When a seek has been initiated the system can free the path from a disk drive to a controller for use by another disk drive, while it is waiting for the required data to come under the read/write heads (latency). This facility usually improves the overall performance of the I/O subsystem.

second-line support

Where the fault cannot be resolved by first-line support or requires time to be resolved or local attendance.

Security Management

The process of managing a defined level of security on information and services.

Security Manager

The Security Manager is the role that is responsible for the Security Management process in the Service Provider organisation. The person is responsible for fulfilling the security demands as specified in the SLA, either directly or through delegation by the Service Level Manager. The Security Officer and the Security Manager work closely together.

Security Officer

The Security Officer is responsible for assessing the business risks and setting the security policy. As such, this role is the counterpart of the Security Manager and resides in the customer's business organisation. The Security Officer and the Security Manager work closely together.

seek time

Occurs when the disk read/write heads are not positioned on the required track. It describes the elapsed time taken to move heads to the right track.

segregation of duties

Separation of the management or execution of certain duties or of areas of responsibility is required in order to prevent and reduce opportunities for unauthorised modification or misuse of data or service.

self-insurance

A decision to bear the losses that could result from a disruption to the business as opposed to taking insurance cover on the Risk.

Service

One or more IT systems which enable a business process.

Service achievement

The actual Service Levels delivered by the IT organisation to a customer within a defined life span.

Service Catalogue

Written statement of IT services, default levels and options.

Service Dependency Modelling

Technique used to gain insight in the interdependency between an IT service and the Configuration Items that make up that service.

Service Desk

The single point of contact within the IT organisation for users of IT services.

Service Level

> The expression of an aspect of a service in definitive and quantifiable terms.

Service Level Agreement (SLA)

> Written agreement between a Service Provider and the customer(s) that documents agreed Service Levels for a service.

Service Level Management (SLM)

> The process of defining, agreeing, documenting and managing the levels of customer IT service, that are required and cost justified.

Service Management

> Management of Services to meet the customer's requirements.

Service Provider

> Third-party organisation supplying services or products to customers.

Service quality plan

> The written plan and specification of internal targets designed to guarantee the agreed Service Levels.

Service Request

> Every incident not being a failure in the IT Infrastructure.

Services

> The deliverables of the IT services organisation as perceived by the customers; the services do not consist merely of making computer resources available for customers to use.

severity code

> Simple code assigned to problems and known errors, indicating the seriousness of their effect on the Quality of Service. It is the major means of assigning priority for resolution.

simulation modelling

> Using a program to simulate computer processing by describing in detail the path of a job or transaction. It can give extremely accurate results. Unfortunately, it demands a great deal of time and effort from the modeller. It is most beneficial in extremely large or time-critical systems where the margin for error is very small.

soft fault

> The situation in a virtual memory system when the operating system has detected that a page of code or data was due to be reused, i.e., it is on a list of 'free' pages, but it is still actually in memory. It is now rescued and put back into service.

Software Configuration Item (SCI)

> As 'Configuration Item', excluding hardware and services.

software environment

> Software used to support the application such as operating system, database management system, development tools, compilers, and application software.

software library

> A controlled collection of SCIs designated to keep those with like status and type together and segregated from unlike, to aid in development, operation and maintenance.

software work unit

> Software work is a generic term devised to represent a common base on which all calculations for workload usage and IT resource capacity are then based. A unit of software work for I/O type equipment equals the number of bytes transferred; and for central processors, it is based on the product of power and CPU time.

solid state devices

> Memory devices that are made to appear as if they are disk devices. The advantages of such devices are that the service times are much faster than real disks since there is no seek time or latency. The main disadvantage is that they are much more expensive.

spec sheet

> Specifies in detail what the customer wants (external) and what consequences this has for the Service Provider (internal) such as required resources and skills.

stakeholder

> Any individual or group who has an interest, or 'stake', in the IT service organisation of a CSIP.

standard cost

> A predetermined calculation of how many costs should be under specified working conditions. It is built up from an assessment of the value of cost elements and correlates technical specifications and the quantification of materials, labour and other costs to the prices and/or wages expected to apply during the period in which the standard cost is intended to be used. Its main purposes are to provide bases for control through variance accounting, for the valuation of work in progress and for fixing selling prices.

standard costing

> A technique which uses standards for costs and revenues for the purposes of control through variance analysis.

stand-by arrangements

> Arrangements to have available assets that have been identified as replacements should primary assets be unavailable following a business disruption. Typically, these include accommodation, IT systems and networks, telecommunications and sometimes people.

storage occupancy

> A defined measurement unit that is used for storage type equipment to measure usage. The unit value equals the number of bytes stored.

Strategic Alignment Objectives Model (SAOM)

> Relation diagram depicting the relation between a business function and its business drivers and the technology with the technology characteristics. The SAOM is a high-level tool that can help IT services organisations to align their SLAs, OLAs and acceptance criteria for new technology with the business value they deliver.

super user

> In some organisations it is common to use 'expert' users (commonly known as super or expert users) to deal with first-line support problems and queries. This is typically in specific application areas, or geographical locations, where there is not the requirement for full-time support staff. This valuable resource, however, needs to be carefully coordinated and utilised.

surcharging

Surcharging is charging business users a premium rate for using resources at peak times.

swapping

The reaction of the operating system to insufficient real memory: swapping occurs when too many tasks are perceived to be competing for limited resources. It is the physical movement of an entire task (e.g., all real memory pages of an address space may be moved at one time from main storage to auxiliary storage).

system

An integrated composite that consists of one or more of the processes, hardware, software, facilities and people, that provides a capability to satisfy a stated need or objective.

tension metrics

A set of objectives for individual team members to use to balance conflicting roles and conflicting project and organisational objectives in order to create shared responsibility in teams and between teams.

terminal emulation

Software running on an intelligent device, typically a PC or workstation, which allows that device to function as an interactive terminal connected to a host system. Examples of such emulation software includes IBM 3270 BSC or SNA, ICL C03, or Digital VT100.

terminal I/O

A read from, or a write to, an on-line device such as a VDU or remote printer.

third-line support

Where specialists' skills (e.g., development/engineer) or contracted third-party support is required.

third-party supplier

An enterprise or group, external to the customer's enterprise, which provides services and/or products to that customer's enterprise.

thrashing

A condition in a virtual storage system where an excessive proportion of CPU time is spent moving data between main and auxiliary storage.

threat

An indication of an unwanted incident that could impinge on the system in some way. Threats may be deliberate (e.g., wilful damage) or accidental (e.g., operator error).

Total Cost of Ownership (TCO)

Calculated by including depreciation, maintenance, staff costs, accommodation, and planned renewal.

tree structures

In data structures, a series of connected nodes without cycles. One node is termed the 'root' and is the starting point of all paths; other nodes termed 'leaves' terminate the paths.

unabsorbed overhead

Any indirect cost that cannot be apportioned to a specific customer.

Underpinning Contract

A contract with an external supplier covering delivery of services that support the IT organisation in their delivery of services.

unit costs

Costs distributed over individual component usage. For example, it can be assumed that, if a box of paper with 1000 sheets costs £10, then each sheet costs 1p. Similarly, if a CPU costs £1m a year and it is used to process 1,000 jobs that year, each job costs on average £1,000.

urgency

Measure of the business criticality of an incident or problem based on the impact and the business needs of the customer.

user

The person who uses the service on a day-to-day basis.

Utility Cost Centre (UCC)

A cost centre for the provision of support services to other cost centres.

variance analysis

A variance is the difference between planned, budgeted or standard cost and actual cost (or revenues). Variance analysis is an analysis of the factors that have caused the difference between the predetermined standards and the actual results. Variances can be developed specifically related to the operations carried out in addition to those mentioned above.

version

An identified instance of a Configuration Item within a product breakdown structure or Configuration Structure for the purpose of tracking and auditing change history. Also used for Software Configuration Items to define a specific identification released in development for drafting, review or modification, test or production.

version identifier

A version number, version date, or version date and time stamp.

virtual memory system

A system that enhances the size of hard memory by adding an auxiliary storage layer residing on the hard disk.

Virtual Storage Interrupt (VSI)

An ICL VME term for a page fault.

vulnerability

A weakness of the system and its assets, which could be exploited by threats.

warm stand-by

See 'intermediate recovery'.

waterline

The lowest level of detail relevant to the customer.

Work-around

Method of avoiding an incident or problem, either from a temporary fix or from a technique that means the customer is not reliant on a particular aspect of the service that is known to have a problem.

workloads

In the context of Capacity Management Modelling, a set of forecasts which detail the estimated resource usage over an agreed planning horizon. Workloads generally represent discrete business applications and can be further subdivided into types of work (interactive, timesharing, batch).

WORM (Device)

Optical read only disks, standing for Write Once Read Many.

XML

Extensible Markup Language. XML is a set of rules for designing text formats that let you structure your data. XML makes it easy for a computer to generate data, read data, and ensure that the data structure is unambiguous. XML avoids common pitfalls in language design: it is extensible, platform-independent, and it supports internationalisation and localisation.

APPENDIX B PROCESS THEORY

B.1 Process theory

This appendix provides a general introduction to process theory and practice, which is the basis for the ITIL process models. One becomes aware of 'process' through process models that define workflows and provide guidance on performing it. A process model enables understanding and helps to articulate the distinctive features of a process.

A process can be defined as:

> **a connected series of actions, activities, changes, etc., performed by agents with the intent of satisfying a purpose or achieving a goal.**

Process control can similarly be defined as:

> **the process of planning and regulating, with the objective of performing a process in an effective and efficient way.**

Processes, once defined, should be under control; once under control, they can be repeated and become manageable. Degrees of control over processes can be defined, and then metrics can be built in to manage the control process.

The output produced by a process has to conform to operational norms that are derived from business objectives. If products conform to the set norm, the process can be considered effective (because it can be repeated, measured and managed). If the activities are carried out with a minimum of effort, the process can also be considered efficient.

Process results metrics should be incorporated in regular management reports.

B.1.1 The product-oriented organisation

Process activities exist in many organisations. However, they are often carried out throughout an organisation, but without any process-oriented coordination. This results in problems that have to be addressed during process implementation. Some examples include:

- processes lacking a clear purpose and focus on business results
- similar processes with inconsistent approaches
- actions or processes performed many times instead of once
- activities that are missing
- no focus on existing business-oriented results.

B.1.2 Moving towards a process-oriented organisation

Since processes and their activities run through an organisation, they should be mapped and coordinated by Process Managers. Figure B.1 shows how process activities may be assigned to people in several different organisational units. The simple box diagram indicates the apparent consecutive flow of processes in a linear sequence. Reality is better reflected in the organisational view, where the flow is clearly non-linear and where it is possible to think of delays and interactions that might take place.

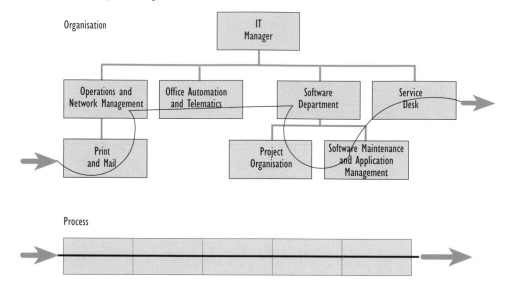

Figure B.1 – Process mapped to organisational unit

In a product-oriented organisation, the flow of activities and processes in Figure B.1 is not generally recognised at all; the focus is on the product, and management and control are often lacking. The evidence is in the lack of any useful metrics related to the production process, because the process activities are not clear or even not identified.

B.1.3   The process approach

The model shown in Figure B.2 is a generic process model. Data enters the process, is processed, data comes out, and the outcome is measured and reviewed. This very basic description underpins any process description. A process is always organised around a goal. The main output of that process is the result of that goal.

Working with defined processes is a novelty for many organisations. By defining what the organisation's activities are, which inputs are necessary and which outputs will result from the process, it is possible to work in a more efficient and effective manner. Measuring and steering the activities increases this efficacy. Finally, by adding norms to the process, it is possible to add quality measures to the output.

The approach underpins the 'plan-do-check-act' cycle of any Quality Management System. Plan the purpose of the process in such a way that the process action can be audited for successful achievement and, if necessary, improved.

The output produced by a process has to conform to operational norms that are derived from business objectives. If the products conform to the set norm, the process can be considered effective. If the activities are also carried out with minimum effort, the process can also be considered efficient. Process measurement results should be incorporated in regular management reports.

'Norms' define certain conditions that the results should meet. Defining norms introduces quality aspects to the process. Even before starting, it is important to think about what the outcome should look like. This enables:

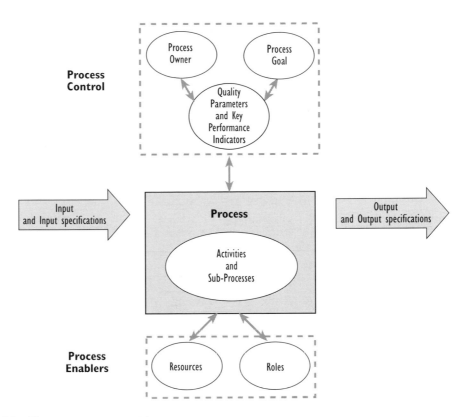

Figure B.2 – The generic process model

- inputs and activities to be considered beforehand because 'what to do' is known
- effective measurement because 'what to measure' is known
- assessment of whether the result fulfilled expectations because 'what to expect' is known.

Defining objective norms is a tedious task and may be very complex, since objectivity can often be subjective (to slightly misquote Woody Allen).

To discover whether activities are contributing optimally to the business goal of the process, their effectiveness should be measured on a regular basis. Measuring allows comparison between what has actually been done and what the organisation set out to do, and consideration of the improvements that may be needed.

APPENDIX C SYSTEMS INSTALLATION POLICIES

This appendix contains guidance on planning and managing site preparation for the installation of new ICT services and equipment. It covers planning for the installation of equipment and services into either a greenfield site or existing accommodation. These activities should be managed as a project and carried out by a project team. Indeed, the size of the project may well necessitate the formation of several sub-projects, especially if there is new building work and new ICT equipment to be procured. However, it is important that all sub-projects should be coordinated by a single project manager.

The projects should be run using a formal Project Management method such as PRINCE2 and adhere to organisational and site standards. The quality of ICT project planning needs to be dramatically improved if the industry-quoted statistics on ICT projects are to be believed:

> '90% of ICT projects only ever reach 90% completion.'
>
> '40% of ICT projects fail, 70% are over budget and many others under-deliver.'

Reference should be made to Figure 1.6 on workflow through ICT processes.

This appendix covers:

- building computer accommodation
- the procurement process
- service planning and acceptance
- equipment planning, installation and handover
- supporting documentation.

The remainder of this appendix has been divided into sections covering:

- general planning and preparation considerations
- planning and preparing accommodation on a greenfield site
- planning to install equipment into previously prepared accommodation.

C.1 General planning procedures and preparation

These activities should be managed using a recognised project method, with sign-off procedures at every stage. The project should use the organisational policies and standards for equipment environment and accommodation. Most organisations will have a number of different accommodation standards ranging from major computer suites, through major equipment and network nodes through to open office and factory environments. Appendix D contains further details on environmental policies and standards.

The first activity to be completed is to identify, document and agree the requirements of the project with all areas concerned. This should not only identify what the immediate requirements are but should also quantify any possible future requirements and allow for those as well.

The general activities required to ensure that projects are successful can be summarised as follows:

- define the scope, terms of reference and objectives of the project
- perform project planning and management, e.g. using PRINCE2, with development of a Project Initiation Document (PID) and fully defined business goals, and the appointment of a Project Board and project manager
- identify and allocate the appropriate resources
- identify project risks and actions to minimise them
- identify external dependencies with other associated projects
- recognition of equipment and software lead times within project time-scales
- negotiate realistic and achievable time-scales and deliverables
- consult with senior Business Management and ICT Management for project sponsorship, commitment, project goals and system acceptance criteria
- identify and plan all required documentation
- make allowances within the project to ensure that all necessary staff are recruited and trained in the appropriate areas, including both central support staff and local support staff
- consult with all the Service Delivery functions
- Service Level Management: transfer smoothly from SLRs to new or modified SLAs
- Financial Management: secure the budget and funding to complete the project
- Capacity Management: ensure sufficient capacity is available in all areas for any new services and that the performance of existing services is not impacted
- Availability Management: check that the changes conform to the Availability Plan and that no security aspects or availability targets are threatened, in either new or existing components or services
- IT Service Continuity Management: review appropriate Business Continuity Plans for any affected services
- Customer Relationship Management: ensure that appropriate liaison and communication with the business, customers and users is performed
- consult with all the Service Support functions, ensuring that:
  - **Service Desk and Incident Management** are kept informed of project progress, provided with the adequate documentation and planned handover dates
  - **Problem Management** are made aware of all known errors and possible service issues
  - **Change Management** – all changes to ICT infrastructure are subjected to all Change Management processes
  - **Configuration Management** – all new components and services are entered into the Configuration Management Database (CMDB) and are subjected to Configuration Management processes
  - **Release Management** – the deployment of all new or amended ICT infrastructure components is controlled by Release Management processes

- consult with all other ICTIM functions, and ensure that:
  - **Deployment** are involved in the project and are responsible for completing all aspects of component installation
  - **Operations** are ready to assume the day-to-day support and monitoring of all new operational components and services
  - **Administration** are involved in the evaluation of any new technology and can assume third-line support and administration functions for any new components or services

- consult with all external parties, including all ICT partners, site management staff, architects, surveyors, project managers, builders, engineers and other sub-contractors.

C.2 Preparing accommodation on a greenfield site

This section deals with the areas of:

- identifying a site
- quantifying computer accommodation requirements
- designing and building the accommodation
- commissioning and testing the accommodation
- handover of the computer accommodation.

C.2.1 Identifying a site

Selecting the location of the site is outside the scope of this book, but if a site has not already been identified, it should be considered during the Feasibility Study. The corporate business plan and the IS Strategy should be examined for factors that may influence the choice of site. Some of the key items that need consideration are:

- availability and cost of land, together with building costs
- availability of suitable staff and staffing costs
- availability of high speed network facilities and network coverage
- availability of maintenance facilities
- resilience and contingency/disaster recovery requirements
- access to electrical power of sufficient capacity and reliability
- proximity to high levels of electromagnetic radiation such as large radar installations
- possible local hazards, e.g., flooding, chemical leakage
- security requirements
- proximity to users and customers.

A risk analysis and management review using, for example, CRAMM (the UK Government's Risk Analysis and Management Method), should be conducted at a high level to determine the outline security requirements and physical security measures to be included in the new accommodation. This review will identify the assets, potential threats, vulnerabilities and countermeasures.

At the end of the Feasibility Study, a report should be published containing costed options and recommendations for the way ahead, project plans and resource plans for the next stage, the full study.

C.2.2 Quantifying computer accommodation requirements

During the full study, more information will be required on the type and amount of accommodation to be built and its layout. A further, more detailed, risk analysis and management review should be carried out. This review will consider the assets in greater detail and refine the threats, vulnerabilities and countermeasures previously identified.

The information required for the full study will include:

- detailed specifications of all equipment to be housed
- detailed specifications of computer environmental equipment (including plant rooms)
- SLRs and SLAs for new and existing services
- Capacity Plans
- Availability and Contingency plans (split building or split site requirements).

The implementation policy should be decided, since this may affect the space and power requirements. For instance, if there is a need to continue running existing applications, are these to be transferred to the new site? Will this require the existing equipment to be housed alongside the incoming new equipment on a temporary or semi-permanent basis? If so, the space requirements must accommodate the existing equipment. In any case, there should be sufficient space to allow for growth in all areas. However, consideration should be given to the continuing trend towards smaller components.

C.2.3 Designing and building the accommodation

Following acceptance of the full study report by senior management, the project team should start preparing an Operational Requirement (OR) for the procurement of new equipment, and an Accommodation Design Brief for the specification of the new accommodation. The design of the computer accommodation can now be started, bearing in mind that it will probably take much longer to design and build the accommodation than to purchase the equipment and that the accommodation has to be handed over in a clean state before the equipment can be installed. During the Design and Build phases for a major equipment location, the following management aspects of planning an environment should be considered:

- reference to environmental standards and policies (see Appendix D)
- planning acceptance procedures and handover criteria
- interface to the OR and suppliers
- interface to the Accommodation Design Brief
- managing changes to the plan and/or construction.

C.2.4 Commissioning and testing the accommodation

Before the accommodation is handed over, it should be complete and clean with all plant having been fully commissioned and tested by the supplier/partner. It is at this stage that the project manager assumes responsibility for performing acceptance tests to ensure that the accommodation and environment meet the requirements specified in the Accommodation

Design Brief. The acceptance tests themselves should have been specified in the brief. Alternative plans and actions should exist to be invoked in the event of acceptance test failure.

The following aspects (depending on the environmental conditions chosen) should be tested to ensure that the requirements are met:

- temperature control
- humidity control
- chilled water/air supplies
- dust levels
- ambient, radiated fields
- mains electricity and stand-by electrical power supplies
- balancing of electrical supplies
- earthing
- fire detection, alarm and suppression
- floor resistance and loading
- environmental monitoring equipment and alarms
- access control and management
- security precautions, prevention and facilities
- health and safety issues, emergency exits, etc.

In order to test some of these it will be necessary to generate an artificial loading in order to simulate normal conditions. For example, the air-conditioning should be tested by using a simulated heat load.

C.2.5   Handover of the computer accommodation

When the acceptance testing has been successfully completed, the acceptance certificate should be signed off and ownership should be transferred to the client organisation. The accommodation is now ready to receive the equipment. Note that this is a significant milestone, the project should not proceed until it has been signed off.

C.3   Planning to install computer equipment in an existing or new environment

Planning for the installation of new equipment should run in parallel with the preparation for any new accommodation, as described in the previous section. If new accommodation is not needed, extension or refurbishment of existing accommodation may be required and planning for this should be in place at an early stage. This may necessitate the conducting of a Business Impact Analysis (BIA) or risk analysis exercise in conjunction with Availability Management, Security Management, IT service continuity or all three. Installation of the equipment will be directly dependent on the availability of the new or refurbished accommodation. Depending on the scale of changes necessary the exercise may involve a complete cycle of Operational Requirement production, potential supplier evaluation and selection and subsequent implementation project.

The cooperation of the customers and users during the project is essential. They should be kept informed as the project plans develop and agreement should be sought for their involvement in the project, including participation in the project team, defining future service levels, Service Level Requirements, supporting trials and cut-over plans. Training plans should be established for all users of new equipment and software.

The first task is to identify the equipment, functionality, targets and service levels required. Statement Of Requirements (SOR), Invitation To Tender (ITT) or Operational Requirement (OR) will identify the equipment and functionality needed and will be used to invite proposals from potential suppliers. Service Level Requirement (SLR) documents will specify the targets and service levels required to meet the business needs. All other areas of Service and ICT Management should be consulted to ensure that all current and future needs are addressed, wherever possible.

The whole process of product and supplier evaluation will then need to take place. This will involve:

- production of a set of:
  - mandatory requirements
  - important requirements
  - 'nice to have' requirements

- supplier evaluation process and criteria
- the production of the evaluation criteria, weighting and scoring system
- production of a 'supplier shortlist'
- identification and attendance at a set of demonstrations and reference site visits
- assessment of contracts and legal terms and conditions
- the selection and decision-making process
- awarding of the contract.

Many organisations have a procurement function whose responsibility is to purchase equipment. They will assist in producing a list of potential suppliers, using their experience. The project team should maintain regular and close contact with the procurement function.

While the procurement organisation manages the quotation and ordering cycles, the project team should maintain close liaison with them and hold regular, minuted meetings in order to track the status of the ordered equipment.

When the quotation cycle has been completed and the successful suppliers have been identified, an equipment order should be submitted through procurement. All the contact points of the suppliers, e.g., Account Manager and technical representatives, must be known to the project team, as frequent contact will be necessary. In addition, lead times for equipment delivery should be agreed, documented and circulated. All new components should be brought under Configuration and Change Management as early as possible during the ordering and procurement cycle.

C.3.1   Physical layout planning

Planning of the equipment layout should be conducted by the organisation's site planning staff in conjunction with the equipment supplier's installation planning engineers. Computer-aided design (CAD) or other suitable design tools should be used to assist with this work and subsequent documentation. The 'space planning' and provision of adequate environmentally secure equipment accommodation may be a full-time occupation in some organisations.

C.3.2 Major equipment rooms and computer suites

Whether the computer suite or the equipment room is new or exists already, consideration should be given to the location of new equipment, taking into account:

- access routes, which must allow the easy relocation of equipment
- clearances between units, including maintenance and cleaning access
- raised floor tiles and cut-outs, for all equipment
- ergonomic layout – it may be possible to locate new equipment near to existing similar items, for example, disk drives and tape units
- provision for future moves and growth
- cable length restrictions – the supplier's installation planning engineers should be consulted
- footprint, floor area and shape
- room height
- raised floor loadings
- placement of air-vents
- electrical and mechanical services
- security requirements
- health and safety requirements
- air-conditioning needs
- network connections and cabling
- fire walls (2 or 4 hour rated), door and routes
- environmental sensors, detectors and alarms
- network connectivity
- backup considerations and off-site or split-site requirements.

All these issues should be addressed during the specification and ordering activities, as additional costs may be involved in the extension of current facilities or the relocation of existing equipment to make space for the new equipment.

Delivery schedules should be carefully planned and reviewed to ensure that equipment moves are kept to a minimum. Where continuity of service is required during the installation period, it may be necessary to install temporary equipment to maintain ICT services whilst equipment moves take place. If this is the case, additional space (including power and air-conditioning) and network connections may be required.

Building drawings and detailed room layouts should be amended to reflect the new equipment as soon as possible.

C.3.3 Building access

Consideration must be given to the way the equipment will be brought in and out of the building. This is particularly relevant if the computer room is not at ground level. The route should be planned carefully, taking into consideration equipment size and weight, vehicle access, and liaison with the police if roads are likely to be obstructed. Special lifting equipment may also be necessary.

It is recommended that a site survey be conducted to establish a plan to manage the delivery of the equipment, including storage space for the equipment whilst awaiting installation.

C.3.4 Additional support areas

Control room/bridge area

IT Operations functions are often controlled from a 'bridge area' or control room, which may well be outside the controlled environment of the main computer suite. The area accommodates equipment consoles. A 'bridge area' often includes the Computer Operations, Network Control, and Service Desk functions, together with their appropriate consoles and equipment.

Telecommunications

Telecommunications equipment, consisting of termination frames, modems and controllers for internal and external communication lines, is usually located together in a telecommunications room. These rooms often form part of the computer suite but, if they are separate, additional environmental equipment may be required. The maximum allowable length of connecting cables and ergonomic considerations will determine the maximum distance of the telecommunications rooms from the computer rooms. The size of the room will be dependent on the amount of equipment that has to be installed.

Media store

The environmental conditions for the storage of all media are often the same as for the computer room. The volume of media to be stored will determine whether a new room, or an extension to an existing one, is needed.

Engineers' room

It may be necessary to provide facilities for engineers to repair equipment and store spares and replacement units. This does not normally require a controlled environment.

Plant room

A separate area should be provided for the housing of all the additional environmental equipment such as switch gear, UPS, generator, air-conditioning, etc.

Printer room and stationery store

The printer room may be adjacent to the computer room or remote from it, depending on ergonomic considerations. It should be separate or screened from the computer room because of noise and dust levels, and preferably air-conditioned.

C.3.5   Security

Consideration must be given to the security of all areas associated with equipment and equipment operations. Equipment should be protected from deliberate and accidental disruption to its availability. Certain sensitive or classified data may require special security controls to maintain its confidentiality and integrity.

Access to areas containing essential engineering services, such as plant rooms, transformers and switch gear, should be strictly controlled.

During the building and installation activities, it will be necessary for suppliers to visit the site. They should ensure that the security countermeasures, which have been determined by risk analysis reviews (e.g. CRAMM), are implemented.

Some of the security countermeasures that should be considered are:

- physical security fences, gates, etc
- badge readers, personal access devices and codes or PINs
- closed circuit television (CCTV) and video recorders
- intruder detectors and alarms
- double, interlocked doors
- electronic operated or programmable key locks
- window locks and alarms
- asset tagging and sensor devices
- area and location (external local risk – e.g., flooding, chemical contamination)
- underfloor access
- radio and electrical interference or monitoring
- flammable materials.

Comprehensive and extensive security procedures should be implemented and any incidents involving security (minor or major, physical or logical) should be reported to the ICT Security Officer immediately.

C.3.6   Health and Safety

National and international legislation (e.g. the UK's Health and Safety at Work Act), and other relevant statutory requirements and standards, apply to all personnel who design, construct, operate and maintain computer equipment.

Safe working practices must be used and all work performed in such a way that no safety hazard is present or likely to arise. Health and safety policies and procedures must be defined, documented, publicised and observed. Access routes to machines must be safe and without risk to health. Safety practices and procedures should be clearly displayed in a prominent position.

The significance of emergency and warning alarms must be defined and consequent action specified. Emergency exits and escape routes need to be clearly defined and indicated. If there are special clothing requirements, their usage should be defined.

All aspects of the workstations used throughout the organisation should comply with the appropriate Health and Safety (Display Screen Equipment) Regulations. Any incident or 'near miss' involving personnel or machines should be promptly reported to the site Safety Officer, at the time of occurrence.

C.3.7   Electrical safety

The electrical installation must comply with the requirements of relevant safety standards. It is recommended that periodic and required legal checks be conducted to verify the safe earthing of machines, that equipment conforms to all Portable Appliance Testing (PAT) requirements and electrical installation regulations, for example, **IEE (Institution of Electrical Engineers) Regulations for Electrical Installations**. Any incident or 'near miss' involving personnel or machines should be promptly reported to the site Safety Officer, at the time of occurrence.

C.3.8   Planning equipment installation

As part of planning for the installation of hardware and software, a team of Operations and Administration personnel should be selected. This team will be involved in preparing for the equipment delivery and planning for acceptance and will act in support of the project team. The following items should be considered at this stage:

New hardware

The project manager should ensure that plans are in place to:

- confirm that the physical environment is completed for the new equipment
- receive the new equipment and documentation
- unpack the equipment and verify that all items ordered have been received
- updated building drawings are available to indicate the positioning of new equipment
- establish if any changes are required to the delivered hardware
- verify that the installation conforms to site standards and supplier/manufacturer standards
- have the supplier's installation engineers available when required
- confirm that appropriate support and maintenance agreements and contracts are in place.

New software

The project manager should ensure that plans are in place to:

- check that all items of software received are as ordered, including supporting documentation
- check that all new software is properly licensed and supported
- establish whether any changes are required to the delivered software
- check that external support of the installation is available, if required
- have appropriate Technical Support staff available to support the installation
- check that appropriate support agreements and contracts are in place.

Network and communications equipment

If an existing major equipment centre is being relocated, plans to provide temporary or permanent network connections may need to be installed during the move. Additionally, upgrades to existing network equipment may be necessary. In either case, continuity of ICT services during the installation period may need to be preserved.

Operations

The installation of new hardware and software will affect operational systems. Plans should be in place to ensure that Operations are made aware of the new equipment and its operation in advance of its installation. They should provide contributions to the definition of acceptance criteria.

Parallel running

It may be necessary for existing hardware and software to continue operation during the installation period. The project manager should ensure that plans are in place to continue providing existing services, with the use of temporary equipment and staff, if necessary.

Where existing applications are to be transferred to the new installation, plans should be made for the cut-over, probably using pilot and trial operations in parallel with existing systems leading to a phased introduction into live operation. Cut-over planning needs to be carried out with extreme care to ensure that existing services are not affected by the new installation. If possible, it should take place during a weekend or other off-peak time. Appropriate regression plans should have been developed and tested prior to cut-over. In any case, cut-over plans must include procedures to keep all affected staff, including customers and users, fully informed.

Decommissioning of equipment

It is possible that the installation will replace existing equipment and software. The decommissioning and removal of the replaced equipment and software should also be reflected in cut-over plans and procedures.

C.3.9 Planning acceptance

The acceptance policy and criteria should be planned, e.g., unit testing, integration testing, system testing, including any network or communications equipment and connections. Will any of the applications under development be ready to run when the equipment is installed? If so, these applications will be available for acceptance testing and can be specified as such and agreed with suppliers. If no suitable applications will be ready in time, some other means of testing the equipment must be found. It may be possible to simulate the new applications by constructing some simplified prototypes or models. However, care must be taken to ensure that any prototype or model is representative of the live system. Alternatively, if there is an existing system, this could possibly be run on the new equipment for acceptance testing.

At a time specified in the supply contract, before the start of the predefined acceptance period, an acceptance testing schedule should be agreed with the suppliers. The schedule should include:

■ the acceptance timetable including start dates, end dates and milestones

- workload details, including specific functional tests, performance tests and benchmark jobs
- any demonstrations required during the acceptance period
- system or unit configuration, including any required media and consumables
- minimum trial and acceptance configurations
- acceptance criteria – functionality, performance, serviceability, security
- incident reporting and support procedures
- full supporting documentation
- agreed responsibilities
- staffing to operate the trial system
- a record of the items under test.

C.3.10 Planning for ongoing management

Plans must be made for the ongoing operation and management of the new hardware and software. These should be developed in conjunction with all other areas of ICTIM, especially Operations. They should include:

- management of ICT services, including, monitoring, measuring, reporting, reviewing and improving the ongoing Service Levels and management processes
- disposal of any replaced and temporary equipment
- transition of new and amended services to the customers and users, all ICTIM and ITSM functions
- signed Service Level Agreement(s) (SLAs)
- fully operational documentation and automated procedures, including all backup and recovery, scheduling, event, exception, incident, problem, change, Release and alert handling procedures. These should also cover all the operational and ongoing procedures for Environmental Management, Security Management, Input Data Management, Output Data Management, Spooling Management, Stationery Management, Accommodation Management, Media Management, Storage Management, File Management, Application Management and all batch processing
- implementation of user and Service Support facilities, including possible external partnership contracts and their management
- project evaluation review – the primary objective of this review will be to ensure that the installation, testing and subsequent handover to live operation was completed as planned (lessons learnt from the project should be included in the review and recorded for future reference) – the review success criteria should be planned at this time
- ongoing reviews of documentation, procedures, skills, roles, responsibilities, knowledge and training
- ongoing Configuration, Change, Release and Deployment Management.

APPENDIX D ENVIRONMENTAL POLICIES AND STANDARDS

Every organisation should produce an environmental policy for equipment location, with minimum agreed standards for particular concentrations of equipment. Additionally, minimum standards should also be agreed for the protection of buildings containing equipment and equipment room shells. The following tables cover the major aspects that need to be considered, with example characteristics.

D.1 Building site

Access Secure

> perimeters, secure entrances audit trail

Building and Site protection

> Security fencing, video cameras, movement and intruder detectors, window and door alarms, lightening protectors, good working environment (standard)

Entry

> Multiple controlled points of entry

External environment

> Minimise external risks

Services

> Where possible and justifiable, alternate routes and suppliers for all essential services, including network services

D.2 Major equipment room shell

Location

> First floor wherever possible, with no water, gas, chemical or fire hazards within the vicinity, above, below or adjacent

Visibility

> No signage, no external windows

Shell

> External shell: waterproof, airtight, soundproofed, fire-resistant (0.5 hours to 4 hours depending on criticality)

Equipment delivery

> Adequate provision should be made for the delivery and positioning of large delicate equipment

Internal floor

> Sealed

Separate plant room

Uninterruptible Power Supply (UPS). Electrical supply and switching, air-handling units, dual units and rooms if business critical

External

Generator for major data centres and business-critical systems

D.3 Major data centres

Access

Secure controlled entry, combination lock, swipe card, video camera (if business critical and unattended)

Temperature

Strict control, $22°$ ($\pm 3°$). Provide for up to $550W/m^2$. $6°$ variation throughout the room and a maximum of $6°$ per hour

Humidity control

Strict control: 50% ($\pm 10\%$)

Air quality

Positive pressure, filtered intake low gaseous pollution (e.g., sulphur dioxide ≤ 0.14 ppm), dust levels for particles > 1 micron, less than $5x10^6$ particles/m^3. Auto shut-down on smoke or fire detection

Power

Power Distribution Unit (PDU), with three-phase supply to non-switched boxes, one per piece of equipment with appropriate rated circuit-breakers for each supply. Alternatively, approved power distribution strips can be used. Balanced three-phase loadings. UPS (on-line or line interactive with Simple Network Management Protocol (SNMP) Management) to ensure voltage supplied is within $\pm 5\%$ of rating with minimal impulse, sags, surges and over/under voltage conditions

False floors

Antistatic, liftable floor tiles 600x600mm on pedestals, with alternate pedestals screwed to the solid floor. Minimum of 600mm clearance to solid floor. Floor loadings of up to $5kN/m^2$ with a recommended minimum of 3m between false floor and ceiling

Internal walls

From false floor to ceiling, fire-resistant, but with air flow above and below floor level

Fire detection/prevention

HSSD or VESDA multi-level alarm with auto FM200 (or alternative halon replacement) release on 'double knock' detection

Environmental detectors

For smoke, temperature, power, humidity, water and intruder with automated alarm capability. Local alarm panels with repeater panels and also remote alarm capability

Lighting

Normal levels of ceiling lighting with emergency lighting on power failure

Power safety

Clean earth should be provided on the PDU and for all equipment. With clearly marked remote power-off buttons on each exit. Dirty power outlets, clearly marked, should also be supplied

Fire extinguishers

Sufficient electrical fire extinguishers with adequate signage and procedures

Vibration

Vibrations should be minimal within the complete area

Electromagnetic interference

Minimal interference should be present (1.5V/m ambient field strength)

Installations

All equipment should be provided and installed by qualified suppliers and installers to appropriate electrical and health and safety standards

Network connections

The equipment space should be flood-wired with adequate capacity for reasonable growth. All cables should be positioned and secured to appropriate cable trays

Disaster recovery

Fully tested recovery plans should be developed for all major data centres including the use of stand-by sites and equipment

D.4 Regional data centres and major equipment centres

Access

Secure controlled entry, combination lock, swipe card, video camera (if business critical and unattended)

Temperature

Temperature control, 22° (± 5°), preferable

Humidity control

Strict control: 50% (± 10%), preferable

Air quality

Positive pressure, filtered intake low gaseous pollution (e.g., sulphur dioxide ≤ 0.14 ppm), dust levels for particles > 1 micron, less than 5×10^6 particles/m^3. Auto shut-down on smoke or fire detection

Power

PDU, with three-phase supply to non-switched boxes, one per piece of equipment with appropriate rated circuit-breakers for each supply. Alternatively, approved power distribution strips can be used. Balanced three-phase loadings. Room UPS to ensure voltage supplied is within ± 5% of rating with minimal impulse, sags, surges and over/under voltage conditions

False floors

Antistatic, liftable floor tiles 600x600mm on pedestals, with alternate pedestals screwed to the solid floor. Minimum of 600mm clearance to solid floor. Floor loadings of up to $5kN/m^2$ with a recommended minimum of 3m between false floor and ceiling

Internal walls

From false floor to ceiling, fire-resistant, but with air flow above and below floor level

Fire detection/prevention

Generally fire detection but not suppression, although HSSD or VESDA multi-level alarm with auto FM200 (or alternative halon replacement) release on 'double knock' detection maybe included if business-critical systems are contained

Environmental detectors

For smoke, temperature, power, humidity, water and intruder with automated alarm capability

Lighting

Normal levels of ceiling lighting with emergency lighting on power failure

Power safety

Clean earth should be provided on the PDU and for all equipment. With clearly marked remote power-off buttons on each exit. Dirty power outlets, clearly marked should also be supplied

Fire extinguishers

Sufficient electrical fire extinguishers with adequate signage and procedures

Vibration

Vibrations should be minimal within the complete area

Electromagnetic interference

Minimal interference should be present (1.5V/m ambient field strength)

Installations

All equipment should be provided and installed by qualified suppliers and installers to appropriate electrical and health and safety standards

Network connections

The equipment space should be flood-wired with adequate capacity for reasonable growth. All cables should be positioned and secured to appropriate cable trays

Disaster recovery

Fully tested recovery plans should be developed for all regional data centres including the use of stand-by sites and equipment where appropriate

D.5   Server or network equipment rooms

Access

Secure controlled entry, by combination lock, swipe card or lock and key. In some cases equipment may be contained in open offices in locked racks or cabinets

Temperature

Normal office environment, but if in closed locked rooms adequate ventilation should be provided

Humidity control

Normal office environment

Air quality

Normal office environment

Power

Clean power supply with a UPS-supplied power to the complete rack

False floors

Recommended minimum of 3m between floor and ceiling with all cables secured in multi-compartment trunking

Internal walls

Wherever possible all walls should be fire-resistant

Fire detection/prevention

Normal office smoke/fire detection systems, unless major concentrations of equipment

Environmental detectors

For smoke, power, intruder with audible alarm capability

Lighting

Normal levels of ceiling lighting with emergency lighting on power failure

Power safety

Clean earth should be provided for all equipment. With clearly marked power off buttons

Fire extinguishers

Sufficient electrical fire extinguishers with adequate signage and procedures

Vibration

Vibrations should be minimal within the complete area

Electromagnetic interference

Minimal interference should be present (1.5V/m ambient field strength)

Installations

All equipment should be provided and installed by qualified suppliers and installers to appropriate electrical and health and safety standards

Network connections

The equipment space should be flood-wired with adequate capacity for reasonable growth. All cables should be positioned and secured to appropriate cable trays

Disaster recovery

Fully tested recovery plans should be developed where appropriate

D.6 Office environments

Access

All access should have the appropriate secure access depending on the business, the information and the equipment contained within it

Lighting, temperature, humidity and air quality

> A normal clean, comfortable and tidy office environment, conforming to the organisation's health, safety and environmental requirements

Power

> Clean power supply for all computer equipment with UPS facilities if appropriate

False floors

> Preferred if possible but all cables should be contained within appropriate trunking

Fire detection/prevention and extinguishers

> Normal office smoke/fire detection systems and intruder alerting systems, unless there are major concentrations of equipment. Sufficient fire extinguishers of the appropriate type with adequate signage and procedures

Network connections

> The office space should preferably be flood-wired with adequate capacity for reasonable growth. All cables should be positioned and secured to appropriate cable trays. All network equipment should be secured in secure cupboards or cabinets

Disaster recovery

> Fully tested recovery plans should be developed where appropriate

APPENDIX E DISTRIBUTED SERVICE ADMINISTRATION

The roles and responsibilities of DSAs and DSAC are specific to each organisation. In some organisations, they will be part of the ICT section, whereas in others they will belong to the individual business units. However, some ideas and guidelines have been incorporated here to indicate the sorts of activities that need to be addressed. It should be borne in mind that the role of DSAs may vary in scope from having responsibility for a number of desktop systems, laptop systems and phones to being responsible for a substantial regional or national data centre.

E.1 Distributed Service Administration Coordination (DSAC) – roles and responsibilities

- formulation and implementation of DSA policies and strategies
- coordination and support of all DSAs, with regular meetings and communication
- coordination of all DSA activities and responsibilities
- development of all organisation-wide DSA processes and procedures
- production, distribution and maintenance of all central and distributed DSA documentation
- development, maintenance and distribution of a single manual covering all aspects and procedures of the DSAs and DSAC
- circulation of regular newsletters and service updates
- provision of training, technical advice and guidance for DSAs
- monitoring, measurement, reporting and reviewing the success of the DSAs and the DSA processes
- control and maintenance of centralised spares for distributed systems
- rapid distribution of workarounds, incidents, problems and known errors
- assurance that DSA responsibilities are documented and agreed within SLAs
- liaison between DSAs and all central ICT Management and staff
- information and advice on the deployment of all major new services and upgrades to existing services.

E.2 Distributed Service Administrators (DSAs) – roles and responsibilities

- operation and delivery of local services to agreed service levels
- administration, maintenance and housekeeping of local services
- local user liaison, training and support providing local coordination for ICT services
- local equipment operation and support
- control of access to local equipment and services

- liaison with central ICT and Service Management staff and processes
- maintenance of local documentation and procedures
- on-site contact point for support staff and maintenance engineers
- maintenance of a catalogue of local services
- coordination and procurement of consumables
- assistance to Configuration Management and Change Management with the control of all distributed ICT infrastructure components
- control and maintenance of local on-site spares
- logging, reporting, filtering and correlation of local events, incidents and problems
- implementation of local alternate, redundant or recovery ICT processes
- liaison for local customers and users on all major deployments of new or updated services, assisting with the deployment where necessary with any on-site activities
- development, maintenance and application of all local conditions and procedures for internal and external staff visiting the site and using ICT services, including local security procedures
- being 'the local eyes and ears' for all central ICT staff and Management.

APPENDIX F IMPLEMENTATION SCHEDULE FOR A NEW SERVICE

F.1 Introduction and project initiation

This appendix describes the planning and implementation of new or enhanced network services. This procedure should be carried out using a formal project method, such as PRINCE2. The scope and Terms of Reference (TOR) for the project must clearly highlight the business issues involved and include a statement of objectives within the Project Initiation Document and the initial project documentation. In addition, the documentation must outline:

- the breadth and depth of consultation expected with existing IT processes, such as application development, Capacity Management, etc.
- the intended use of the new network services
- the service levels required within a Service Level Requirement
- the budget, cost profiles sought, and cost constraints
- the criteria that will be applied to determine the viability of any proposed solutions
- how the network systems and services are to be supported and managed after the implementation is complete
- whether the provision of support and management forms part of the project (which is usually the case).

F.2 Appoint a project team

The next step in the project is to appoint a team to carry out the planning and implementation of the new services. When selecting individuals for the team, it is important to ensure that:

- the correct breadth and depth of both business and technical skills are included
- staff from business planning, technical ICT planning and ICT Service Management are included in the team
- those selected do not have conflicting workloads or responsibilities.

All areas of ICT and Service Management should be included within this process, especially Operations, Service Level Management, Financial Management, Capacity and Availability Management, Service Continuity and Security Management, the Service Desk, Incident and Problem Management, Change, Release and Configuration Management. All staff must be kept informed during the planning process and should be considered for involvement in the project team. Input from these functions is an essential component of the planning process and involvement at this stage will help create improved assistance and cooperation later on.

Having appointed the team, the following major steps are involved in the planning process:

- establish precisely what is required by the business, customers and the end users, i.e., carry out a user requirements analysis – this must conform to the ICT strategies and the overall aim of the business as stated in the TOR for the project

- carry out a gap analysis – analyse the existing systems and services and identify the shortfalls in meeting the proposed user and business requirements
- conduct an outline application sizing exercise on what is required
- review alternative approaches and options
- carry out an initial costing exercise
- prepare a formal business case
- obtain business and ICT Management approval
- prepare a formal ITT or SOR
- prepare an outline implementation plan and schedule.

F.3   Requirements analysis

Unless the project forms part of a larger infrastructure project, for which user requirements have already been analysed and documented, it will be necessary to carry out a detailed analysis of user requirements. The analysis can be achieved by using well-established techniques such as:

- interviews with representative users and Managers
- written questionnaires
- industry reports and consultants
- user group and industry forum reports and seminars
- industry and customer surveys.

The analysis must cover not only functions, but also the service levels and the support required. In the analysis, it is important to separate out the business requirements (wants and needs) from the preferred and wish-list type of request ('nice to haves'). It must identify what users currently find unsatisfactory and why. All requirements must be documented, but it is important that their priorities and weightings are clearly defined by Business Managers.

F.4   Gap analysis

Once the analysis of business, customer and user requirements is complete, these should be compared with the results of the review of existing systems and services. The comparison will indicate whether the project requirements are completely new or enhancements of existing facilities. The latter is more likely, unless some new business function, change of working practice or exploitation of new technology is being considered. If the analysis indicates that the requirements are new, it is worth attempting to locate similar types of installation elsewhere. This enables the project team to validate the requirements (and assumptions) on which the current project plan is based by undertaking reference site visits (RSVs) and seeing similar sites already operating. See Appendix J for guidance on carrying out an RSV.

F.5 Conduct outline application sizing exercise

The business process, job or task types to be supported by the planned new services should be identified. This will enable required usage patterns, performance and availability requirements to be predicted for new or changed services. By accumulating this data, the design team can predict the service levels and traffic volumes required. These activities should be completed in collaboration with the Capacity Management process.

In order to complete this process, a knowledge is needed of the:

- new service, the application and their needs
- number of existing and planned locations
- new infrastructure components and design
- organisational mix at each location
- number of people per job function; users and their usage patterns.

In the case of the implementation of a completely new service, the only source of information may be outline plans and designs. This will require that the impact of the new service can only be simulated or modelled. This modelling should be refined and developed throughout the application design and development process. In all cases, the information collected must cover the planned period that the project is to address. For existing services, the overall analysis of existing volumes and usage may indicate that the demand can be met by enhancing current services or infrastructure components. The next step is to obtain detailed information on the current usage patterns and volumes. With this information, it will be possible to formulate maximum, minimum and probable values for the proposed new usage. This data will form the basis for an outline application sizing. Further detail on application sizing techniques can be found in the *Service Delivery* book within ITIL. Accurate figures on current usage can be obtained by such monitoring tools as response time monitoring systems and protocol monitoring. Previous invoices from the use of external network services are also useful as indications of volumes and costs.

F.6 Produce alternative designs, approaches and options

A number of alternative designs for the new services or infrastructure should be produced. These should all conform to the overall existing ICT strategies, policies and architectures. Each design should be evaluated for its advantages and disadvantages both to ICT and the business. This evaluation should not only include the advantages during the design, development and implementation but should also consider the ongoing operational aspects as well. All the Service Management processes and the ICT processes should be part of this evaluation, as well as the business requirements.

Coordination between the design team, the implementation team, Technical Support staff and Operations staff is essential for a successful implementation. In the case of a greenfield site, it is particularly desirable for the designers to also plan the operational support and managerial structures, methods and procedures that will subsequently be required.

F.7 Carry out an initial costing exercise

Once the user requirements analysis and outline sizing exercises are complete, the overall cost of the new service and the alternative infrastructure solutions can be calculated. This will reflect the full scope of the project. Each service required by users or for Management purposes must be clearly identified, prioritised and costed.

It can be useful to allocate an initial cost based on typical industry values to each service if possible. This cost can be on a per-user basis or a per-service basis depending on how it affects the overall costs. The costs derived are not an accurate estimate of the final costs of the project. The final costs depend on the design and implementation chosen. Nevertheless, it is important to obtain an estimate of the costs involved, in order to allow a decision to be made as to whether to proceed with the project and which particular design alternative should be implemented.

Typical costs and performance information for the base infrastructure chosen for each potential design can be obtained from suppliers. From this, a complete cost analysis for each design should be carried out. Estimates should be made, either on a per-user basis or for the system as a whole. In some cases, it may be necessary to include variable costs where, for example, scale of use has an effect on the cost structure.

This cost analysis provides the project team, and hence the users, with a guide to the costs associated with each aspect of the SOR/ITT. This is essential if the projected costs exceed the currently allocated budget. The information can be compared with the user's priority for each function to best match the design with the budget constraints of the project.

It is important to consider the business benefits of each service and quantify any cost savings. A cost-benefit analysis may be required to obtain an estimate of the final net value of each service and facility provided. From the results of this costing exercise, the project team can prepare a detailed cost analysis and benefit profile for the project. This will enable Business Managers to evaluate the business worth of the proposed new service(s) and select the most appropriate business solution.

F.8 Select the most appropriate solution

The result of considering various design options should be a range of design solutions, each with its advantages, disadvantages and costs. A final comparative evaluation must then be carried out based on the business and user requirements, the cost profiles and the technical and business issues involved. In carrying out the evaluation, it is essential to consider all aspects of the solution including the operational and support issues such as:

- the required skill levels for support staff
- the maintenance, support and training costs over the period of operation (say three years)
- the costs of new test and development equipment for support
- projected ongoing hardware and software maintenance costs.

The design of the infrastructure must be clearly shown to conform to the capacity, availability, contingency and security requirements. In a number of cases, it may be difficult to decide upon a single solution because of unknown variables. In these cases, refine each solution by modelling or simulating the criteria concerned and use comparative analysis techniques on the results.

F.9   Prepare a formal business case

Once the most appropriate business solution has been selected, a formal business case should be produced. Details of the contents of a business case are included in Appendix G. The business case should concentrate on the business aspects and advantages of the solution rather than the technological aspects, to enable senior business and ICT Management to approve the development and implementation of the chosen solution. The business case should include:

- a description of the requirements
- details of the proposed solution
- the business and ICT advantages of the proposed solution
- the development, implementation and ongoing costs of the solution
- supplier, contractual and legal issues.

F.10   Obtain business and ICT Management approval

Once produced, the business case should be circulated to senior business and ICT Management. The ISG or even the organisation's Board may take the decision on whether or not to proceed with the solution.

F.11   Prepare a formal ITT or SOR

The authority to proceed allows the project team to finalise the infrastructure design and prepare a formal Statement Of Requirements (SOR) or Invitation To Tender (ITT). Guidelines on the contents of these can be found within Appendix H.

Once the costs have been analysed, and the options and integration with existing systems have been considered, it is possible to finalise the infrastructure design to provide the required functionality for the period of the plan. The design must:

- support users' requirements for service levels, i.e., performance, reliability and availability (including resistance to failure). Ideally, a provisional SLR should be developed
- allow for the monitoring of service levels and targets
- provide for existing capacity and facilitate enhancement to accommodate projected growth in the use of existing services and for projected new services
- provide for alternative facilities to be made available if any part of the solution suffers from major or prolonged failure
- meet all regulatory requirements
- be supportable by Technical Support staff

■ facilitate the provision of the required support levels from suppliers and maintainers

■ facilitate the provision of customer support via the Service Desk, Incident and Problem Management staff.

The maturity of the technology (i.e., how well proven it is) and the reliability of the suppliers must be taken into account. Where possible, a formal Reference Site Visit (RSV) should be arranged, to talk to other similar users of the proposed infrastructure and customers of the potential suppliers. Guidelines for carrying out RSVs are given in Appendix J.

The SOR/ITT must clearly identify the business needs being satisfied with each function or facility identified and the business benefits associated with them. The SOR should then be validated by the business and the users to ensure that it still meets their requirements. An important step in validating the SOR is to give a formal presentation of how the data and associated assumptions were obtained and used to project the final values. This allows users to fully understand the derivation of the data and challenge any erroneous assumptions made by the project team. If the SOR is accepted, the project team can proceed to the detailed design stage with confidence.

If the SOR is not approved the requirements and the SOR must be reviewed in order to ensure objectives of the business are satisfied. This may require a redefinition of requirements or a change in the technology or the allocated budget.

While all this takes time, the process must occur to ensure that:

■ the business objectives and benefits to be realised are known and documented

■ all parties involved in the project understand what functionality is proposed

■ all parties understand why this functionality is being proposed

■ the proposed levels of service are known

■ the resources required to support the project are understood.

This exercise may be iterative to take account of multiple services if the project is addressing more than one requirement. Each service should be considered individually for business benefit in order that each service may be assessed independently.

F.12   Prepare for the review process and selection method

Once the ITT/SOR has been produced and circulated to prospective suppliers, the supplier review and selection process should be prepared and planned before starting the selection process.

A good method for comparison of suppliers, services and components is to produce a list of:

■ mandatory facilities or requirements (Wants)

■ important facilities or requirements (Needs)

■ optional facilities or requirements ('Nice to haves').

A spreadsheet can be produced containing scores and importance weighting factors. A formalised evaluation can then be completed automatically for each of the selection panellists. The total evaluation score can be used to select the most appropriate supplier, components or services.

The selection panel should agree all the list of facilities, the scores, weightings and decision-making process before the starting the selection process. This will minimise the need for subsequent discussions and differences of opinion. A supplier can then be selected and the purchase authorised.

F.13   Prepare an outline implementation plan and schedule

Once a final decision has been made on the design and the set of suppliers has been selected, the implementation must be planned in detail. The distributed nature of ICT infrastructure makes the task of project managing implementations or enhancements very demanding. The implementation project team needs to be organisationally separate from the operational staff to ensure that:

- the current operational workload does not interfere with implementation work
- the implementation project is properly managed; this requires skills which may not be fully developed in the operational teams
- there is a defined end-date by which the project must be completely finished and signed off
- separate teams exist to allow independent quality reviews to be undertaken.

A detailed project plan must be produced and submitted for Management approval (e.g., PRINCE2 Project Board). The plan should contain:

- details of what needs to be done
- an estimate of the time-scales, skill levels and budget required for the remainder of the project
- deliverables and milestones
- activities, roles and responsibilities
- provisional costs
- provisional cost-benefit analysis
- the results of the sizing exercise(s)
- a risk register of the risks involved and actions taken to minimise those risks
- project reports and stage reviews.

The material in the plan must be sufficiently detailed to allow decisions to be made on which aspects of the project should proceed to the implementation stage.

The implementation project manager must liaise with other areas affected by implementation, such as staff from the business, Operations, Deployment Management and Distributed Systems Administrators, Change and Release Management. The manager of the implementation project must also:

- maintain regular contact with any suppliers involved in the project
- hold regular meetings throughout the implementation period with the business, service suppliers, hardware/software suppliers, as well as with contracted staff, e.g., installers or consultants
- ensure that the review and communication procedures are agreed prior to the implementation phase and form part of any contract – see OGC's Management guide: *How to Manage Service Provision* for further details.

The order in which the implementation should be undertaken, if this is significant, should be agreed and specified. Practices and procedures must be defined before the implementation of new systems to ensure existing services are not disrupted. These practices and procedures are covered in more detail in Section 3.5.3, under the sub-heading *Documentation*.

The activities to which these procedures apply affect operational staff both during and after the implementation work has been completed. It is, therefore, advisable for operational staff to check at this stage that the procedures are satisfactory, and later, that the activities have been completed satisfactorily before the service is made live. These activities should be included within the plan. Operations and Technical Support staff have the final authority to accept or reject any aspect of the installed systems and services at the handover period, before the systems have been made operational.

The Bring into Service (BIS) procedures detail the order in which systems and services become live and how the cut-over to live working takes place. The BIS procedures also identify relevant documentation about the installed systems and services that must be presented to the Operations and support staff.

APPENDIX G THE CONTENTS OF A BUSINESS CASE

Key message

It is worth remembering that financial approval bodies are not primarily interested in technical arguments. To be successful, a business case must relate costs to business benefits, using sound methods of investment appraisal.

Each organisation should have its own standards and format for business cases. A business case should be logical, well structured and concise. It should contain, where appropriate:

- identification and quantification of all the benefits to the business and its customers
- the overall scope, objectives, Critical Success Factors (CSFs) and business benefits of the proposed solution
- the business sponsor/owner and the stakeholders
- a description of the current situation, including strengths, weaknesses, opportunities and threats
- the strategic fit and details of how the preferred solution conforms to, or deviates from, existing business and ICT policies, strategies and plans
- the implications and impact of not proceeding with the business case (do nothing)
- a description of the proposed new services, components or technology being considered
- a table of contents
- details of all constraints and dependencies
- an overview of how this proposal support the key strategic objectives of:
  - the corporate strategy
  - the business strategies
  - the ICT strategy
- how those key strategic objectives and benefits are to be achieved
- the level of authorisation or approval necessary and the required time-scale for approval
- market considerations:
  - the markets involved and their possible geographical variations
  - external opportunities and threats
  - market share and competitors
  - the key customer segments and business sectors
  - present and forecasted volumes, revenues and profit
  - regulatory and legislative constraints
  - trends in price, quality, standards and technology
  - competitive services and products, their quality and performance

- proposed Bring Into Service (BIS) date
- details of how the objectives, CSFs and business benefits will be measured
- details of the Project Management methods and approach
- details of all impacts on, and benefits to:
  - ICT organisations and processes
  - the business organisations and processes
  - the market
  - internal customers
  - external customers
  - market share and competitors
  - other ICT systems and services
  - human resources: headcounts, operational support and responsibilities

- details of anticipated business volumes and ICT volumes
- identification and quantification of all risks:
  - description of the risk
  - probability of the risk
  - the impact of the risk
  - analysis of the risk
  - steps taken to manage and minimise the risk
  - any necessary contingency plans and expenditure

- the preferred solution with its advantages, disadvantages, benefits, risks, costs, resources and time-scales, including ongoing requirements and costs
- alternative solutions considered and their advantages, disadvantages, benefits, risks, costs and time-scales, including ongoing requirements and costs, including the 'do nothing' option
- the reasons for selecting the preferred suppliers and rejecting alternative suppliers
- details of key milestones in the implementation process and the overall dependency upon them
- details of parent programmes or projects and their interfaces and approval status
- details of any dependent programmes or projects and their dependencies and approval status
- the authorising, owning or sponsoring body and budget(s) to be used
- details of the approach to be adopted (e.g., in-house development, contracted-in development or outsourced development)
- what levels of service are expected from the new services, components or technology and whether they are consistent with all existing levels and targets
- procurement plans and policies with details of the preferred suppliers and their costs and comparative alternatives and their costs
- financial analysis:
  - financial assumptions
  - initial costs
  - ongoing costs
  - financial constraints and budgets

- – payback period and return on investment (ROI)
- – tolerances and sensitivities
- – funding and stakeholders
- – the effect on the organisation's financial performance and profitability

■ the requirements for resources and finances from other Departments and Organisations

■ contractual, legal and regulatory issues

■ environmental issues

■ summary and recommendations, clear, concise and unambiguous.

APPENDIX H THE CONTENTS OF AN INVITATION TO TENDER (ITT) OR STATEMENT OF REQUIREMENTS (SOR)

The following is a reference checklist of a minimum set of contents that should be included in an ITT or SOR:

- a description of the services, products and/or components required
- all relevant technical specifications, details and requirements
- an SLR where applicable
- availability, reliability, maintainability and serviceability requirements
- details of ownership of hardware, software, buildings, facilities, etc.
- details of performance criteria to be met by the equipment and the supplier(s)
- details of all standards to be complied with (internal, external, national and international)
- legal and regulatory requirements (industry, national, EU and international)
- details of quality criteria
- contractual time-scales, details and requirements
- all commercial considerations: costs, charges, bonus and penalty payments and schedules
- interfaces and contacts required
- Project Management methods to be used
- reporting, monitoring and reviewing procedures and criteria to be used during and after the implementation
- supplier requirements and conditions
- sub-contractor requirements
- details of any relevant terms and conditions
- description of the supplier response requirements:
    - format
    - criteria
    - conditions
    - time-scales
    - variances and omissions
    - customer responsibilities and requirements
- details of planned and possible growth
- procedures for handling changes
- details of the contents and structure of the responses required.

APPENDIX J GUIDELINES FOR REFERENCE SITE VISITS

A Reference Site Visit (RSV) is an excellent way of gaining insight and valuable information about components and services that are being considered for use. When undertaking an RSV it is important to be clear about what is to be achieved through the visit. Examples of objectives are assessments of the:

- supplier in terms of meeting the costs, time-scales, quality and functionality required for installation
- supplier or third party maintainer in terms of supporting the components or services
- the ability of the components or services to cater for growth
- the overall performance, security, availability, reliability and maintainability of the components or services
- strengths and weaknesses of the components or services
- the suppliers', the components' and/or the services' adherence to standards
- the usage and availability of components and services and their interoperability.

It is important for someone undertaking an RSV to understand the differences between the infrastructure and business of the reference site and those of their own organisation. They should take account not just of differences in models and versions if there are any, but also differences in the use of the components and services. These questions should, therefore, be asked about the reference site usage:

- are they the same models, releases or versions as the components and services being considered for the organisation?
- what is the current and proposed use of the reference components and services?
- how do the size and use of the reference components and services compare to the size and use being considered for the organisation?
- what is the level of current use (e.g., percentage load factor)?
- how long have the components and services been in use?
- what criteria were used to select the reference components and services and have they been met?

To obtain the maximum information from the RSV it is important to plan for the visit. A detailed questionnaire that covers all aspects of the components and services to be assessed should be prepared. As well as covering the points listed above, the questionnaire should also elicit the following information:

- components and services details:
  - length of the implementation and the installation date
  - initial configuration
  - who installed the components and services
  - resources required
  - number of users
  - percentage load factors

- – performance criteria
- – connections to other systems
- – availability, reliability and maintainability
- – usability and quality
- – documentation and training
- – support and maintenance
- – support of open interfaces and standards

■ management capabilities:

- – details, reports and information provided
- – length of the implementation and the installation date
- – initial configuration
- – integration with other related management systems
- – level of automation of administration and maintenance tasks
- – usability and quality
- – documentation and training
- – support and maintenance
- – support of open interfaces and standards

■ supplier details:

- – quality of Project Management
- – quality of method and work
- – quality of personnel
- – level of liaison with organisation's staff
- – whether the supplier met the planned dates
- – time required for installation
- – whether all aspects were delivered as required
- – quality of training
- – quality of new releases

■ internal support:

- – who supports the system
- – level and skill of staff required
- – number of incidents handled
- – number of underlying problems
- – types of problems
- – ease of modification
- – ease of growth
- – Systems Management features
- – diagnostic abilities

■ supplier support:

- – number of incidents and problems handled
- – types of incidents and problems
- – quality of response
- – level of commitment
- – expertise of support staff
- – availability of system
- – reliability of system
- – spares levels and requirements

- organisational issues:
  - reasons for selection of system
  - main areas of use
  - type and expertise of users

- Security requirements – some organisations may not be prepared to supply answers to these questions; therefore, sensitivity will be required:
  - what security mechanisms, physical and logical, are available?
  - what security mechanisms, physical and logical, have been implemented?
  - what tests are applied to the security mechanisms and what are the results?
  - how many security violations have occurred?
  - how severe were the security violations?

A good method for comparison of suppliers, services and components is to produce a list of:

- mandatory facilities or requirements (Wants)
- important facilities or requirements (Needs)
- optional facilities or requirements ('Nice to haves').

These can be fed into a spreadsheet together with a score and importance weighting, and a formalised evaluation can be completed. The total evaluation score can then be used to select the most appropriate supplier, components or services.

APPENDIX K   THE SERVICE LIFECYCLE

An overview of the major stages involved in the lifecycle of a service and the responsibilities are illustrated in Figure K.1.

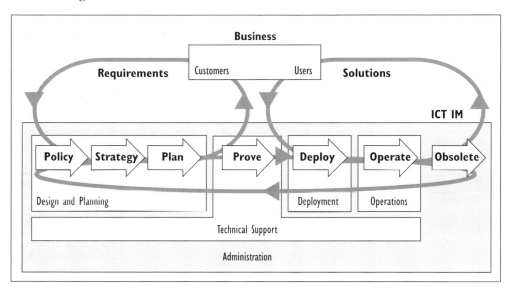

Figure K.1 – The stages in the lifecycle of a service

These can be expanded into the activities and deliverables that constitute each of these stages, as shown in Figures K.2 and K.3.

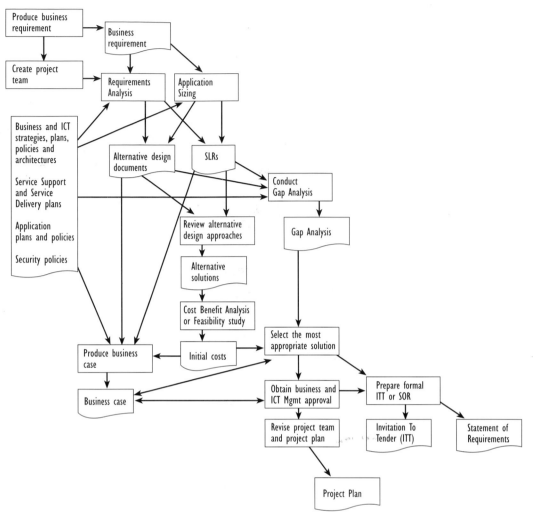

Figure K.2 – The service lifecycle (Part a)

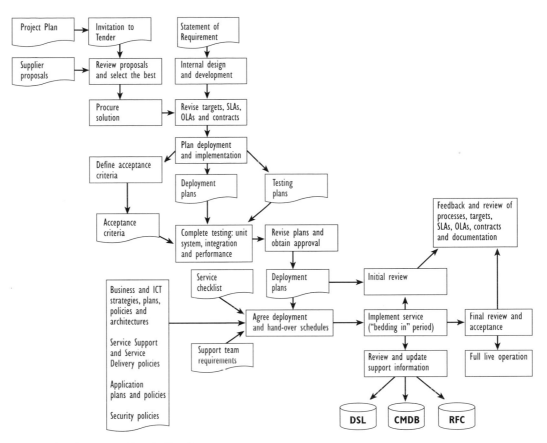

Figure K.3 – The service lifecycle (Part b)

The current status and progress of a service through the stages of its lifecycle should be recorded within the Configuration Management Database (CMDB). A checklist of acceptance activities for bringing a new service into operation is included within Appendix M.

APPENDIX L   THE CONTENTS OF A FEASIBILITY STUDY/GAP ANALYSIS

The following are typical contents of Feasibility Study and gap analysis exercises. The two exercises are often linked together, the gap analysis identifying the 'gap' to be addressed and the Feasibility Study addressing the decision to proceed or stop.

L.1   Gap analysis

A gap analysis typically contains:

- business requirements, needs and likely usage
- scope and terms of reference
- identification and quantification of the current situation, often derived as the output from a review, assessment or SWOT analysis
- definition and quantification of a desired future state(s)
- priorities, interfaces and dependencies
- evaluation and comparison of alternatives
- the business and IT benefits accruing from the desired state(s)
- outline plan and estimation of the following:
  - roles and responsibilities
  - activities and resources
  - time scales
  - costs

  required to achieve the defined desired state(s).

L.2   Feasibility Study

A Feasibility Study may often include, or follow on from, a gap analysis exercise, and typically contains:

- business requirements, needs and likely usage
- scope and terms of reference
- evaluation of alternative options
  - resources, costs and benefits
  - priorities, interfaces and dependencies
  - risks and probabilities
  - impacts and costs associated with the risks
  - cost of risk reduction

- restrictions and constraints
- likely future knock-on effects and developments

■ benefits and time-scales
  - short-term
  - long-term
  - ongoing operational

■ costs and time-scales
  - short-term
  - long-term
  - ongoing operational

■ cashflows, financial justification and recharging options

■ additional justifications
  - business benefits
  - customer and user benefits
  - IT benefits

■ a recommendation or set of recommendations.

APPENDIX M A CHECKLIST FOR THE ACCEPTANCE OF NEW SERVICES

The following is a reference checklist of a minimum set of activities that should be completed before a new or amended service is made live:

- a 'pilot phase' or 'bedding in' period has been agreed with all parties together with a Bring Into Service (BIS) date
- the implementation schedule has been agreed with all affected parties
- the service and its components conform to all business and ICT strategies, standards and policies
- the appropriate business, customers and user contacts have all been consulted and have all the necessary documentation and procedures
- all essential customer, user and support staff training has been completed and future needs have been identified and planned
- the service has been added to the Service Catalogue
- the new or amended SLA has been negotiated, agreed and signed by all parties, including agreed responsibilities
- all necessary OLAs that underpin the SLA targets are in place and agreed and signed by all parties
- all necessary contracts that underpin the SLA targets are in place and agreed and signed by all parties
- processes are in place to monitor and review all aspects of the SLA and SLA targets, OLA and OLA targets and contracts and contract targets
- all Service Desk documentation and procedures have been produced and agreed and the Service Desk is ready to support the new service
- all components of the service are covered by OLAs and/or contracts
- all components of the service are supportable and all
  - Technical Support
  - Service Desk
  - Incident Management
  - Problem Management
  - DSAC and DSA

  procedures and support documentation are in place, including any new incident and problem categories and classifications
- all relationships, interfaces, dependencies and integration with other existing and future services have been agreed, documented and tested
- all downtime has been agreed with all affected customers
- all necessary components have been added to the backup schedule
- all security requirements, policies and procedures have been reviewed and completed

- all operational procedures, Operations and batch processing schedules have been documented and agreed with Capacity Management
- all tests and testing plans have been completed and signed by all parties including all quality aspects, which should include:
  - component and unit testing
  - systems and integration testing
  - management procedural tests for alerting, performance, etc.
  - facility and functional testing
  - performance and response time testing
  - stress testing and load testing
  - regression testing
  - user acceptance testing
- all deficiencies, variations, problems and known errors have been recorded in the Configuration Management Database (CMDB) and the known error database has been updated, completed and is available to everyone
- all performance aspects of the service and its components are being monitored and stored within the Capacity Management Database (CDB) with agreed thresholds and alerts in place
- the service and its components have been incorporated into Capacity Management, the Capacity Plan and their associated activities, including current and future usage volumes
- all the project costs and service costs have been accumulated and agreed by all parties as well as the ongoing operational costs
- the service charges are documented within the SLA and procedures are in place for their calculation and recovery
- all the availability criteria are documented and agreed and processes are in place to monitor all aspects of availability with corresponding alerts and alarms
- maintenance times and procedures have been agreed
- all relevant suppliers and contracts have been reviewed and any additional suppliers and contracts have been added to the Supplier Catalogue (preferably within the CMDB). Agreed procedures are in place to review supplier performance and contract performance
- a risk analysis has been completed on the new service and its possible impact on existing services
- all continuity and recovery processes and procedures have been completed and tested with supporting Business Continuity Plans and have been signed off by the business and ICT
- service resilience tests have been added to the overall resilience testing schedule
- the service and all of its components have been added to the CMDB and accurately reflect their current status
- all Change Management procedures have been agreed and completed and all Requests for Changes (RFCs) have been correctly authorised, updated and reflect their current status
- all software components have been lodged within the DSL

- all Release Management procedures have been agreed and completed. All Release records have been updated to reflect their current status
- release policies and frequencies have been reviewed, agreed and documented
- all other service and component management processes, agents, reports and procedures are in place
- the implementation project has been reviewed, agreed and signed off.

APPENDIX N QUALITY

N.1 Quality Management

Quality Management for IT services is a systematic way of ensuring that all the activities necessary to design, develop and implement IT services which satisfy the requirements of the organisation and of users take place as planned and that the activities are carried out cost-effectively.

The way that an organisation plans to manage its Operations so that it delivers quality services is specified by its Quality Management System. The Quality Management System defines the organisational structure, responsibilities, policies, procedures, processes, standards and resources required to deliver quality IT services. However, a Quality Management System will only function as intended if management and staff are committed to achieving its objectives.

This appendix gives brief details on a number of different Quality approaches – more detail on these and other approaches can be found on the Internet at www.dti.gov.uk/quality.

N.1.1 Deming

> **Quote**
>
> 'We have learned to live in a world of mistakes and defective products as if they were necessary to life. It is time to adopt a new philosophy...'
>
> (W. Edwards Deming, 1900–1993)

W. Edwards Deming is best known for his management philosophy for establishing quality, productivity, and competitive position. As part of this philosophy, he formulated 14 points of attention for managers. Some of these points are more appropriate to Service Management than others.

For quality improvement Deming proposed the Deming Cycle or Circle. The four key stages are 'Plan, Do, Check and Act' after which a phase of consolidation prevents the 'Circle' from 'rolling down the hill' as illustrated in Figure N.1.

The cycle is underpinned by a process led approach to management where defined processes are in place, the activities measured for compliance to expected values and outputs audited to validate and improve the process.

Example

Excerpts from Deming's 14 points relevant to Service Management

- break down barriers between departments (improves communications and management)

- management must learn their responsibilities, and take on leadership (process improvement requires commitment from the top; good leaders motivate people to improve themselves and therefore the image of the organisation)

- improve constantly (a central theme for service managers is continual improvement; this is also a theme for Quality Management. A process led approach is key to achieve this target)

- institute a programme of education and self-improvement (learning and improving skills have been the focus of Service Management for many years)

- training on the job (linked to continual improvement)

- transformation is everyone's job (the emphasis being on teamwork and understanding).

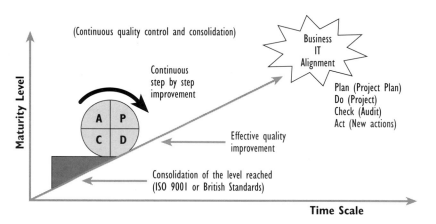

Figure N.1 – The Deming Cycle

N.1.2   Juran

Joseph Juran became a recognised name in the quality field in 1951 with the publication of the Quality Control Handbook. The appeal was to the Japanese initially, and Juran was asked to give a series of lectures in 1954 on planning, organisational issues, management responsibility for Quality, and the need to set goals and targets for improvement.

Juran devised a well-known chart, 'The Juran Trilogy', shown in Figure N.2, to represent the relationship between quality planning, quality control, and quality improvement on a project-by-project basis.

A further feature of Juran's approach is the recognition of the need to guide managers; this is achieved by the establishment of a quality council within an organisation, which is responsible for establishing processes, nominating projects, assigning teams, making improvements and providing the necessary resources.

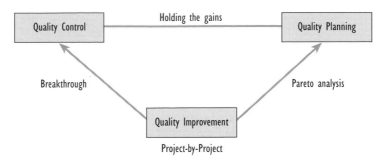

Figure N.2 – The Quality trilogy

Senior management plays a key role in serving on the quality council, approving strategic goals, allocating resources, and reviewing progress.

Juran promotes a four-phased approach to quality improvement, namely:

- Start-up – creating the necessary organisational structures and infrastructure
- Test – in which concepts are tried out in pilot programmes and results evaluated
- Scale-up – in which the basic concepts are extended based on positive feedback
- Institutionalisation – at which point quality improvements are linked to the strategic business plan.

N.1.3 Crosby

The Crosby TQM approach is very popular in the UK. However, despite its obvious success in the market, it has been subject to much criticism, primarily due to poor understanding, or a blinkered application of the approach in some organisations, using a limited definition of quality. The approach is based on Crosby's Four Absolutes of Quality Management, namely:

- Quality is conformance to requirement
- The system for causing quality is prevention and not appraisal
- The performance standard must be zero defects and not 'that's close enough'
- The measure of quality is the price of non-conformance and not indices.

The Crosby approach is often based on familiar slogans; however, organisations may experience difficulty in translating the quality messages into sustainable methods of quality improvement. Some organisations have found it difficult to integrate their quality initiatives, having placed their quality programme outside the mainstream management process.

Anecdotal evidence suggests that these pitfalls result in difficulties being experienced in sustaining active quality campaigns over a number of years in some organisations.

Crosby lacks the engineering rigour of Juran and significantly omits to design quality into the product or process, gearing the quality system towards a prevention-only policy. Furthermore, it fails to recognise that few organisations have appropriate management measures from which they can accurately ascertain the costs of non-conformance, and in some cases even the actual process costs!

N.1.4 Six Sigma

This is commonly described as a body of knowledge required to implement a generic quantitative approach to improvement. Six Sigma is a data-driven approach to analysing the root causes of problems and solving them. It is business output driven in relation to customer specification and focuses on dramatically reducing process variation using Statistical Process Control (SPC) measures. A process that operates at Six Sigma allows only 3.40 defects per million parts of output.

The Six Sigma approach has evolved from experience in manufacturing, and is therefore not readily applied to human processes and perhaps other processes that are not immediately apparent. The approach relies on trained personnel capable of identifying processes that need improvement and who can act accordingly. It does not contain a systematic approach for identifying improvement opportunities or facilitate with prioritisation.

Six Sigma perhaps offers another path toward measurable improvement for CMM Level 3 organisations, but this alone may make it difficult to apply in the context of Service Management compared to software engineering.

There are research reservations on applying validation and measurement to process improvement and particularly in the application of SPC to non-manufacturing engineering processes. It has been found that a Goal, Question, Metric (GQM) approach provides suitable measures, rather than a statistical method. It is still somewhat a controversial area, and even the SW-CMM at the higher levels (4–5) has come in for some academic criticism in this area. However, there are indications that Six Sigma is being applied in the service sector and, with good Service Management support tools, tracking of incidents, etc., would allow this approach to be used for process improvement.

N.2   Formal quality initiatives

N.2.1   Quality standards

International Standards Organisation ISO 9000

An important set of International Standards for Quality Assurance is the ISO 9000 range, a set of five universal standards for a Quality Assurance system that is accepted around the world. At the turn of the millennium, 90 or so countries have adopted ISO 9000 as the cornerstone of their national standards. When a product or service is purchased from a company that is registered to the appropriate ISO 9000 standard, the purchaser has important assurances that the quality of what they will receive will be as expected.

The most comprehensive of the standards is ISO 9001. It applies to industries involved in the design, development, manufacturing, installation and servicing of products or services. The standards apply uniformly to companies in any industry and of any size.

The BSI Management Overview of IT Service Management is a modern update of the original document, PD0005, which was published in 1995. The Management Overview is a management level introduction to Service Management, and in fact can be used as an introduction to ITIL. This is also now supported by a formal standard, BS 15000 (Specification for IT Service Management). ITIL is in many countries the *de facto* standard and, with the help of BSI and ISO, it is hoped that a formal international standard based on ITIL will soon be in place. The BSI Standard and Management Overview cover the established ITIL Service Support and Service Delivery processes, as well as some additional topics such as implementing the processes.

N.2.2 Total Quality Systems: EFQM

Quote

'...the battle for Quality is one of the prerequisites for the success of your companies and for our collective success.'

(Jacques Delors, president of the European Commission, at the signing of the letter of intent in Brussels to establish EFQM on 15 September 1988.)

The EFQM Excellence Model

The European Foundation for Quality Management (EFQM) was founded in 1988 by the Presidents of 14 major European companies, with the endorsement of the European Commission. The present membership is in excess of 600 very well-respected organisations, ranging from major multinationals and important national companies to research institutes in prominent European universities.

EFQM provides an excellent model for those wishing to achieve business excellence in a programme of continual improvement.

EFQM mission statement

The mission statement is:

> To stimulate and assist organisations throughout Europe to participate in improvement activities leading ultimately to excellence in customer satisfaction, employee satisfaction, impact on society and business results; and to support the Managers of European organisations in accelerating the process of making Total Quality Management a decisive factor for achieving global competitive advantage.

Depiction of the EFQM Excellence Model

The EFQM Excellence Model consists of 9 criteria and 32 sub-criteria; it is illustrated in Figure N.3.

In the model there is explicit focus on the value to users of the 'Plan, Do, Check, Act' cycle to business operations (see Section N.1.1), and the need to relate everything that is done, and the measurements taken, to the goals of business policy and strategy.

Self-assessment and maturity: the EFQM maturity scale

One of the tools provided by EFQM is the self-assessment questionnaire. The self-assessment process allows the organisation to discern clearly its strengths and also any areas where improvements can be made. The questionnaire process culminates in planned improvement actions, which are then monitored for progress.

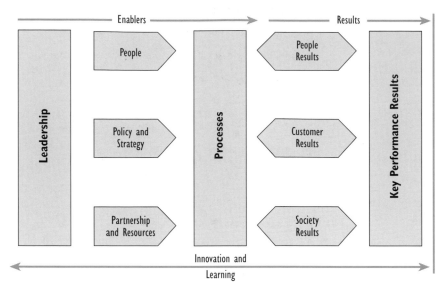

©EFQM. The EFQM Excellence Model is a registered trademark

Figure N.3 – The EFQM Excellence Model

In this assessment progress can be checked against a five-point maturity scale:

1. Product orientation

2. Process orientation (the maturity stage aimed for by the original ITIL)

3. System orientation (the maturity target for ITIL-compliant organisations in the new millennium)

4. Chain orientation

5. Total quality.

N.2.3 Quality awards

To demonstrate a successful adaptation of the EFQM model, some companies aim for the European Quality Award, a process that allows Europe to recognise its most successful organisations and promote them as role models of excellence for others to copy.

The US equivalent to this award is the Malcolm Baldridge Quality Award for Quality Management. The Malcolm Baldridge National Quality Improvement Act of 1987 established an annual US National Quality Award. The purpose of the Award was (and still is) to promote awareness of quality excellence, to recognise quality achievements of US companies, and to publicise successful quality strategies.

For the Malcolm Baldridge Award, there are three categories:

■ Manufacturing companies or sub-units

■ Service companies or sub-units

■ Small businesses.

The criteria against which firms are judged are:

1. Leadership

2. Strategic planning

3   Customer and market focus

4   Information and analysis

5   Human resource development and management

6   Process management

7   Business results.

For the European Quality Award, there are four possible categories:

- Companies

- Operational units of companies

- Public sector organisations

- Small and medium enterprises.

The criteria against which candidate organisations are measured are:

1   Leadership

2   People

3   Policy and strategy

4   Partnerships and resources

5   Processes

6   People results

7   Customer results

8   Society results

9   Key performance results.

In the EFQM Excellence Model, the first four criteria are defined as enablers. Best practice in ITIL process implementations show that placing proper emphasis on these topics increases the chances for success. The key points for the four enablers are listed below.

Leadership

- Organise a kick-off session involving everyone

- Be a role model

- Encourage and support the staff.

People management

- Create awareness

- Recruit new staff and/or hire temporary staff to prevent Service Levels being affected during implementation stages

- Develop people through training and experience

- Align human resource plans with policy and strategy

- Adopt a coaching style of management

- Align performance with salaries.

Policy and strategy

- Communicate mission, vision and values
- Align communication plans with the implementation stages.

Partnerships and resources

- Establish partnerships with subcontractors and customers
- Use financial resources in support of policy and strategy
- Utilise existing assets.

INDEX

Other Information Sources and Services

The IT Service Management Forum (itSMF)

The IT Service Management Forum Ltd (itSMF) is the only internationally recognised and independent body dedicated to IT Service Management. It is a not-for-profit organisation, wholly owned, and principally operated, by its membership.

The itSMF is a major influence on, and contributor to, Industry Best Practice and Standards worldwide, working in partnership with OGC (the owners of ITIL), the British Standards Institution (BSI), the Information Systems Examination Board (ISEB) and the Examination Institute of the Netherlands (EXIN).

Founded in the UK in 1991, there are now a number of chapters around the world with new ones seeking to join all the time. There are well in excess of 1000 organisations covering over 10,000 individuals represented in the membership. Organisations range from large multi-nationals such as AXA, GuinnessUDV, HP, Microsoft and Procter & Gamble in all market sectors, through central & local bodies, to independent consultants.

How to contact us:

The IT Service Management Forum Ltd
Webbs Court
8 Holmes Road
Earley
Reading RG6 7BH
Tel: +44 (0) 118 926 0888
Fax: +44 (0) 118 926 3073
Email: service@itsmf.com
or visit our web-site at:
www.itsmf.com

ITIL training and professional qualifications

There are currently two examining bodies offering equivalent qualifications: ISEB (The Information Systems Examining Board), part of the British Computer Society, and Stitching EXIN (The Netherlands Examinations Institute). Jointly with OGC and itSMF (the IT Service Management Forum), they work to ensure that a common standard is adopted for qualifications worldwide. The syllabus is based on the core elements of ITIL and complies with ISO9001 Quality Standard. Both ISEB and EXIN also accredit training organisations to deliver programmes leading to qualifications.

For further information:

visit ISEB's web-site at:
www.bcs.org.uk

and EXIN:
www.exin.nl